AT THE
BIRTH OF
BOWIE

LIFE WITH THE MAN WHO BECAME A LEGEND

AT THE BIRTH OF BIRTH OF BOWIE

PHIL LANCASTER

JOHN BLAKE

Published by John Blake Publishing,
2.25, The Plaza,
535 Kings Road,
Chelsea Harbour,
London SW10 0SZ

www.johnblakebooks.com

www.facebook.com/johnblakebooks 🇫
twitter.com/jblakebooks 🇪

First published in hardback in 2019

ISBN: 978 1 78946 062 9

British Library Cataloguing-in-Publication Data:

A catalogue record for this book is available from the British Library.

Design by www.envydesign.co.uk

Printed and bound in Great Britain by Clays Ltd, Elcograf S.p.A.

1 3 5 7 9 10 8 6 4 2

Papers used by John Blake Publishing are natural, recyclable products made
from wood grown in sustainable forests. The manufacturing processes
conform to the environmental regulations of the country of origin.

Every reasonable effort has been made to trace copyright-holders of material
reproduced in this book, but if any have been inadvertently overlooked the
publishers would be glad to hear from them.

John Blake Publishing is an imprint of Bonnier Books UK
www.bonnierbooks.co.uk

*For Christine, Stefan, Jenny
and David Jones*

CONTENTS

FOREWORD
BY
DENIS TAYLOR

When we met him for the first time, David Robert Jones was a fresh-faced lad, just turned eighteen, from a small terraced home in Plaistow Grove in Bromley, Kent.

In early May 1965, we – The Lower Third – were holding auditions at a club called La Discotheque in Wardour Street, in the West End of London, where we had a residency. Many musicians and singers turned up that day, but more for a jam session than for an audition, I think.

Among the gathered assortment of musicians were a couple of sax players and another drummer (which we didn't need at that time or even advertise for). In among all these people there were also singers (which we did advertise for) including Steve Marriott, later of Small Faces fame but at that time in a band called Marriott's Moments. He sang with us that afternoon, with others joining in, on an old rock-and-roll standard called 'Rip It Up'.

As the afternoon drifted on and people meandered away, among those who stayed was David, who had also brought along his alto sax and had apparently started out at the audition just playing that. He had probably been hanging around in the background, checking out the competition first, as you do. In fact, I hadn't noticed him at all until he asked to sing (he was still wearing the leather collar and clip he attached to his sax). We let him, of course, but partly because we were getting desperate by this time. Suffice to say that we were all impressed, not only with the range of his voice but also with his distinctive 'look'. Shortly after, and following a bit of thought and discussion, we unanimously decided that 'This is the guy.' In retrospect, I think we chose rather well!

Anyhow, a couple of days later we formally asked him to join us. I thought he was a good singer, but I have to admit I didn't think he would last the distance in the world of professional music. I wasn't sure if he was strong enough. But I thought we would be OK with him.

I was a lot older than he was, so I already knew what was in store for him. It wasn't going to be a bed of roses. All this, of course, before I knew he was already a minor star, or certainly known, due to his very long, blondish hair and appearance in a BBC2 TV interview.

A man with long hair in those days just wasn't the thing. It's difficult to imagine today, but it really was shocking and even upset many people back then. It certainly got him noticed, though.

He was new to songwriting at that time, so would experiment with ways to write songs. I remember strange times when he was at our flat in Pimlico, London (which certainly wasn't a posh area of town in 1965), and he would ask me to come into the bedroom with my guitar. We would sit on the bed and he would say, 'Just place your fingers anywhere on the fret and hit the strings.' So I would, and from that he would attempt to come up with a new song on his twelve-string, just from the random sounds it made. This didn't always work out and more often we would just laugh a lot and create daft songs from the 'noise' (as noise is all I can call it) that we made. This gave us a lot to chuckle about and possibly led to a few ideas for David to develop further. We had some great moments, all the same, but I don't know what the others must have been thinking in the other room, hearing the racket we made.

David and I used to go to Denmark Street almost daily. Next door to La Gioconda – our favourite café – was a small demo studio that producer Shel Talmy had allowed David to use at any time. So we were often dragged in there with no idea of what David was going to play on his acoustic after our impromptu 'noise' jams. The ideas seemed to change a bit by the time we got there. He must have been thinking about it during the journey to the studio. It was always interesting and I never knew what he would finally come up with. It was a nice little set-up where David and the rest of us could experiment with and listen back to the results. If the session worked, we might take away some demo discs.

About a month after David joined us, our drummer, Les, decided he was homesick and really missed his girlfriend in Ramsgate. David said it was no problem, he would find us another drummer straight away. He certainly did, and what a drummer! That was Phil Lancaster, who just happens to be the author of this book. What are the chances of that!

When Phil joined us, for some reason I was under the impression that he had previously been in a large Mexicano-type band, or something like that. I haven't a clue why I thought that or why that stayed with me!

There is no need for me to tell you any more, as Phil has a far better memory of these events than me.

From here on, he will tell you how it all went for us – the highs and the lows, and some of the bits in between. It's a great read.

Over to you, my friend…

Denis 'T-cup' Taylor
Lead Guitarist – The Lower Third

INTRODUCTION

So there we stood, like a face-off in a B-movie: all the characters fixed firm with their own agendas, looking for things to work out as we hoped they would. The equipment – our drums, guitars and amplifiers – was already partly unloaded in the car park outside the venue.

The scene in this particular movie has Ralph Horton, manager of David Bowie and The Lower Third, trying to face us down – me (Phil Lancaster, the drummer), lead guitarist Denis 'T-cup' Taylor and bassist Graham Rivens. Meanwhile, David is schoolboy-like, walking back and forth along the top of a hotel's boundary wall, listening as the exchange becomes more and more heated.

Of all the places this could have taken place, it probably didn't help that it was an important location for David – his old haunt, The Bromel Club in Bromley, just a short hop from his family home. Significantly, David has separated himself from us and remains clear of the argument, but

1

neither is he standing alongside Ralph. He wants the gig to go ahead, dearly wants it to go ahead. He can't openly agree with Ralph and alienate us completely, as that would aggravate the situation, but at the same time he is pissed off, upset that we three are making a stand at this venue – a hometown event.

It was an impasse. We weren't going to budge, but nor was Ralph. 'No pay, no play,' we stated. This was our mantra, agreed earlier that same afternoon at the Marquee when, once again, we left the venue without payment. Our courage to do the unthinkable, renege on a gig commitment, came as the last straw in our dealings with Ralph and the changing relationships between him, David and the rest of us.

'Well if you are not going to play, then I want the equipment I've paid for,' said Ralph.

'So that's it, then,' said Denis.

With that, Denis and Graham unloaded the remaining amps due to Ralph from the ambulance (our tour bus). We were finished as David Bowie and The Lower Third. I offered my hand to Dave as a parting gesture, but he declined it. He was torn between Ralph and us, or more likely between playing what was to him an important homecoming gig and ditching the Third.

Or was there more to it?

Was it actually the outcome they had been working towards all the time, or had it, rather inconveniently, occurred more prematurely than they had planned?

*

INTRODUCTION

The year 1965 was one of exciting change both for record companies and the fashion industry alike (particularly London-led fashion). The music that was coming through was certainly more individual, more idiosyncratic than at any time before. Legendary early sixties pioneers such as The Beatles and The Rolling Stones had already paved the way and had defiantly broken away from the conventional format that pop music had once had. Up to this point, British pop had been characterised by ballads and show tunes, older types of music that were beginning to sound dated to the new, younger generation (or 'baby boomers', as we post-war kids were labelled in the fifties). The UK may have taken its time to adapt, but it was now – or so it felt at the time – ripe for a damn good shake-up.

One particular group (for that's what 'bands' were called then) that I heard one day on the radio in Germany was like nothing I'd heard before. It was an epiphany. I immediately thought, 'That's it, that's the sound, that's what I want to do.' It was The Who, one of their early releases with Keith Moon thrashing hell out of his drums in a sort of manic free-form style against the tremendous energy of Pete Townshend's frantic guitar, John Entwistle's thumping bass and Roger Daltrey's urgent, rebellious vocals. I didn't know who they were at that point, but I still remember the amazing buzz it sent through me, which immediately made me want some of what they were doing. As soon as I heard it, I knew it was time to get back to London.

By this time, I was totally ready for a complete change of direction, having paid my dues gigging over the previous decade, mainly covering the hits of the day in various bands and styles. But I had my own ideas too, and an equal ambition to create something different. I just needed some like-minded musicians to work with.

This proved to be the start of a fascinating period of my life. I would meet David Jones and become a member of Davie Jones and The Lower Third – and life would never be quite the same after that.

I thought I would share my story.

Phil Lancaster
2018

CHAPTER 1

LITTLE DRUMMER
BOY

I was born in 1942 on a rather grey and misty afternoon on Boxing Day in Walthamstow, London E17. Not a bad place to arrive, although there was actually a war going on outside our front door. As it happened, I was lucky: it turned out to be a very artistic area. A number of famous visionaries and creative types associated with the district had already made an impact on the world. For example, Walthamstow had been the birthplace of William Morris, who came into the world 108 years earlier at nearby Elm House on Forest Road, opposite where Walthamstow fire station is situated today and approximately at the site where, aged fifteen, I got a job at the factory that took its place.

I grew up on Chingford Road, which junctions with Forest Road. On Forest Road is the Walthamstow Assembly Hall, where I would later play many times. Very near the Assembly Hall stands Walthamstow

College of Art, where Sir Peter Blake taught from 1961 to 1964. His students were pretty special too and included Vivian Stanshall, Ian Dury and Peter Greenaway. Ken Russell also attended. As a teenager, I went to evening art classes there for a while, but found nude geezers boring to draw, and only once did we get the more interesting female form to ponder on and submit to paper. So, while I was doing my own thing, many future highly creative luminaries were being fledged around the corner from my house. Vivian Stanshall and Peter Blake actually lived in Walthamstow too.

*

It seems that the traditional British art college is a rite of passage for budding musicians. I'm not thinking about my brief artistic sojourn here, but the aforementioned Ian Dury and Vivian Stanshall, who were both incredibly inventive, plus the likes of Keith Richards, John Lennon, Pete Townshend, Jimmy Page and, of course, he who shall be referred to heavily in this book: our Dave.

Other notables born in Walthamstow include Geoffrey Wellum DFC – Battle of Britain ace fighter pilot (his compelling memoir *First Light* has you strapped in his Spitfire alongside him), plus author and artist Robert Barltrop. The latter was actually a cousin of mine and something of an early mentor, giving me a combination of philosophical works and other serious material to read and engage with. He wrote books about Jack London, cockney English, and an autobiographical account of growing up in north-east London between the wars.

Other important local musical links include Spider From Mars/key Bowie collaborator Mick Ronson, who often stayed at his sister's home in Walthamstow. And, of course, there was the boy band E17. . .

*

My earliest memory of being on the stage is when I was five years old. My maternal grandfather, David Pope (an entertainer himself), was a resident performer at a venue known as the Buxton Club, which was sited just off Walthamstow High Street. I remember being passed across by my father, Wally, and then over the heads of other punters, to be placed on the stage, where I sang a popular song of the day called 'Open The Door, Richard'. The song was initially an old black vaudeville number, recorded by The Three Flames in 1947 and also by saxophonist Jack McVea and His All Stars, who had a big hit with it at around this time.

My grandfather was a clog dancer and comedian whose stage name was Larry Norman. I still have his greasepaint and clogs, and I would wear his sequinned velvet stage costume to play-act in from time to time, during my teenage years. I would have worn it with the Lower Third if we had changed our name to The Toys, as was once suggested! It wouldn't have raised an eyebrow amongst the ever-changing styles and costumes Dave was eventually to adopt.

Before my Buxton Club stage debut, my family and I, like thousands of others, had been regularly plagued by Hitler's V2 rocket menace while huddled inside our intimately sized Anderson shelter. Our back garden, where this corrugated outhouse stood, was equally bijou.

My memories of these bleak Anderson shelter nights are few, though I remember it being very dark and lit by candles. It was so small that, with all the adults resting inside, we were hemmed in very tightly. When our shelter became flooded, we shared next door's, which is probably why I remember us as being so crowded in. I was too young to be scared and I can't actually remember any explosions, so I must have slept through most of World War II.

Many years later I was to gig at the Buxton with a guitarist from a band called The Outlaws, an outfit who were also known as Mike Berry and The Outlaws. We thought it best not to include 'Open The Door, Richard' in our set this time, however.

One other funny memory I have of the Buxton is as a sixteen-year-old, when I was with a band that backed a duo drag act for part of the show. As one of the performers took a bow and was leaving the stage he/she turned around, smiled, ran his fingers through my hair and said, 'Hello, curly locks.' As a reasonably naive teenager, I suppose something like that could have been a bit disconcerting, but I just remember being flattered. By the way, I've still got my curly locks, though admittedly I'm slightly greyer today.

*

My passion for showing off (a running theme in this book) picked up again when I was around eleven years old and took up ventriloquism. I was a big fan of Peter Brough and Archie Andrews.

Brough had made his name as a ventriloquist on BBC radio starting in 1944, and introduced his slightly frightening-looking Archie Andrews character in 1950 with his own dedicated series called *Educating Archie*. It sounds silly today – a popular ventriloquist with his own radio show – and I can clearly hear you asking 'How would anyone know whether he moved his lips or not?' Of course, these shows were all recorded in front of a live audience and it was their appreciative response that made he and Archie all the more believable. It really seemed to work and I loved it. Also, you have to bear in mind that radio back then was our form of television. We used to make up our own pictures with pure imagination.

By 1956, Archie Andrews had his own TV show and, although the screens were very small then, you could easily see that Brough was a damn good ventriloquist.

Anyway, I wanted to be Walthamstow's very own Peter Brough and worked hard at it, actually getting to a level where I could speak without moving my lips nearly as well as a pro, certainly well enough to make my ventriloquist dummy appear to be the one who was actually talking. At around the same time, I also started to develop an escapology act, already with one eye on becoming a consummate all-rounder.

My mother, an equally consummate seamstress, made the little fella a corduroy suit and a neat shirt and tie, so he really looked the part. I still have this little chap, and years later a lady in my life completely freaked when I introduced her to my Archie. Of course, guys, little Archie isn't something you can whip out on a first date!

Starting out with this lark as a solo performer, I put on a show for the neighbourhood kids at my parents' house, with all the chairs we could muster set in rows to create the auditorium. Oh dear. It all ended in tears (for me) when one kid accepted my challenge to break out of being bound and padlocked. I had started this part of my act by example, by deftly picking the padlock that was restraining me with the aid of a secreted old nail. I pretended to free myself with a flurry of dramatic gestures, then jumped free of my restraints to smugly accept the applause from my small but appreciative young audience.

Then I repeated this trick on my friend, whom I fully expected to struggle and eventually give in and ask to be released. What I hadn't banked on was my friend's no-nonsense approach to the problem. With complete nonchalance he just snapped away the plastic bindings and instantly released himself, to even greater applause.

Boo-hoo. That was my escapology act firmly put in its place.

Actually, I can't have been that bad, as I regularly performed my whole act at Winns Avenue junior school in Walthamstow. In fact, I have a copy of the school magazine, called *The Acorn*, which includes a short article by yours truly about ventriloquism. The editor's note explains how, at age eleven, I'd already given shows in school. Indeed, with the help of my friend Jack White I formed a troupe of performers and craftily got out of lessons by putting on shows for different classes at my school. I also did magic tricks as well as the escapology (the latter was added after seeing Tony Curtis in the film *Houdini*), and hand and string puppetry. Jack played guitar and the other kids played instruments of one sort or another. What a precocious little sod, I hear you say. But no, in reality I was quite shy and just wanted to entertain; on stage I could literally be someone else and hide behind that. Actually, that way of thinking reminds me of a guy I would meet a few years after I turned pro as a drummer. He had a very similar approach to performing in public and went on to do very, very well for himself. I wonder who that could be?

*

Unbelievably, our headmistress advised all under her domain not to enter the eleven-plus. Some belief in us that showed. Of course, if you saw the original spelling of the book you are currently reading (before spellcheck zapped it), you would probably not blame her. And, if you saw my old school books (I still have some of them) the writing looks like the trail of a spider that has climbed out of an inkwell and tried to form words at my behest. Oh well, I suppose that rests her case.

But in spite of all of that, what my creative chums and I achieved – with various degrees of success and recognition – was to get out of the stereotyped mould we were poured into and make a real stab at things. My good pal Denis Payton – I actually went to three different schools with him – was told by one teacher he would never get anywhere playing the saxophone. What did he know, anyway? Particularly as Denis went on to become one of the founder members of one of the UK's most successful sixties groups, The Dave Clark Five.

Walthamstow was also well equipped to supply great live music, including regular visits by the top music idols of the fifties and sixties. The Granada Cinema, for example, conveniently doubled as a venue for concerts and was one of the main destinations for top music acts, such as The Beatles and the Stones. It also often featured major American bands and artists, such as Count Basie and Duke Ellington. Buddy Holly and Roy Orbison also appeared at the Granada. I played there regularly with one of my early bands, The Blue Dukes – but before that I had to learn to play.

*

It all started out very innocently at first, as these interests often do. I began playing drums at the age of fourteen, at the behest of a school friend with terrific motivational and cajoling qualities. The friend was (and is) Jack White, who himself was full of natural creative talent and wanted his mates to take up instruments and form a band. I was already starstruck by the likes of Eddie Calvert – a trumpet player of note – and Tommy Steele, the big name of the time and Britain's first bona fide pop star. I saw myself as a front man of some kind, just like one of those fifties stars. Well, we can all dream.

Anyway Jack, with his immense powers of persuasion, got me on to and into drumming. Quite frankly, I was blown away by any skill in the field of music, though drumming in particular thrilled me when performers like Gene Krupa let loose. So Jack got his way and I took up the instrument.

My first 'kit', if you could call it that, would probably have put most sensible people off practising music for life. But I had to begin somewhere. With barely a few old pennies to rub together we had to be somewhat creative, so I started off with an arrangement of Oxo tins on my dad's stepladder. Actually, it wasn't unusual to see makeshift instruments of all types at the time, like washboards and tea-chest bases etc. My set-up was kind of Pop Art style before Pop Art; Mr Warhol and company would have been proud of me.

Pretty soon we got hold of a miniature drum kit, but it arrived without skins. No problem! Not to the highly inventive, practical Jack – 'We'll use old shirt material,' he declared when he saw my disappointment. 'Then we'll starch it to stiffen it up.' And so we did just that and it kind of worked. Meanwhile, Jack got on with learning to play the trumpet (my previous desire).

We also encouraged, nagged and pleaded my mate (but Jack's inseparable pal – they might as well have been twins) Denis Payton to get an instrument. Denis's dad was the doorman at the Savoy Hotel in London, so maybe they had a couple of bob more than my family. It was also Denis's father who drove us up to Selmer's music store in Charing Cross Road to buy Denis a clarinet. Not a bad move on his father's part, as Denis eventually swapped the clarinet for a tenor saxophone before joining The Dave Clark Five. Very sadly, Denis passed away in 2006. Our little band of brothers still misses him greatly.

Denis had an older neighbour who played the drums well. One time, when he was changing a car tyre at the kerb, he knocked out a terrific rhythm on the tyre and wheel rim. It enthralled me. I watched on, wishing I could play like that. It made me want to practise all the more.

Although Jack was the driving force in us taking up these instruments, I suppose it was always meant to be. We were a group of like-minded boys who were all just itching to do 'something' in music and Jack was the first out of the blocks. He became our catalyst.

Another pal (and dear friend still to this day) who was ripe and needed no encouragement from Jack or anyone else to take up an instrument was John Urquhart. John had been enamoured by my mum's ukulele skills and she readily taught him to play (she also played the piano – I had quite a talented mum). Thinking about it now, a lot of my passion for music and performance must have come from both my mother and grandfather, but I never consciously had this in mind. John's tuition in the ukulele seemed a natural path to the guitar, which he eventually excelled in. It later brought him much success in the sixties band Nero and The Gladiators, who at one time even supported The Beatles at the Cavern (and whose chart successes included 'In The Hall Of The Mountain King'). We were all Walthamstow boys and attended school together: William McGuffie Secondary Modern – locally referred to as William McScruffy, perhaps due to the right load of herberts like us that attended the place.

*

I have to admit that in our school music lessons I was not academically gifted, whereas my friend Denis definitely was. I remember him sitting opposite me in the next aisle responding to a task that we had been set. While I was struggling with the whole concept, he was busily and expertly filling in the staves on the page of his manuscript book, complete with detailed notation. I remember being somewhat in awe of Den's effortless musical aptitude.

In fact, it is easy to see where we were destined to end up when looking back at my school notebooks, which we made in craft lessons at the time. There are pages and pages of drawings of musical instruments, made by me and my mates, our dreams and desires already starting to show through.

Funnily enough, many of these pages are a mixture of *Goon Show* quotes and character drawings, plus drum kits, saxophones and guitars. (The radio helping to create those pictures, again.)

As was the norm, we all left school at the age of fifteen, mostly destined for factory work, although a few of us harboured more long-term, glamorous ideas. As Denis Payton once commented, many years later, 'We were just thought of as factory fodder.' But that wasn't our dream, certainly not for my band mates and I. Nothing could hold back our creativity and we continued on our path regardless. An early example of us actually bringing our old school-book drawings to life would be our first set-up, The Renegades – our very own skiffle group, no less. This was our first step to glory.

The Renegades included Jack White, Denis Payton and John Urquhart on guitars and yours truly on drums. We felt like kings, even though we could still barely play our instruments. We tried to dress the part too, though there was no set standard skiffle attire at the time, apart from a cowboy-like neck scarf and possibly a checked shirt and jeans. The main thing was that you just had to look a bit different, and we didn't find that too hard to achieve.

Our moment of glory (well, almost) came within weeks of forming, when we entered a prestigious local skiffle competition at Walthamstow's Granada Cinema. We didn't win but it was an excellent experience, and we got our first real taste of performing to a large audience. We got a huge buzz – it was intoxicating. I've always enjoyed showing off and the best place to do that, in my humble experience, is undoubtedly in a band.

Actually, we had a good excuse for not winning that day, as I had caught my hand in the car door on the way to the gig, so I can claim we were at a big disadvantage. My squashed fingers were also one of the main reasons

I wouldn't forget that show in a hurry. I was sure I had cracked a bone or two. It hurt for weeks.

The experience also told us that we had a way to go, that there were a lot of great musicians out there and we had to up our game if we were going to get anywhere. All four of us were like-minded and no doubt this also drove each of us further, to practise more and play the best we could. We studied our instruments and practised relentlessly until we felt we were good enough to hire ourselves out for functions. That was our goal, and we actually got there quite quickly.

From The Renegades we went on to form a number of other groups, quickly moving on from the basic skiffle sound we had cut our teeth on to other styles. These new outfits were far more adventurous and included bands such as The Phil Lancaster Quintet and Les Heath and His Music (Les Heath being yet another musically inclined William McGuffie classmate). They proved a great learning curve for me, particularly as we gained more assurance in our abilities. In fact, we were soon playing – with some confidence – popular swing and jazz numbers. We sounded pretty good, too. I know we did because my parents, whose house we sometimes used to practise in, could hear us getting better week-on-week and would comment on it.

We quickly progressed and started to pick up the odd local gig. It was at this point that my father, who was obviously convinced we were now up to it, arranged our most prestigious gig to date. He belonged to the Walthamstow council social club (like my grandfather, he was also a very funny comedian) and managed to get us an engagement to play at their annual dance. That wasn't the best of it either, as we were to share the billing with Sid Phillips and his band, which was quite a step-up for a group of local herberts.

Phillips was definitely 'big time' and the booking proved a significant early highlight for us, helping to spread the word locally about the band's abilities. Going down well that night was a great relief for all of us. I certainly didn't want to let my dad down and neither did any of my band mates.

This young band of fledgling musicians continued in various forms and style combinations into the early sixties. From our humble beginnings as an amateur skiffle combo, we progressed – through swing and jazz – to become a semi-professional dance band, mostly playing weddings. Then we became an early rock band: John Urquhart, Denis Payton and myself played as a locally respected outfit called The Blue Dukes (by this time I had proper drums, by the way).

The Blue Dukes were an established group with a very good reputation. They were particularly well known in north London, and we were soon playing residencies such as the 59 Club in Yorkton Street, Hackney, sharing bookings with groups such as Neil Christian and The Crusaders, featuring Jimmy Page on lead guitar (he often swapped riffs with John, our lead).

I remember when Dave Clark was on the trail trying to lure Denis for his new group. He brought Mike Smith into The Blue Posts pub in Soho to meet us and introduced me to Mike, with some reverence I remember, as a member of The Blue Dukes. I was later to play with The Dave Clark Five myself, depping for Dave when he was ill (but not too ill to stop him giving me a pep talk on the phone before the gig). Ever attending to business, was Dave. In fact, I apparently blotted my copybook with Dave Clark before I really got started.

The night I stepped in was during the big freeze of early 1963. We had gathered earlier in the day, Denis and myself going to Mike Smith's home. I remember seeing, for the first time, a TV remote control, albeit one connected to the TV by a wire. Mike's dad was using it.

We all set off for the Locarno, Basildon, in Dave Clark's Ford Zephyr Zodiac. The roads were atrocious and we were skidding and sliding all over the Southend Road; it was pretty scary at times. We eventually got there in one piece and the performance went well, the rest of the band actually commenting on how good it was going during the gig. I felt like royalty for a night, as Dave was the group's main man and central to proceedings and here I was sat in his seat, though this was just before their first No.1 single.

The condition of the roads had got so bad that we got the train home. I was due to play with them again the next night but declined, having been scared out of my wits during the previous night's ride. Later, Den told me I'd lost an opportunity by letting them down, as Dave had been considering offering me the drum seat so that he could get up front with the others. Oh well, I would probably have got bored doing so many Ed Sullivan TV shows.

*

The Blue Dukes turned out to be an important group for all concerned, and our good reputation brought in the bookings, which came in from all around the capital, but mostly in our east London neck of the woods. One of our regulars was a very well-known gig on the circuit at Leyton

Baths. This was a swimming pool that was covered over for Saturday night dances (very similar to the one in the film *It's A Wonderful Life*).

At Leyton Baths we played alongside quite a few quality acts, some high in the charts at the time, such as Emil Ford and The Checkmates, who had a big hit with 'What Do You Want To Make Those Eyes At Me For?' On another night, we shared billing with singer Jimmy Justice (real name James Little). He did quite well and enjoyed a couple of UK Top 10 singles, including 'When My Little Girl Is Smiling', but by this time he had also become a significant star in Sweden and wasn't over here enough to capitalise on his growing success. Today you would rely on a video to help promote a record while you are working elsewhere, but video promos hadn't been invented back then, and even if they had been there wasn't a half-decent music programme on TV to feature them. We only just had a second national TV channel to watch in the UK (ITV, launched in 1955), let alone a dedicated twenty-four-hour music channel such as MTV.

In the dressing room that night, Jimmy Justice asked me what stage shirt he should wear out of the two different brightly coloured, sparkling, puffed-sleeved jobs lying nearby. He went with my choice. That's my main memory of Jimmy, though I do remember he had a good voice and stage presence.

The first guy (out of three) to occupy The Blue Dukes' drum seat was Dave Groves. Dave went on to tour with Jimmy Justice and had some good stories to tell.

Another hit band we worked with was Mike Berry and The Outlaws. That was cool because their drummer was Don Groom, who had been The Blue Dukes' second drummer and had left to join The Outlaws (I was the third and last drummer), so there was a bit of a reunion that night.

Playing with Geno Washington and The Ram Jam Band was especially good at the Baths. There were some bands, like Geno's, that I really enjoyed watching from the wings. Their drummer was a friendly guy who tipped me off to putting a sticking plaster on the bass-drum skin where the beater hits to provide extra protection.

Another Leyton Baths gig brought us into contact with singer Michael Cox, who was a surprise guest (both for us and the audience), suddenly appearing on stage midway through our set. As he had a hit at the time – a song called 'Angela Jones' – the audience were naturally excited to see him and we duly backed him as if we had rehearsed it.

There probably was some talk about this before the gig, but I can't remember that, though I do recall his guitarist was none other than Big Jim Sullivan. Big Jim arrived with him and assumed the role of lead guitarist for this impromptu performance, plugging into our lead guitarist John Urquhart's amp. John, no mean guitarist himself, was visibly put out as he stood to one side. But we did the number.

Afterwards, to his credit, Big Jim apologised to John and suggested they have a guitarists' get-together in the near future, and partake in some wacky backy at the same time. I'm pretty sure this never happened, unless the hash later did John's memory of it all. I've read that Big Jim also worked with David Bowie on Dave's first album – but then, Jim worked with everyone, he was a prolific and very much sought-after talent.

Yet another very cool hit-making band we shared billing

with around that time was Brian Poole and The Tremeloes. We played with them at Barking Town Hall, which happened to be Brian Poole's hometown (east London boys, like us). Like The Beatles, Brian and the Trems had covered and also had a hit with the Isley Brothers song 'Twist And Shout', theirs making No.4 in the UK and selling a truckload of records at the same time. But they really hit the jackpot in September '63 when their single 'Do You Love Me' knocked The Beatles' 'She Loves You' off of the No.1 slot. No mean feat. They had a lot more hits after this too. It's also worth noting that they had auditioned for Decca, their label, at the same time as The Beatles, and the Trems won out. The Beatles/Decca audition story is now legendary, of course.

Working alongside all these bands was not only great fun, it was also an essential learning experience. Everyone was keeping an eye on what everyone else was doing. Drumming may seem like a fairly regimented process, but everyone has a style and technique of their own and there are always new tricks and tips to pick up. I've no doubt that each musician in our group used to check out our counterparts in the other bands, as I did, to see what they were up to and what techniques we could possibly steal for our own use. Later on, Dave made no secret of stealing from everyone who inspired him. The main difference with Dave doing something so brazen was that he was so gifted himself that his talent overshadowed everything else. But basically everyone does it and that's how we learn and discover our own style.

*

During my semi-pro years in the very early sixties, my mates and I were huge fans of Georgie Fame and The Blue

Flames. We would catch Georgie whenever we could, particularly when he was booked at the Manor House Pub in north London, which was one of our favourite hang-outs and was a comfortable place to see acts.

I loved the material Georgie Fame did, which included a lot of Mose Allison and jazz-based stuff. During the interval at one of these gigs, two of us were at the bar getting a drink and found ourselves standing right next to the sax player from The Blue Flames. Barry, my bandmate, started talking to him, and he was friendly enough and happy to chat so I joined in.

During the conversation I discovered that they were looking for a drummer. Being a fan of the band, I was quite aware of the chopping and changing of drummers in The Blue Flames' set-up. It was quite intriguing, and we all wondered why it was still going on. That aside, I said I would definitely be interested in the job if it was available and was amazed when the guy encouragingly said, 'Yeah, go and have a word with Clive,' and nodded in the direction of this chap stood just along the bar behind me.

Just as I turned around I could see Georgie Fame himself close by, whose real name I quickly realised was not Georgie at all, but Clive. So I approached him, said hello, and repeated the conversation I just had with his sax player.

He was very friendly and explained a little about the drummers who had come and gone, and that they currently had Phil Seamen in the hot seat. This I knew. I also knew that Phil Seamen was a top-of-the-tree jazz drummer; he was someone I looked up to. I'd actually seen him play many times over the years. Under normal circumstances, there was no chance I could outmatch Phil, no way. But Phil, I discovered, was not staying with the band.

Georgie (who was given his memorable stage name – alongside the likes of Adam Faith, Billy Fury and Marty Wilde – by the legendary music impresario, Larry Parnes) offered me a Gauloises cigarette and as we lit up, told me to come along to audition for the job. I said I would, thanked him and left with a spring in my step to allow him to enjoy the rest of his break.

Boy, was I elated. I couldn't believe my luck.

The thought of being in the very band I had revered for so long was beyond my wildest dreams. I didn't get much sleep that night imagining what the future might bring. However, not long after I finally fell asleep I was suddenly disturbed by a terrible thought. I woke up in a cold sweat when it dawned on me. In my excitement I hadn't actually thought it through and actually asked him where or when the audition was set for. What a plonker! You couldn't make it up.

So that was it, no audition for me.

When I thought about it, I imagined that Clive had perhaps intimated that the audition would be announced in the music press. So, in some desperation, the following morning I went to see a pretty well-connected jazz musician friend who I thought might have his ear to the ground and know of this audition. He, seeing my fresh young face, decided to put me off going by suggesting the lifestyle wouldn't suit me. So that was that. I never did try out for Georgie Fame's band.

Not many months ago, I was chatting with Chris White, drummer with the excellent band Mother Earth. Chris is my mate Jack White's son. I helped Chris get started on the drums when he was a nipper, and he got pretty good on them too. Anyways, Chris has an amazing knowledge of the sixties music scene and we got talking about, among other things, The Blue Flames and my missed audition, etc.

'You know why they came to call themselves The Blue Flames, don't you?' said Chris. 'They used to light their farts in the van and it gave off a blue flame.'

Good enough, I thought. I could have lived with that, but I think the guy who warned me off over fifty years ago was really thinking about what else they lit up in the van after gigs.

*

Through all of my time with the Dukes, we were all just semi-pros, each holding down our regular day jobs. I was in an apprenticeship, making briar pipes, of all things, for a company called Hardcastle in Forest Road, Walthamstow. It was regular money, not too far from home, and I joined straight from school.

My journey thus far with The Blue Dukes was essentially my musical career from the age of fourteen until I was twenty-one. And it was shortly after my twenty-first birthday when my beloved drum teacher, Frank King, told me it was about time I turned fully professional. Putting this book together has started to bring back all kinds of happy memories for me, and Frank was certainly one of them. Funnily enough, I recently read an old Phil Collins interview and discovered that he too had studied with him. He revealed: 'I went back to Frank King when I was about seventeen. I was with him for a couple of years. I liked the way he taught. He taught a lot of people – Brian Bennett of The Shadows, Bobby Elliott of The Hollies and Bill Bruford [Yes] went to him for a while.'

I'm nearly ten years older than Phil Collins, so I'm not surprised I hadn't known of this connection, and have never met Phil (a great name for a drummer, by the way). But I did meet Brian Bennett once at Frank's when I arrived for a lesson, and I also met Bobby Elliott when I was with Frank at a BBC TV *Crackerjack* recording at Shepherds Bush Theatre. Bobby was a great drummer and it was really interesting to meet him. But Phil Collins's endorsement gives you an idea of the great esteem many, many professional drummers held Frank in, and I am delighted he is being remembered for the truly excellent teacher he was.

And so, when Frank turned to me after a lesson and told me I was now ready to go pro it was 'Wow', I really hadn't expected that at all. Frank was a smart guy and knew first-hand how tough the business actually was, but genuinely felt that I had reached the point where I could make a real go at it. It was a revelation. I was both gobsmacked and overjoyed – more than anything else that he thought I was actually good enough to move up to this new league.

If Frank thought I was ready to turn pro, then I really was, and it was all the assurance I needed.

CHAPTER TWO

GERMANY CALLING...

Frank, my sage drum teacher, had been a professional big-band drummer for many years; he was a super musician and very well respected by the fraternity. Not only was he encouraging me to progress, he quickly found me a job, six nights a week, at the Van Gogh bar, which was in the Latin Quarter in Rupert Street, Soho. To illustrate how long ago all this was – early 1964, to be exact – I was able to park my car directly outside the club all night, with no meters, restrictions or worries of any kind. It was virtually all night as well, as we started at 7pm and finished at 3am.

Playing at Van Gogh's was just the thing to help me get on in the business. Playing those long hours, night after night, gave me the opportunity to hone the techniques I had rehearsed every day for years on a practice pad. It was my entrée into the professional world of the musician, a venue where people such as Eric Burdon and Hilton

Valentine of The Animals would stop by for a listen and a friendly chat. It was a very good place to start out.

The three-piece group I'd joined at Van Gogh's played an odd combination of songs. For starters, Eddie – our leader (whose residency this was) – was a Jim Reeves fanatic, so he provided a much-honed Reeves repertoire, singing all the man's hits whilst also playing rhythm guitar. Ted, our lead guitarist, was an out-and-out rocker who alternated between Eddie's favoured 'Distant Drums' and 'I Love You Because', and his own preferred uptempo choices that included 'Roll Over Beethoven' and 'Johnny B. Goode'.

This band's kaleidoscopic musical catalogue didn't end there either, as Eddie was also an accomplished accordionist and would give our transient audience renditions of the day's standards, especially numbers suited to that particular instrument.

So, depending on what time of the night, or morning, you dropped into the Van Gogh bar, you may have discovered a Jim Reeves country band with Eddie gently explaining 'I Won't Forget You', or a Parisian trio featuring great flourishes of classical keyboard from Eddie, or a wildly rocking group led by Ted – replete with rockers' hairdo and Cuban heels, giving his all to 'Maybellene'.

By the time Charles Hawtrey (of *Carry On* films fame) arrived with his mother, quite regularly and always late in the hour, we would be playing at a more sedate pace, which Charles must have appreciated. As we completed each number (generally to a muted, slightly sozzled late-night audience who barely knew we were there), Charles would loudly instruct his elderly mum to 'Applaud mother, applaud.'

*

This bizarre juxtaposition of musical types followed me into my next professional job – or should I say, awaited me. It might have been that Ted simply had a wide interest in musical styles, as the next group he chose for me to work in was certainly unusual. More likely, it was the only group he could find that had a suitable vacancy – musicians' sources of work not always being plentiful, of course. Or was it that Ted simply had a mischievous sense of adventure?

In any event, Ted left The Eddie Ricardo Trio to find fame and fortune on the continent (as we used to call it pre-'Europe'), though my engagement at Van Gogh's continued with a new guitarist filling his shoes. This replacement had not long been in the lead guitar spot (two or three weeks at the most) when I received a letter from Ted inviting me to join him in his new band. Their drummer, it seemed, was returning to the UK. At the end of his invitation was a crafty postscript added as though the decision for me to up sticks and join him abroad had already been made: 'P.S. When you come over please bring my girlfriend Ruth with you. Thanks.'

I was suddenly faced with a big dilemma – not particularly about whether I should give up my job at Van Gogh's, but about Ted's offer conflicting with another that had just been confirmed.

A day or two previously I received an exciting invitation from an American group to join them as their token 'British' musician. Their only requirement for this job was that I had long hair. It was urgent too, as they informed me I was to appear with them within a couple of weeks on American telly. So they seemed to be going places and I was naturally seriously tempted. My mate John Urquhart had also applied, but a guitarist they didn't need.

The arrangement was that they were sending over my flight tickets but I was to bring my own drums. This would have been ironic, as my new Ludwig kit had only just been shipped across from America and had taken weeks to arrive. My drum teacher, Frank King, while pleased for about my chance to progress in the States, was also very sensible about such things and pointed out that, as there was no time for a work permit to be obtained I would be drawing attention to the fact that I intended to work by turning up at customs with my drum kit.

I rang the American group to say they would have to find me a kit, that I might not be let in the country if I tried to bring mine in, etc. Instead, they said they were going to call me 'Candy Man', as this would somehow get me around any work permit problems. Quite how it was going to work was never fully explained. This all sounded too dodgy and Frank finally said he didn't think it was a good idea taking this kind of risk. If the Musicians' Union found out, and in particular the American authorities, I could spoil my chances of ever working in the States again. Things were very strict in those days. An American musician could not work in the UK if reciprocal work was unavailable for a British artist, and vice versa. So, after much deliberation, I rang them and cried off.

Instead I decided to join Ted over the Channel.

As things turned out, I never did get the chance to work in the States again anyway. Had I done so, though, I wouldn't have answered David's *Melody Maker* advert in 1965 and would probably not be writing this book! Thank goodness for Ted's invitation, then.

*

I had never flown before. Nor had Ted's girlfriend Ruth, who was quite nervous about the idea. Work permits were still also required for the continent, but this could be arranged after you arrived and wasn't an issue. I was seen off at London Airport by my parents and duly jetted off to Paris, with Ruth, whom I had never met before.

As she was nervous I knew I had to play the confident guy on this, our first flight, but was as alarmed as she was when the stewardess seemed to lose her step walking through the cabin. A sudden loud, disconcerting thump accompanied her missteps and I thought for a split second that we might have copped it. My first flight, too! In fact, we had landed. We, in our ignorance, hadn't a clue that we had even left British airspace, let alone had already touched down on French soil. Outside it was pitch black, so we couldn't see what was going on either.

After reclaiming my drums and our luggage we successfully made our way though customs (just in case I needed it I had learned to say 'drums' in French) and looked out for Ted and the band who were to meet us. Sure enough, and much to our relief, they were there. After all the introductions and greetings were complete we set off to find the van. My first exciting continental adventure had now begun.

Group vans have quite an underplayed part in any band's story – more of that later. This vehicle was not exceptional in my memory, apart from its general refusal to move forward in anything but second gear. The band had now been on the road for a month or two and were well settled into their routine of batting around France and Germany from venue to venue.

We headed through the darkness, getting acquainted

with each other while we travelled. Of course, I knew Ted, who played lead guitar, and then there was Rick, who was quite an intellectual and played bass. Vicki, a Scot, was our singer. She had appeared on one of Carroll Levis's *Discovery* TV talent shows (Levis being the 1950s' equivalent of today's Simon Cowell).

Then there was the leader of our merry band: Jay Lapaka, a smoothly spoken, half American with half an American accent to go with it. His instrument of choice was the Hawaiian guitar. Hawaiian, or steel guitars, have featured in country music for a long time, but Jay didn't do country, he did *Hawaiian*. This again made for another interesting mixed musical repertoire.

As always, Ted was doing his own thing on stage. Just as with The Eddie Ricardo Trio, he had already staked his pitch in the group's programme with his own favourites, so we would segue from 'Roll Over Beethoven', with just a hint of hula behind Ted's Chuck Berry solos, to the full-blown familiar Hawaiian instrumental 'Love Song', led by Jay wearing his luau, eyes closed and totally in his element as he stylishly swept his steel bottleneck up and down the strings. He was a good musician too, but the cultural diversity of our performance must have, from time to time, been more than a little baffling for some of our continental audiences.

We emerged at dawn, via Belgium, into the snowy terrain of Germany and it was pretty cold in the van. The tour was playing 'the camps'. By that I mean the American military bases. US bases were par for the course for groups in those days and an awful lot of pop bands used to cover them. Initially I found these places fascinating. It was a revelation for me to see and experience the facilities these young American soldiers and airmen enjoyed. I mean, they were far from home but they were given as many home-from-home comforts as possible.

We were allowed different levels of access to these facilities, depending on the base. Usually the bars and restaurants were open to us, and the cinema and pool tables too, but the 'PX' stores (where cool imported US goods were sold) were out of bounds, all except for one base. This was not a problem, though, as we usually made a few friends amongst the GIs at each base and they would make our purchases. In this way I was able to get hold of a number of records directly imported from the States. Jay and I even bought the latest portable record players. We were in our element.

*

So we would perform during the evenings, and sometimes afternoons too, and on certain nights we would share the billing with a cabaret act. One of these touring acts was the fifties hit singer Vaughan Monroe. What particularly thrilled me about his band was that the drummer was the very same guy who had had an amazing drum battle with the legendary Gene Krupa in the 1956 film *The Benny Goodman Story*.

Unfortunately I soon went off him as, after I'd agreed to let him use my kit, he split the skin on the snare drum and then denied that it was his fault. This resulted in me having to take an unscheduled trip to Frankfurt to buy a new one.

We became friends with some of the guys on these bases. One of them, a great guy called Chuck, visited me in England when he was over and we kept in touch for years. Another guy, a master sergeant who ran one of the facilities we worked at, took us all home one evening to meet his ex-pat English wife. I was most impressed to be riding in his Chevy Impala, a great-looking car and favourite make of mine at the time. He and his wife, like most Americans I've met, were most hospitable and the drinks flowed endlessly.

I found a Paul Desmond album in our new friend's record collection that I'd never heard of in England, as we only had recordings of him playing with Dave Brubeck. As a great admirer of Desmond's work I was well away, listening to great jazz and drinking Canadian Club whisky like it was going out of fashion. The only thing was, I had no real experience of drinking whisky and was soon completely plastered.

When it was time to get us back to base, off we went in the Chevy with our host, who took his glass of Canadian Club with him and placed it directly on the dashboard. The suspension of these cars was so good that it sat there without spilling a drop throughout the journey. So much for drinking and driving.

I was just about keeling over and finally succumbed to shutting my eyelids but would stir, misty eyed, every so often and lift my head up to see what was happening. From the back seat I could see that we were driving in the complete darkness of the German countryside with a glass of whisky on the dash. Then my eyes dropped down to the speedo, which was alarmingly touching 90 mph. I just lay down across the back seat, closed my eyes and hoped for the best.

It's a night I'll never forget, as it was the first time I drank too much and spent the rest of the night wishing I hadn't, culminating with my head down the toilet. Never again, I thought. But then, don't we all say that...

Our accommodation varied from a hotel in France with paper-thin walls, where the bird next door hammered angrily on the wall at Rick's record of Bach's 'Toccata and Fugue' – played, admittedly, at full volume – to a hotel in Germany where the cockroaches were sent stampeding in all directions on the stairs when we returned each evening. Wildlife aside, this hotel fed us gorgeous hamburgers, some of the best I've ever had. On reflection though, it was probably for the best that we never saw the kitchens.

By far the best accommodation we had was during our final month in Germany, which was something of a compensation considering how it all ended there. We were allocated Junior Officer's quarters on a US base; splendid indeed, compared to the hostelries we had experienced thus far on our tour. It was in this accommodation that something important happened, which would ultimately lead me to meet David Bowie. In fact, I can remember the exact moment when I heard a new sound coming from the radio in the next room.

I had for a while known that I wanted to branch out musically and find a group where I could help develop a new musical expression – that is, 'let rip'. On the radio was a group I had never heard of previously but one I would later play alongside and spend some time with: The Who. It was an almost free-form type of playing that I loved and was something that I had also nurtured in the back of my mind for a while. This was a long way from the formulaic rock and pop of The Blue Dukes or the predictable, eclectic tunes of The Eddie Ricardo Trio. Today, we are all used to the early Who sound, so much so that I think it's important to remind everyone just how different they were at the time. Pete Townshend and his band were pioneering a new, more aggressive experimental sound that had never been attempted before. In so many ways they were far braver than most of the punk and new wave bands that followed them about ten or twelve years later (who thought they were the first to be radical).

I was just one of many thousands of professional, semi-pro and amateur early sixties musicians who were inspired by their work. Dave Jones from Bromley, who I would soon become acquainted with, had also picked up on their significance.

From the age of fourteen, my first love had been modern jazz and the most exciting part of it for me was its inventive nature, where creations grew before your ears, so to speak. Now, the music of The Who can in no way be called jazz, but it certainly seemed inventive and highly spontaneous to me when I heard it that first time in Germany in early 1965. That was what I wanted to be involved in. It was a revelation.

*

If I had learned anything thus far on the professional circuit, it was about money. One of the ongoing problems of bands, as my experiences were beginning to reveal, was the rather important matter of getting paid. The group I joined in France had a problem with this even before I arrived (as I would later discover). When we met a new agent, one who would handle the rest of the tour for us, we were assured that he would not let us down on payment. This was a great relief all round, particularly as we were all so far from home with no support network to hand. Sadly, he would let us down badly too, and towards the end he also owed us money.

Apparently he was also having problems with the management company we were under, who were based at the US base where our tour was ending. We were not a happy bunch, of course, but held out some hope that it might be resolved at that camp.

The accommodation we had at this US base wasn't for free either and we were presented with a bill when we were signing out. As we had been badly let down financially, we decided that our agent could swing. We unanimously decided that he should settle our bill and, calmly informing the accommodation official of this so as not to raise any suspicions, quickly made off in our van post haste, travelling swiftly through the night to the French coast and home.

Annoyingly, this backfired for one of us. Rick, our bass player, had decided to stay on in France to go travelling and had stored his equipment at the base. It seems the agent didn't even cough up for our accommodation bill in the end, so poor old Rick was nailed for it, with his amplifier and gear being held to ransom. I felt pretty bad about that, as it wasn't how we intended it to pan out. His story was later relayed to me via the grapevine and I sadly never saw Rick again to help resolve it.

Back in the UK we were all dropped off at our respective homes and bade each other farewell. Now I was out of work.

CHAPTER THREE

'MEET OUR SINGER, DAVIE JONES...'

I took a little time to settle back in the UK, see my girl-friend and get together with my mates, and then I started looking for work. A good place to find it in those days was the *Melody Maker* music paper, so I placed an ad and waited. I soon received a call from a friendly chap called Graham Rivens, who told me, 'Our drummer's leaving...'

'What kind of music do you do?' I asked.

'Oh, we do Kinks stuff and some of our own. We play loud!'

That sounded good to me.

The conversation with Graham was brief and the arrangement to meet up straightforward.

'Go to the Gioconda café and meet our singer, his name is Davie Jones. You can't miss him.'

So this, it seemed, wasn't going to be an audition but a meeting. Up to that call I had never heard of either

Davie Jones or The Lower Third, so I had no more than that to go on.

*

The Gioconda was, until not many years ago, located at No.8 Denmark Street, which is off London's busy Charing Cross Road. Denmark Street itself was known in the music business as 'Tin Pan Alley', as it was a street of music publishers, instrument shops and all manner of offices connected to the industry. The music publishers were generally based in Denmark Street and Charing Cross Road, with booking agents positioned all around there and Oxford Street. It was definitely one of the best places to pick up work.

Also in Denmark Street was a small recording studio called Regent Sounds, where some years before The Phil Lancaster Quartet had recorded selections from our repertoire on a demo record. The Rolling Stones famously used this studio in the early sixties and I was to record there many times again with my next group.

So I pitched up at the Gioconda to look out for Davie Jones, based on Graham's rather intriguing description of 'a skinny guy with bleached hair that you couldn't miss'. I can't have looked that hard when I walked in, as I remember quickly walking up to the counter at the far end of the café to ask if they knew of a bloke called Davie Jones.

'That's him on the phone by the door' came the reply; I'd walked right past him on the way in. Standing by the door was indeed a skinny bloke with bleached hair that had partly grown out, his darker roots giving a sort of 'half and half' look.

I went back to where Dave was standing, by now having

finished his call, and introduced myself. He was very friendly and enthusiastic. We found a table, ordered a cup of tea – and perhaps even egg and chips (later one of our mutual meals of choice) – and then settled down for a chat about music and all sorts of other interests, such as our mutual love of the work of Beat writer Jack Kerouac. Naturally, we talked about musical tastes, what kind of music we preferred to play, and so on. This led us on to Bob Dylan, who was a fairly new name in the UK at this point, so pretty hip to reference. As if to prove he knew exactly who Dylan was, Dave gave me an excellent Robert Zimmerman (Dylan's real name) impersonation right there and then, and he was very convincing.

This was indeed an audition, by conversation, and it went well. So well that I got the job without any formal musical audition whatsoever. This was actually quite unusual, but I'm positive (though I can't remember the exact detail) that I reassured Dave I could work intuitively and pick up what was needed for each number as it was called.

I instantly had a very good feeling about this guy, and it was only much later that I would discover that my haircut had played an important part in my selection too. So much for all my years of drum training.

Before I left for home, though, Dave gave me a potted history of what he and the band had done so far, that he hadn't been with them very long himself and so on. But he had an exciting plan of action already mapped out and seemed very together. It appeared to be exactly the sort of group I was looking for. Apparently, they too were into the expressive end of rock and pop and were keen to push that further. Dave had also even made a couple of records before joining The Lower Third – records that had actually been released by established labels, no less – with the promise of more to come. I couldn't have asked for more, it was just the sort of set-up that suited my own ambitions. I had landed on my feet and was more than happy.

Dave had been immediately engaging, had a great sense of humour and carried himself with a real sense of style. The guy 'had it' even then, though of course I hadn't a clue that he would become one of the most famous and recognised musicians in the world while we were tucking into our all-day Gioconda café breakfast specials.

That was it. The deal was done and not a musical note exchanged.

It was agreed that he and the band would pick me up from home for my first gig with Davie Jones and The Lower Third on the Saturday coming, when they were booked to play at Brighton.

The Lower Third had started life a few years earlier as a group in their native Margate, formed by school friends including Graham and Denis, Terry Bolton (who later became Denis's brother-in-law) and Robin Wyatt.

Cutting their teeth on the local circuit, the boys began to increase in confidence and, having built a solid local following, a couple of years later decided the time was right to try to 'make it' in London. This was all before they met up with Dave, though he too, they would later discover, had been on a similar musical journey.

But the band's dreams of instant London recognition were soon dampened when (not unlike the experiences many other performers and groups coming to the big city in search of work before and since) they realised that even sourcing basic, regular gigs was a major job in itself. As the work dried up, disillusionment set in. One by one the members retreated to Margate, leaving Graham Rivens (bass), Denis 'T-cup' Taylor (lead) and Les Mighall (drums) to find a replacement singer.

*

David Jones had turned up for the busy Lower Third audition with his squeaky little alto saxophone – not very trendy or impressive at the time – and a record (Denis remembers a lot of different musicians dropping by that day). Also attending was Steve Marriott – which later partly explained David turning to me at a venue one day and saying, 'He's a mate of mine,' while nodding towards a foyer poster advertising Steve and his new band, The Small Faces.

As hinted above, it's not widely known that Dave had rather wisely brought a copy of 'Liza Jane' with him to the audition, no doubt slipping in that he was now under contract with another label (I guess he didn't bring the more recent single he made with The Manish Boys as he wasn't individually credited on that). Perhaps flashing the single explains why Dave got the job instead of Steve Marriott, or anyone else who turned up that day. That said, Den is adamant that Dave was clearly the most suited to them at the audition.

Historically, of course, everything worked out just fine, particularly for David in the long run, and for Steve too, as he immediately went on to form The Small Faces and raced well ahead of the pack in the success stakes. In fact, it was within a week or so of this Lower Third audition that Steve met Ronnie Lane at the J60 Music Bar in Manor Park, where Steve had a Saturday job, not far from his parents' home in Strone Road. Just a few months after that meeting, The Small Faces had formed, rehearsed, found a manager (Don Arden) and signed a record deal with Decca. By September '65, they had a Top 20 single, 'Whatcha Gonna Do About It?' and were up and running.

Shortly after Dave joined the band (within a month, in fact) the Third's drummer Les departed, and that's when I was drafted in. By this time, however, Dave had already worked some of his cuckoo-like magic on the boys and The Lower Third had become 'Davie Jones and The Lower Third', complete with little blue stickers showing caricature sketches of the group drawn by Dave, to prove it.

So Saturday came and David, Denis and Graham turned up at my parents' house in Walthamstow – my first meeting with the complete band. They arrived in the new group van, which was an ex-London County Council ambulance, still emblazoned with its sign above the windscreen and the bell on the front (illegal, of course, and something that would get us pulled over more than once by the police in the coming months). It had only been purchased that day, so this was the vehicle's maiden voyage, so to speak.

Graham's dad, a publican, had stumped up the money for this lovely vehicle, though he did expect to be repaid at some future date. Amazing what our parents used to do for us in those days. In my case, it was putting up with my continual practising and the house being the venue for various rehearsals and auditions.

The band's previous vehicle, an even older Atlas van, had recently given up the ghost just outside York on the Tadcaster Road following an appearance nearby, stranding Dave and the boys. Getting stuck like that was an occupational hazard in this game and if you let it get you down you would go crazy.

*

My mum's front room played host to many such future noteworthies, including guitarist Alan Parker, later of Blue Mink (and Frank Sinatra recording sessions) and Tony Rivers, later of Harmony Grass and also Cliff Richard's vocal arranger and back-up singer for many years. I was later to record a demo at Regent Sounds with Dave of a song he wrote with Tony Rivers in mind. Sorry, but I can't remember the name of that particular song now, or where the demo went. I wish I'd kept a diary...

Alan Parker came to my mum and dad's house to audition as a second guitarist for The Blue Dukes. His father brought him from where they lived in Leyton (or was it Leytonstone?). But on meeting us it was figured (maybe by his dad) that, at sixteen years old, he was too young for the band. He was only about eighteen months younger than me, but the Dukes' average ages would have been eighteen-and-a-half years old. What a loss to The Blue Dukes. Even then, we could immediately tell he possessed a great talent.

Before moving on from Alan Parker, it's worth mentioning some of his achievements, including how he too got to know and work with David Jones (or Bowie as he would be by then) – once with other Blue Mink session musicians on a rare single called 'Holy Holy', and later as a session guitarist on Dave's amazing *Diamond Dogs* LP. Alan plays the famous guitar riff on 'Rebel Rebel', among other important contributions to that album.

Although he sadly didn't become a Blue Duke in the

end, Alan's above-average ability gained him a place at the Royal Academy of Music. A great achievement in itself, of course, but even more so when you consider that his teacher turned out to be Julian Bream (Elton John would also develop his prodigious skills at the Royal Academy a couple of years after Alan was there). As well as some important Bowie recordings, Alan can be heard on many hundreds of other sessions. Some of most famous were for Donovan's 'Hurdy Gurdy Man', The Walker Brothers' 'No Regrets', Blue Mink hits such as 'Melting Pot', 'Banner Man' and 'Randy', and the *Top Of The Pops* 'Whole Lotta Love' main theme by CCS, as well as hundreds of TV and film scores (the theme to BBC's popular *Coast* documentary is also Alan's work).

So the boy done good – and once played guitar in my mum's front room!

*

The Lower Third's ambulance has since taken on legendary status and is something I'm often asked about. You will be hearing a lot of stories about it in this book, but I'll provide an overview of it to get you acquainted.

It wasn't the most comfy ride in the world, believe me, but it managed to transport us from A to Z. Most of the time. At this point it still had its seats in a row along each side. There was no space for a stretcher, so I guess this was for transporting the walking wounded rather than dealing with horizontal ones, or taking patients back home from hospital. Later on, Graham did an amazing job converting it into a mobile home for the band.

The boys came in and met my parents, Wally and Norah, and I could feel an immediate friendly camaraderie developing. We lived in a typical terraced house at 70 Chingford Road (very similar looking to David's Bromley home, in fact).

All three guys were outgoing and we seemed to hit it off right away, this also being my first meeting with Denis and Graham. My parents, who were used to having a house that resembled Piccadilly Circus, with my mates and musicians coming and going at all hours, were pleased to meet my new associates. Dave immediately made himself comfortable, sprawling out in one of the fireside chairs with legs outstretched. Conversation flowed while we all consumed a pot of tea, and at one point Dave said to Graham, 'I'll introduce you to Jack Kerouac,' meaning his writings.

Then came time for us to get on the road (that's the Kerouac influence again) and we left the house and loaded my gear into the ambulance. I can still picture my mum and dad standing at the front door to see us off. Dave stood at the kerb, not far from my mum and, with his legs firmly apart, gave her a hearty theatrical wave – like a departing mariner would do from a distance towards family and friends waving back on a quayside. I knew then I would have a laugh in this group.

I was buzzing with excitement and, I'm sure, with some anticipation. It certainly wasn't the usual thing to start in a new band without any rehearsals, but that's how it was. Bear in mind, however, I was very used to playing in 'scratch' bands for one-off events, often without knowing any of the other musicians, so playing in this way wasn't completely alien to me. The only time I would get a feel of what was needed was in conversation with David during the journey and at a brief soundcheck at the venue, which turned out to be the Starlight Rooms, a trendy music venue in Brighton. Why it was called the Starlight? I'm not sure, as it was a rather damp, claustrophobic hotel basement that offered no chance of daylight, let alone sky.

All I can remember of that night is that the show went well, especially as we'd had no actual rehearsal. It was probably even more of an achievement considering some of the songs were Dave's own compositions, not instantly recognisable chart hits. The majority of the material we performed that night had never been heard by me before, I just responded to quick directions given to me either by Dave or Graham before each song to create the right tempo and adjust to the overall feel and phrasing and quirky chord changes. If I was lucky, Graham and Denis would start a number with an intro. This would then give me an insight into what was coming and I could immediately find my feet. If we were all counted in together, the count would provide me the tempo and the rest I would create during the first few bars as I picked up what that song required.

It might seem a bit strange to many of you reading this, wondering how musicians can work in this way, but many just can. I was very lucky to be very intuitive in this way, which is why I was able to keep myself busy in the business for many years playing in numerous 'scratch' bands.

When necessary, David would look at me and use his hand to create the beat, baton style, to set the tempo. The rest of the night is a blur, though I've no doubt Dave introduced me to the packed audience as the band's 'new boy'. In any case, it was a good one to get under my belt.

As time went by, of course, it would fall to me to set the tempo (by tapping my drumsticks together above my head and calling out, 'One, two, three, four…') once David had announced what number he had decided to do next. We were soon working together like a well-oiled machine.

While we were setting up, Dave told me he was glad to have another Londoner in the group. I think he must have felt outnumbered by the original three Kentish blokes. I later learned that he had previously been in another band, even larger in number, called The Manish Boys, who had also hailed from Kent.

On that first trip to Brighton our seating arrangements, which remained the same thereafter, were: Graham driving, Denis – his old Margate mucker – next to him, and Dave and I plus all the equipment in the passenger seats in the back. The driving cab of the ambulance was partitioned off at this time, but with a sliding glass window to communicate through. (Graham picked up the nickname 'Death' at some point, though none of us could work out exactly why that was – he himself surmised that it might have had something to do with his mad driving.) He also wore a cool military-style peaked cap offstage a lot of the time. This, coupled with the 'Ambulance' insignia, made us look even more like a working emergency vehicle. No wonder the police got so hacked off and pulled us over regularly.

On one occasion, a particularly zealous motorcycle cop stopped us. He wouldn't allow us to move until we had fully disabled the bell and covered up the 'Ambulance' writing. This we fixed as soon as he let us go and we had put a bit of distance between him and us. Bear in mind, though, this signage could be particularly useful if we got caught up in traffic and were late getting to a venue. We even rang the bell when we had to. Very naughty, I know, but very effective.

Which reminds me of another joke Dave and I particularly enjoyed when the chance offered itself in central London, or any busy town. If Denis and Graham spotted a busy bus queue in the distance they would alert us so that, as Graham pulled up next to the queue, either Dave or I would be ready to drape an arm out of one of the vehicle's sliding, smoked windows. At this point we would start moaning loudly for a few seconds to make sure our audience had taken note before the other would then snatch the arm in and quickly slam shut the window. Graham would then casually pull away as if nothing had happened. Agreed, simple things please simple minds, but it used to make our day a little more enjoyable.

*

I was a bit curious about the band's name and wanted to know about its origins, so Denis gave me a potted history during one of our early trips. He told me they had known each other since school, that the 'Lower Third' was a reference to schooldays and that their original name had included a deliberate Charles Dickens link – Oliver Twist and The Lower Third. Dickens had spent many years in the Thanet area, particularly at Fort House in Broadstairs, which was renamed Bleak House shortly after his death and still stands. Thanet is also the most easterly tip of the UK.

Over time, I would winkle out some of Dave's musical history too, though he wasn't always the easiest person to get a straight answer from. He always retained an area of mystery about himself and that, I think, is one of the reasons people find him so fascinating today.

This was still the 'getting to know you' stage when maybe we wanted to impress each other. Anyway, Dave was full of gossip about Mick Jagger and also David Bailey. Actually, Dave had been rubbing shoulders with quite a few people who had made it in the industry by then. This was demonstrated later when he asked me to pull my car over in Denmark Street and wind down the window so he could call over Ray Davies, whom he spotted walking towards us. I believe they had previously been on the same tour together and Ray seemed friendly enough and told us what he was up to.

*

During the time I knew Dave well I would sometimes hear stories, or the shared experiences, of his time in earlier bands. In fact, Dave was quite proud of telling me about the group he had been in called The King Bees. I got the impression from the way he spoke that it had been his own group. Naturally he was quite proud of the record he made with them, or probably more that he had actually already had a single released. Also I believe the record had even been featured on TV's *Juke Box Jury* show and that Dave had been introduced to the panel after their verdicts were delivered. This was in the year before I met him, so it was all very recent history at that point and a pretty impressive achievement for him.

However, I don't remember Dave talking about The Manish Boys at all. In fact, we picked up an ex-Manish Boy called Johnnie Edward in the ambulance one day. Dave said he was going to make a radio commercial for him, as he was now something to do with Radio City (a pirate radio station). Anyway, we arrived at a recording studio somewhere in town, where Dave quickly got to work and made up a ditty, on the spot, to record straight away. I still remember him singing these simple lyrics:

> *Any time, coffee time…*
> *Coffee time, any time…*
> *Any time is coffee time…*

Thinking about it, that actually wasn't a bad maxim for David himself. He did like his coffee – though it was the hip drink of the day, of course, particularly the frothy kind.

This very basic lyrical mantra we repeated in a loop. We were going to provide some instrumentation, but in the end just David and Denis sang what actually turned out to be a rather monotonous tune with no musical accompaniment at all. I, or maybe we, tapped out a rhythm or just clapped along, but nothing more. I don't think it took more than an hour or so to knock together, but it seemed to do the job. From then on for quite a while, when any of us felt like stopping for a brew the call would go up: 'Any time, coffee time?'

I believe Dave also made some jingles for Johnny Edward's radio show too (he broadcast as Johnny Flux, I think) and he also made a couple of commercials with Denis Taylor's brother-in-law, Terry Bolton, just before I joined. Through Channel Radio in Kent, the radio station I broadcast with today, I came into contact with another ex-Manish Boy, Bob Solly (Bob also had a show with Channel at the time). While attending a party at Bob's house fairly recently, I was pleased to discover Johnny Edward was also there (it was a bit like an old Bowie musician's reunion). Funnily enough, it was only while making notes for this book that I remembered I had previously met Johnny, way back in the day. I completely forgot we had worked together, and with Dave, on that basic commercial. Writing this book has revived so many old memories, it's been quite a revelation.

Before moving on from Johnny Edward, it's worth noting that he's kept himself very busy over the years. He created the children's TV show *Metal Mickey*, which was directed and co-produced by ex-Monkees drummer Micky Dolenz, and co-penned 'Save Your Love', a No.1 for Renée and Renato in 1982. He still writes music at his London home studio.

*

As I was now a group member again, my former schoolmate Roger Seamark, now a professional artist who'd created professional caricature drawings for Dave Clark and his band's promotion, painted 'The Lower Third' on my bass drum – as was the style in those days. Significantly, this also helped to denote the group's separate identity, which Dave always respected and was happy with (similar, I suppose, to the Cliff Richard and The Shadows arrangement).

Over the years, Roger has been very successful in his profession and today is particularly well known in Sweden, where he made his home in the 1970s. When I left the band, somewhere along the line the drum skin was changed and I lost the original. Naughty of me, I know. I occasionally get asked about the drumhead design, and someone suggested to me that I should recreate it for posterity. As Roger is still an active artist, I decided to ask him whether he would consider remaking it for me, and he kindly agreed to give it a go. With the aid of some enlarged photos of the original drum kit, he got to work and bloody brilliant it is. Thank you, Roger!

*

Returning now to 1965, I was starting to settle in with Dave and the boys. Very quickly it felt like we had been working together and had known one another for months and months, rather than a few weeks. This happens when you genuinely feel comfortable with the people you are with: camaraderie develops.

We continued to gig like this, playing at places ranging from La Discotheque in Soho to, bizarrely, Streatham Ice Rink at 390 Streatham High Road (yes, ice and skates, with people skating around trying not to brain themselves as we performed). The rink was part of the Silver Blades franchise, which was part of the Mecca organisation. I remember thinking it felt odd performing to people who were gliding aimlessly past our bandstand, mostly looking down at their feet, though we did have quite a few gathered in front of the stage just watching us too.

On the outside, apart from an Art Deco, cinema-style frontage and a few colourful flags positioned along the rooftop, Streatham Ice Rink looked a bit like a large bingo hall. Inside, however, it revealed a surprising grandeur, and was certainly a lot more luxurious than you would expect to find in a similar establishment today (in fact, exactly what you would expect to find in the very average-looking building they've replaced it with). Although the original structure and rink was constructed in the early 1930s, the plush makeover had only been completed two or three years before our arrival, and everything still felt new and even a little futuristic in places. The addition of live pop acts once a week was one of the management's many promotional investments, which also included booking The Kinks a few times (whose work, you will recall, we often included in our own set).

Sadly, the old building, like so many of the band's favourite haunts – including the wonderful Marquee Club before it – bit the dust and was redeveloped in 2012.

Our gear was set up almost at the level of the ice itself, midway along one side of this cavernous space, next to a rather smart-looking white grand piano – something we never had any reason to utilise ourselves, sadly. As the room was so big, we could even play as loud as we wanted (as it wasn't a problem for the mums worried about their kiddies' ears). This was an added bonus. It would take a lot for us to compromise on our volume.

Overall, our stint at Streatham Ice Rink was a bit more relaxed than our normal club bookings, so I've little doubt that we just chucked in some extra random chart hits to help suit the broader-aged clientele. We did this gig a couple of times, so the management must have thought we were good enough to invite back.

*

By the late sixties, the live music scene would become a lot more sophisticated, particularly regarding presentation, as specialists in lighting, sound balance and back-line support gained a firmer foothold. The main live circuit that we and most other bands played at the time offered no such luxuries, however – not unless you were playing the big theatres, and even then it might only be the lighting that was a bit more advanced. Saying that, the Streatham

Silver Blades set-up was a rare exception: they had at least one 'follow spotlight' that I can recall.

This kind of demonstrates just how primitive things were, both on- and offstage, back in our day. For example, the set-up at the Marquee was typical and may surprise you, considering it was one of London's premiere music hangouts. While the overall space conveyed an undoubtedly unique atmosphere, up on stage there were absolutely no technical frills on offer, no special lighting that I can recall, and no technical support either.

The stage lights were either on or off and featured no sophisticated coloured lighting, dissolves, strobes or follow spots; in fact, nothing dramatic at all. The house lights would be up before and after bands performed, and when they were dimmed a few white lamps would illuminate the stage. Job done.

There wasn't even a mixing desk or stage monitors (we never toured with such things either). We never used monitors at any time and I know we never even considered 'sound balance' beyond turning up our amps to eleven. The only thing The Lower Third had were a few effects pedals to alter the sounds of the guitars. That was it. Stone-age rock or what?

'Oh man, look at those cavemen go, it's the freakiest show...'

(If you don't know which Bowie song that that line comes from then it's back to Bowie school for you, I'm afraid.)

As a rule of thumb we would arrive at the designated venue, unpack our gear, set it up on stage and then settle into what dressing-room facilities we were provided with until show time. These dressing facilities were often little more than big cupboards.

Apart from turning the amps on and off to make sure

the power was OK and the microphones were properly connected, that was it. We rarely did any soundchecks or pre-show rehearsals of any kind and didn't need to coordinate with the backline crew, as we never had any backline sound men or lighting technicians to coordinate with. It seems crazy by today's standards, but that's how most bands on the circuit did things in those days.

Today, monitors are particularly necessary to help each musician directly hear what the audience is hearing, enabling them to keep a tidy sound balance and, more importantly, remain in the same key as their fellow musicians. The Lower Third's monitors were just the main speakers that stood behind us. Far from ideal, but that's the way most bands played at the time.

I'm not even sure what health and safety rules were in place for the performers either, though there must have been some. Quite how that impacted on the safety of our equipment is also up for debate, as I clearly remember Graham once – mid-show – successfully repairing a blown amp's fuse with the use of some silver paper from the inside of a cigarette packet (without isolating any of the power). We didn't have the cash to keep luxuries like spare fuses! Luckily for us Graham was a trained electrician and so, like most things to do with the band's welfare, we generally looked to him when hit with a problem. In this respect I would definitely say that Graham was the most practical of us all. Quite how we would have survived without him I really don't know.

*

Eventually we set up regular rehearsals at the Roebuck pub, 108a Tottenham Court Road, London. This became a kind of HQ for a while. It would be quite a busy pub at times, particularly at night, but we could work away during the afternoons doing our own thing without being disturbed.

We rented the room upstairs, on the first floor, and there we practised and modified the current releases by groups such as The Kinks and The Yardbirds (whom we would later do a gig with), and Dave's own material too, of course. We eventually developed this repertoire to include experimental and even quite bizarre material. An incredulous Rikki Farr (one-time actor, promoter and brother and manager of Gary Farr and The T-Bones) once pulled me to one side at the Marquee to ask, 'What the hell is he doing this sort of song for?' The song in question was 'Chim Chim Cher-ee' from the recently released Walt Disney film *Mary Poppins* – albeit nothing that really resembled the Dick Van Dyke original. Dave put his own particular 'spin' on it, though we retained the primary three-four time signature. The original, clearly based on the styling and meter of a faster waltz, had been written by Disney's favourite composers, the brilliant Sherman brothers (who scored most of his classic animations).

It might seem very strange now to hear that we were doing a song like this, but remember it had a strong London connection, which David loved, and a lot of the songs Dave was writing at the time were about the city. I can still hear some of Dave's Anthony Newley-like expressions coming through in his delivery of this number. It was the perfect show tune, even though I'm still not sure it really suited our loud makeover.

Film music was actually something we all generally liked, including our manager, Ralph. I remember looking at a copy of the 1962 Maurice Jarre *Laurence Of Arabia* soundtrack album at his flat one day. It had a memorable, boldly designed graphic of Peter O'Toole on the cover, which I studied as Ralph played us the album. When we left the flat shortly after, the main theme tune was on all our lips, but it was Dave who started to whistle it first. It was very catchy.

Having just mentioned Rikki Farr (who got into the business after meeting The Silver Beatles in Germany in the early sixties), I also remember, at another Brighton gig, Rikki giving me his insight into Dave's popularity with the girls in the audience. He had clocked how many of them just stared at him, kind of transfixed, during our sets. 'You know why they go for him, don't you? They want to take him home and feed him' – a reference to Dave's emaciated physique. I only weighed 9 stone myself at the time, but I am much shorter than Dave. He was pallid, with almost translucent skin. Saying all that, he was a strikingly handsome chap even then, and skinny was still very rock and roll.

Rikki obviously quite liked what we were doing as, later in the year, he booked us to play at a new club he had helped set up called the Birdcage, in Eastney Road, Portsmouth. He was a very good promoter and many of the best acts of the day played at that club. Rikki really had his finger on the pulse and went on to promote the legendary 1968, '69 and '70 Isle of Wight festivals. (The final one, which famously featured Jimi Hendrix just a few weeks before his death, pulled in a larger audience than had attended Woodstock.) Rikki certainly knew a thing or two about staging an event.

*

Time with Dave was always interesting. I felt that he was way ahead of me generally, older in many ways, even though he was actually younger in years. When we were together I had developed an ambition to write and this would eventually lead me to try my hand at scriptwriting for television (never accepted). But while I was working with Dave, I was writing humour – possibly to get published or for radio submission, I'm not sure now. Anyway, I had a spiral-bound exercise book that I carried around and regularly wrote nonsense poetry in, often scratching ideas into it when the muse hit me.

When we were gigging in Birmingham one time, we all took a regular bus journey across town somewhere and I happened to have this notebook with me. As I was sitting next to Dave on the top deck I, somewhat cautiously, decided to ask him if he would cast an eye over my latest efforts. I remember that I tried to gauge his reaction as he flicked through a few of the pages, no doubt in the hope of a positive response; like a slightly raised eyebrow, an amiable smile or maybe even a laugh. I remember this so clearly I can even recall the pages and titles he read, which included 'Bob's Bell':

The bell on my bike got bent,
So I borrowed Bob's.
I bent Bob's and he bashed me back.
I told his dad and he bashed Bob's bonce.
I don't talk to him no more.

Also, this untitled bit of nonsense, which I probably wrote while we were en route to a gig in the ambulance:

There goes the cow,
There goes the fence,
There goes the trees, the sheep and the tents.
Here come the chimneys,
Here come the cars,
Here comes the office, the house and the bar.

There is no doubt most of these ideas were inspired by John Lennon's recent tomes *In His Own Write* and *A Spaniard In The Works*, which I knew Dave was fond of too. Also, that eternally wacky genius Spike Milligan was a great favourite of mine and made a significant impact on my writing. *The Goon Show* radio scripts and early sixties TV spin-off *The Telegoons* were all written by Spike.

As I looked at Dave while he read through some of this material, I suppose I was really hoping he would turn to me and say, 'Wow Phil, that's brilliant...' or something equally edifying. In fact, he didn't pass much comment at all. As we pulled up at our stop, he just handed the book back to me. On reflection, it obviously wasn't up to much, but I thought he would be the one to try it out on first. If anyone could recognise any potential, I surmised, it would almost certainly be Dave. He was 'cool'.

On the nights we were working well away from London (where at least Dave and I had homes we could return to), there was generally no accommodation arranged between gigs. In these circumstances, the only thing we could do was turn our vehicle into a mobile hotel room. This wasn't as straightforward as you might think, as much of the space was taken up with bulky amplifiers, cabling, power-lead blocks and pedals, microphone stands and my drum kit.

We were all seasoned enough to make sure we had a good supply of blankets and pillows so that we could at least create some level of comfort, the cold being the main problem (although cloudless summer nights could get quite cold too). Normally, we parked up on a quiet city centre side street, perhaps devouring any fast food we could find at that time of night before grabbing a few hours' sleep.

After a little careful rearrangement to create suitably flat surfaces, Dave and I would generally sleep on the amplifiers in the back of the vehicle. Denis and Graham slept in their seats in the cab, each of them having just enough legroom to stretch out. It was far from ideal, but on reflection I think Dave and I had the more comfortable set-up.

When we gradually stirred in the morning, dishevelled and stiff as posts (Dave and I with the outlines of Marshall amp logos stamped into our backs), we turned on the radio.

'I love this, turn it up,' said Dave one morning while still half asleep, his hair all over the shop. I can see him now, focusing on the music to stir himself to life, still wrapped up snugly in a large blanket to retain the warmth. Listening to this track with him, I quickly concurred. It wasn't rock or pop, but something very haunting and atmospheric – it turned out to be a jazz standard called 'Harlem Nocturne'. Originally written in 1939, the version we listened to that day was a sixties take on the tune, complete with an attractive, updated arrangement.

Dave and I in particular shared a wide taste in music, and jazz had been high on both of our agendas. I think a lot of people would be surprised just how much Dave liked his jazz, and how knowledgeable he was on the subject too. I know this had a lot to do with his love of the saxophone (which he never played with The Lower Third, by the way, even though he had brought it to his audition). I also know it was due to working in a Bromley record shop when he was quite young. I believe it was only a Saturday job and in the back of my mind I'm sure that Dave once told me that they paid him with records, which is why his jazz collection was so good. This must have been when he was still at school. This record shop had a lot of specialty imports as the owner was well connected and knew his stuff. It would have been my dream job too. I'm sure David lived a charmed life.

*

Our rehearsals at the Roebuck sometimes revealed Dave's serious intent to make it in the business. Denis sometimes had trouble remembering things, and his mistakes weren't suffered quietly. As musicians, both Denis and Graham were very good, though; they knew how to play. If you listen to the recordings we made, you can hear this for yourself. Our energy was terrific and this comes over on those early tracks, but never so much as when we performed live.

However, Dave expected a lot from the band and poor old Denis copped it a few times when he messed up. Dave just wanted to put on the best show he could, so he kept the bar raised high all the time.

In his foreword for this book, Denis recalled his writing experimentation with Dave, where Dave would ask him to put his fingers randomly on his guitar fret and strum, in the hope that something interesting would happen that he could then write around. Graham and I joined these experiments later on in our own style, playing the way we felt the song should best be played. Dave always left Graham, Denis and I to help develop something he had written in this way, and he always seemed content with our input.

As a rule, Dave would compose on his twelve-string guitar, then play the song to us and we'd take it from there. I don't recall him ever asking me to play in a particular way, he just went with what I did. It was great to have such freedom but also, looking back – particularly after all that he achieved – I also feel proud that he considered me an equal in the whole creative process.

Once, while setting up for a gig, I went to a piano and played a little tune of my own I'd recently been working on. David, walking by, stopped and asked what it was. When I said it was one of mine he said, 'Hmmmm... I might use that.' I don't think he ever did, though.

In 2016, I spent a few days at a hotel in Tottenham Court Road and it was only on the last day that I realised that the old Roebuck pub was right across the road from our hotel window. It's now called The Court and still looks the business. I was so pleased to see it still standing, and still a vibrant pub.

It was only while I gazed across the street at it that an amusing memory came back to me. We would park our ambulance right outside the Roebuck, as you could in those days (well before double yellow lines, red routes and bus lanes). Once, when we were loading our gear in, we were suddenly showered with sugar lumps. Looking up, we saw lots of smiling girls – probably secretaries – hanging out of various nearby office widows, trying to get our attention by cheekily throwing these lumps of sugar down at us. I wouldn't have minded, but I don't have a sweet tooth.

*

Another thing that impressed me about David Jones was that he had a manager, though I have to admit we didn't see an awful lot of him. Leslie Conn, who had an office in Denmark Street publisher's building, had managed Dave before the Third arrived on the scene, and was still working with him when I first joined the group. Through this arrangement Leslie had already set Dave up with a two-singles deal with Parlophone Records, the first of which, titled 'I Pity The Fool', he had already recorded with The Manish Boys earlier in the year. It was due to that handy contractual arrangement that we would make our first single together – as Davie Jones and the Lower Third – even though only Dave's name would ultimately appear on the label when it was released.

Ray Davies wrote a great little song called 'Denmark Street', which very much summed up the funny little road Dave and the band got to know so well – and the attitude of the music publishers who hung out there:

You go to a publisher and play him your song
He says I hate your music and your hair is too long
But I'll sign you up because I'd hate to be wrong...

CHAPTER FOUR

ONE FOURTH
OF A THIRD

While it became our routine to demo record Dave's new compositions for potential release, or for possible cover by other artists, we also demoed songs by other songwriters and recording artists (including The Pretty Things), for them to consider rerecording and then releasing themselves. These demos were invariably made at Regent Sounds in Denmark Street, where The Phil Lancaster Quintet had nervously committed their junior efforts to acetate a few years before. Indeed, the studio owner that I'd met while with my early group was still running it when I returned with Dave. Dave was also well known to the management there, having regularly used the studio in the past.

Some of the demos we made back then have turned up on a CD called – *David Bowie–Early On (1964–1966)* (see 'Recordings' at the end of the book for a list of the unreleased demos we made). Listening to them for the first time, thirty years later, was a weird experience, like discovering a walled-up memory or finding a book of old family photos.

Regent Sounds was part of the insular rock and pop community based around Charing Cross Road. You had The Gioconda café just a few doors along from the studio, where everybody on the scene met before going off to gigs or to socialise or look for work. Also available for recording in the same street was Central Sound Studio, another small but efficient set-up, this one owned by a vocal coach and producer called Freddie Winrose. Then, literally just around the corner in Charing Cross Road, was Lew Davis, the guitar shop frequented by anybody who was anybody. Ray Smith, guitarist in Head, Hands & Feet, who worked in that shop, would also introduce me to the next group I joined after departing The Lower Third. You would always bump into someone you either knew or recognised in the business at Lew's place. For example, I was just hanging around there chatting to the staff one day when The Kinks' bass player Pete Quaife wandered in for a chat, carrying a couple of fully loaded shopping bags. 'Look what I bought,' he said, holding out a pile of colourful jumpers with a look of real pleasure on his face. Definitely newfound wealth, I thought to myself.

My big pal John Urquhart still has fond memories and a high regard for the folks who worked in Lew's shop in the sixties. In fact, he and I called in there years later for a trip down memory lane, chatting with the staff and spending time reminiscing about 'the good old days'. On reflection, I'm sure they would have preferred to make a sale instead, but we certainly enjoyed ourselves. Good old Lew Davis. Never knew him, but loved his shop.

I remember us sitting in the Gio one afternoon, all very excited and a bit apprehensive as we were due to meet an agent who had an interesting offer for us (or so we thought). He was the brother of Al Saxon, a singer popular at the time. We were excited because there was possibly a chance of gigs in New York. This was going to be the big time and we all felt a glow of excitement at the prospect.

The guy never came and the three of us never did make it to New York, so we had to settle for the Gio's amazing coffee instead. You have to get used to a lot of disappointments like that in the music business.

*

The date for the Parlophone single recording was set for early July 1965 and was to be recorded at IBC (the International Broadcasting Company) Studios at 35 Portland Place, just along from BBC Broadcasting House. Dave also had a 'name' recording manager called Shel Talmy at the time, an American who was successfully producing hits for The Who and The Kinks. He was a perfect fit for our sound – and it was his sterling production work with The Who that had excited me so much in Germany.

The recording engineer was Glyn Johns, who had started his career at IBC and went on to work with some of the biggest names in the industry. As did our session pianist, who was brought in to beef things up, an interesting guy called Nicky Hopkins. Quite an array of talent in one studio, as musical history bears out.

We had two numbers slated for release, 'You've Got A Habit Of Leaving' and 'Baby Loves That Way', both of which we had rehearsed earlier that day in preparation for this important session. After an initial run-through, we decided my bass drum was booming a bit, so I draped Dave's (one and only, I think) double-breasted tweed jacket over the front of the drum. That deadened the offending boom nicely. After a few takes Shel seemed to have had enough and got up, slipped on his jacket and said, 'Nice cut' before departing for a bite to eat and leaving us in the capable hands of Glyn Johns.

Denis only recently told me how Dave 'rubbed a wine glass up and down the frets for extra effect' to get the scratchy 'string noise' effect during 'You've Got A Habit Of Leaving'. I personally can't remember any of that as I was no doubt solely concentrating on my own input, though I was very pleased to hear an alternative take that Shel Talmy had kept hold of and issued in 2017 on an excellent CD compilation of his work. Fifty-two years on and our recording still sounds pretty good to me.

As time went by, and particularly as we established ourselves in London, we soon picked up the reputation for being the second loudest group in the capital, with no prizes for guessing that the first was The Who. I mention that here, as apparently we were so loud at IBC that day that an EMI publicist, who had stopped by to see how we were getting on, told Denis and Dave that we 'sounded like a Lancaster bomber flying through the studio'.

'Baby Loves That Way' was meant, by Dave, as a tongue-in-cheek take on Peter Noone and Herman's Hermits, and he informed us before we left that morning's rehearsal that he planned to fill out the chorus with as many people as he could at the studio to emulate 'chanting monks', of all things. I could never really make out the chanting monks part of it on the end result, and I don't think it sounds like Herman's Hermits much either, though we did indeed bulk out the backing vocals with as many people as we could rope in. This included Shel, who returned from his lunch just in time to join in on vocal backing – a backing which pretty much runs the length of the track, not just the chorus. I was standing next to Shel and to Les Conn, who also joined in on these vocals, along with Glyn Johns, Dave and the band, and another IBC technician. Boy, were both Shel and Les out of tune! You can hear it if you listen carefully (or maybe I just can't erase it from my memory). Not that I was in a position to offer an opinion of any kind – something I would particularly discover later on, when working with another high-profile record producer.

'Baby Loves That Way' opens with these lyrics:

Baby likes to go outside, so I let her
Wants to fool with other guys, so I let her
Wants to be bad, so I let her be bad
But fooling around, it will make me sad
She fools around with other boys and treat me like
an unwanted toy…

I only really remember Les during the recording of this single, funnily enough, though I'm sure he must have stopped by the Roebuck to see Dave once or twice. I mostly remember seeing him that day, however, as it was an important event for me, being my first professional recording and all. I just wanted to take in as much of the detail as I could. It wasn't long after this recording that Dave changed management anyway, so Les wasn't part of our set-up for too long. Dave also seemed to be losing interest in the arrangement, though it was probably a mutual decision as there was no dramatic parting of ways in the end. But it's well worth remembering, and noting here, that Leslie Conn did get Dave his first-ever record deal, and the first three singles that Dave ever released were due to deals that Conn had arranged for him, so the chap certainly played a significant part in the David Bowie story.

On a final note about Les in this chapter, during the writing of this book I came across a fabulous piece of Bowie memorabilia – a slightly yellowed napkin, of all things. This strange keepsake had almost certainly originated from the Gioconda, and Dave had written on it:

> *I, Davie Jones*
> *Hereby promise not to*
> *become too big-headed*
> *when I am famous.*
> *Signed this glorious day*
> *10th May '65 in the presence of*
> *Signed*
> *Davie Jones.*

Under Dave's signature it is endorsed, witness style, by Les Mighall and Les Conn, plus an unidentified hand.

Putting the rarity value of this most unusual item aside, Dave's early prediction of fame, together with his declared promise not to let himself become a big-head when it did arrive, was really bang on the mark. If there was one thing that David Jones was not, even when he became the mighty and world famous David Bowie, it was conceited or arrogant.

Casually recording Dave's intention to become a big success like this was obviously an idea that came to Les while they chatted about their future business relationship together. But it also offers us an insight into Conn's own ability to spot a possible star of the future (he was also working with a certain Mark Feld around this time too, who I'm sure I'll mention again at some point).

Leslie Conn passed away in London, aged seventy-nine, in 2008.

One last thing about this rather delicate and fascinating piece of music memorabilia (a photo of which is included in this book's picture section). It was dated 10 May 1965, and the Les Mighall endorsement helps clarify another interesting detail, most important for the many Bowie aficionados around the world who treasure such information. No one in the band could remember exactly when Dave made contact with The Lower Third originally, just that it was most probably in early May. This item now confirms that to be true, and that the first known date that Dave could have performed live with the band was on 17 May. We can now, with reasonable confidence, confirm that Dave's debut appearance with The Lower Third was on 17 May 1965, at the Grand Hotel in Littlestone (a small seaside village on the edge of New Romney).

Not long ago, before my new partner Christine moved home, I would spend weeks at a time at her home in St Mary's Bay, which is only about three miles along the coast from Littlestone. We would often drive past the exact location. Unfortunately the aptly named Grand Hotel, a large and impressive Victorian building that faced out across the English Channel, was demolished in 1973 and replaced with flats. As the booking for this gig had been made before Dave joined the band, the poster only mentioned The Lower Third, and no one was previously sure whether he had even met the band yet. So hopefully that's another useful detail put to bed.

When in 1983 David was asked for his memories of The Lower Third and the type of material they did, he replied:

I guess it wanted to be a rhythm 'n' blues band. We did a lot of stuff by John Lee Hooker, and we tried to adapt his stuff to the big beat, never terribly successfully. But that was the thing: everybody was picking a blues artist as their own. Somebody had Muddy Waters, somebody had Sonny Boy Williamson. Ours was Hooker.

My response to this statement by David is that I think he was a little confused with his bands. I can't remember us doing any John Lee Hooker numbers at all. However, I know that both of his previous groups, The King Bees and The Manish Boys, were drawn more to this R&B sound. I just think he has mixed this up, which of course was quite easy to do considering the amount of groups David experimented with during the 1960s.

*

When 'You've Got A Habit Of Leaving' was released in the height of summer 1965, we eagerly awaited our imminent success. We all felt that, with Shel Talmy's sage assistance and what we thought was a good enough song, the A-side at least had enough of a contemporary edge to get some attention. But it wasn't to be. In fact, we felt a little deflated before it was even released.

When we each received a copy, a tinge of disappointment set in among the band when we discovered we weren't credited on the label, which simply read 'Davy Jones'. (For a few weeks he changed the spelling from Davie to Davy.)

To be fair, label billing was never actually discussed beforehand. I suppose we just assumed the record would be billed just like our concerts, as Davie Jones and The Lower Third. Looking back on it now, I can understand why this happened. I'm absolutely sure that Dave wasn't having a go at us directly or personally, it was actually more to do with his experience with The Manish Boys. With Les Conn's assistance, together with his own his previous single release acumen, Dave felt he himself had brought The Manish Boys the deal and opportunity to record and release 'I Pity The Fool' with Parlophone. When the band somehow conspired and managed to get Dave's name removed so the single was just credited 'The Manish Boys', Dave was definitely not a happy camper, and I know Les Conn took the brunt of David's disappointment. And so, when 'You've Got A Habit Of Leaving' was being pressed, he made sure that David was clearly credited this time.

And, if proof were needed exactly how Dave felt about his treatment by The Manish Boys, their single had barely been released when he decided to leave the group, without even debating it with them. He then made contact with Den, Graham and Les Mighall in search of a new band and within two months of 'I Pity The Fool' had left The Manish Boys for good and set up shop with The Lower Third.

The message was already clear: don't mess with Dave Jones!

With or without an early single success, we were convinced we were going to make it – so much so that we regularly used say to one another: 'One day we'll be millionaires.' This, of course, was many years before a British TV character called Del Boy Trotter made it a famous catchphrase (and it was also at a time when a millionaire was still considered a ridiculously rich person). We would often shout out his moral-lifting mantra in the ambulance or use it arbitrarily as either an uplifting war cry following a successful gig, or as a much-needed shot in the arm if we had just bombed somewhere.

I always thought that with our early liberal use of this aphorism there was some real irony in that the *Only Fools And Horses* (the BBC comedy that featured 'Del Boy') theme tune conveniently featured David's name in its closing lyric:

> *We've got some half-priced cracked ice,*
> *And miles and miles of carpet tiles,*
> *TVs, deep freeze and David Bowie LP…*

Today it's hard to imagine the phrase 'One day we'll be *miwlionaires'* in anything other than Del Boy's bastardised cockney patois. Of course, after all that we were partly right, one of us certainly made more than a *miwlion* or two in his lifetime – and he earned, it too.

*

With or without a catchphrase, there was little doubt in my mind that I was heading for success. It was what I'd dreamed of as a boy, wanting to be Eddie Calvert or Tommy Steele, and it was with this group, I now decided, that this guaranteed success was to be achieved. No question about it, we were the next quartet who were going to make it *big*, with The Beatles the ideal role models – a perfect example of four lads sharing great success equally.

Our band certainly seemed to be an equal enterprise to

begin with. This ambition was, however, slightly offset by the unavoidable fact that the lead singer always receives most of the attention in a group. This was undoubtedly the reason Dave Clark decided to step to the front of his band. His was a rare example of a drummer successfully taking centre stage in a combo.

On its release, 'You've Got A Habit Of Leaving' received some encouraging music press reviews and did get some radio play too. It felt like a positive start – it was great to finally get commercially released.

The *Record Mirror* review in particular put a smile on my face:

Davy Jones: You've Got A Habit Of Leaving; Baby Loves That Way (Parlophone R 5315). Shel Talmy production for the highly talented singer. It's a curiously pitched vocal sound, with powerful percussion and a slightly dirgy approach. Plenty happening; lots of wailing. Very off beat.

(You did note the 'powerful percussion' praise, I hope!)

One small review that I've only recently seen remained unimpressed by our effort and didn't hold back either. This is from the *Aberdeen Express*:

In recording 'You've Got A Habit Of Leaving' (Parlophone R5315) Davy Jones has concentrated too hard on creating a 'wilder than wild' sound. The result, in my opinion, is a rather boring noise. Not chart material this one.

While the review was spot on in that it would never trouble the charts, any reader that ignored the advice and decided to buy a copy anyway would now have a record worth many hundreds of pounds in his collection. It's a strange business, this rock and roll.

The song's lyric was formulaic, of course, its theme nothing more than your regular, plaintive teenage sob story, with some sudden wild 'T-cup' Taylor guitar noise (and Graham doesn't hold back on the bass here either) rounded off with a touch of demented drumming from yours truly. Dave even throws in some random harmonica at one point, which he would sometimes do live on stage when we started to get into a real groove.

Girl trouble was a subject central to much of David's writing at the time (and the majority of other male songwriters too, for that matter), and quite possibly central to David's own life when he wrote it. He always seemed to be hung up on this girl or that.

The A-side also contains a line that has always stood out for me: *'You could grow up – if you wanted to, wanted to, wanted to…'* If you listen carefully towards the end of the track, after about 2'5", you can hear Dave's wine-glass effect on Denis's guitar strings. It's quite an inventive play-out effect.

I first heard 'You've Got A Habit Of Leaving' played on the BBC, on the 'midday spin' section of the *Sam Costa Show*, curiously enough, Costa, who was also a well-known radio actor, was in his mid-fifties at the time and our record was not a particularly mainstream kind of disc. But I'm very grateful he gave us that first-ever airing, all the same; it was quite something to be played at all by the BBC and I can still remember the thrill of hearing a record I had helped make being broadcast nationally. There's nothing like it.

We were played every week on Radio London's chart

show, it being one of the pirate stations with whom we had worked and built up a good relationship. They also read out our current position in their own singles chart. Actually, we were regularly promoted on the station, probably because of *The Inecto Show* (an advertorial-type gig I will get to soon), and also because quite a few people did see David as a potential star and wanted to help him make it. Saying that, one afternoon while listening to Radio London with my mum, the DJ unexpectedly announced: 'Get down to the Marquee this Friday to see David Jones and The Lower Third. Check out the drummer...' I was amazed and elated to be singled out in that way: not even Dave was highlighted on this occasion (though we were getting many plugs as a group too). But to hear this guy compliment me like that, completely out of the blue, was quite something. Impressing my mother at the same time was a double bonus. We all want to do that.

Due to their help, I started to regard the band as a fully badged, Radio London-endorsed act. Certainly as far as airplay went. I don't remember Radio Caroline playing our records, but I may have just missed it as I always had Radio London on. It was a fascinating time for radio and there are many people out there, me included, who feel very nostalgic about these old pioneering stations. It's very much in the spirit of Radio London, in particular, that I do my own radio show today. Channel Radio, who I've been with for a few years now, give me complete freedom to play the tracks I want to play – I'm not confined to any set disc rotation. I even play my old Lower Third records from time to time, and often share an old on-the-road story or two.

Apart from the *Sam Costa Show*, I've barely mentioned

BBC Radio yet, and particularly the pressure the Corporation was under in regard to pirate radio broadcasting. As pirate stations like Caroline, Luxembourg and Radio London were starting to do so well – not only playing the type of modern music younger audiences really preferred to hear, but also working with a younger, dedicated selection of DJs who knew all about the latest sounds – the BBC could do nothing more than try and offset it with a similar station of their own. But that wouldn't come until 1967, after our band had been and gone, so we had to make do with the few pre-Radio One BBC shows broadcasting that might play us – and, of course, we were up against a lot of established artists too.

In the sixties and seventies, the best way to get more plays on the BBC than regulation airtime allowed was to pass an audition. This was all due to something BBC broadcasters referred to as 'needle time'. The Corporation could only afford to play so many records in a day and to get around that they would invite approved bands and artists in to rerecord their songs in a BBC studio. In this way, producers were not restricted in how often they could play that recording, as it wouldn't be credited as needle time. What no one had even considered back when these BBC sessions started was just how valuable some of these recordings would eventually become. For example, David's *Bowie At The Beeb* (his BBC sessions collection) proved to be a big-selling asset for both BBC Worldwide and for David's own catalogue when issued in 2000. Most major recording artists with a similar BBC archive have also done well too, The Beatles not surprisingly being the most successful to date.

But before a producer could invite you in to record a

session for his show you had to be BBC accredited, which meant you had to pass an audition. All will be revealed in a chapter or two about this, as our own memorable close encounter of the Broadcasting House kind occurred towards the end of the year – and the result may surprise you.

*

Returning to the time of our first single release, Dave and I were walking up Oxford Street one sunny afternoon (which sounds like a Kinks song) when we bumped into Chris Farlowe. Dave had a copy of the single with him but apparently had already made his mind up about its potential – or maybe was just being defensive? As he showed it to Chris he quickly added, 'You won't like it.'

I don't know what Chris Farlowe made of it in the end, or if he ever heard it at all. Whatever, the record didn't really get us noticed anyway, so it was kind of back to the drawing board for all of us, and I had to put my bid for stardom back on hold again. Bummer!

Relating this memory also reminds me of other days spent in Oxford Street with Dave. He and I would sometimes traipse in and around that busy thoroughfare thanklessly calling in on booking agents in search of work for the band. It was a bit soul destroying at times, but we needed the money – and David could turn on the charm when he wanted to. We did pick up a few bookings this way (particularly last minute 'fillers', where we replaced acts that had pulled out of a gig late on), though more often than not we came away empty-handed.

On another similar occasion, I was driving Dave along Oxford Street in my car and just as we pulled up outside the agent's office we were going to visit, Dave said, 'Look

Phil, there's Rod Stewart...' and pointed along the road. Sure enough, there was Rod, in full Rod-the-Mod style, walking towards us. We figured that the guys he was with must have been The Steam Packet. As we didn't know Rod or his band nothing was said, but I'm sure Rod must have clocked Dave at least, and may have recognised him too (Dave and The Manish Boys had shared billing with one of Rod's early bands at least once). In later years, Rod certainly recalled seeing David around town in the mid-sixties.

When Dave first joined The Lower Third and rapidly assumed leadership, one of the first things he decided to do was write a promotional letter, which he then posted to a few venues around the country. He titled it *'Truth Shows – A very fair show for a very fair price'*, and being the only one with a permanent base at the time, added his home address as the band's main HQ: '4 Plaistow Grove, Bromley, Kent.'

The letter, which was posted together with some of Dave's Lower Third caricature stickers, went on to say:

> *Reputation wise, Davie has a spotless chart. Having picked up the gauntlet in the legendary 'Banned Hair' tale, he stormed into BBC2's 'Gadzooks', leaving such an impression that he has been contracted for yet another appearance this month.*

This dispatch, which went on to point out that the Third's three-piece powerful backing actually sounded more 'like a twelve piece', also mentioned 'Davie's earthy vocals and tenor/alto sax and harp (harmonica) work' and that the next single would be called 'Born Of The Night'. While neither a second *Gadzooks!* TV show appearance nor 'Born

Of The Night' actually came to pass (at least beyond a basic demo of the song), Dave's promotion pulled in a couple of valuable gigs and scored him a few early Brownie points at the same time. But our need had become desperate and, realising the dilemma and with no time to wait on another mail-shot, Dave decided the direct approach was the only way.

One agent we called on one particular day did offer us a gig I remember, at a venue that he, the agent himself, promoted – though he tried to disguise it as an audition. So, in other words, he invited us to play for him for nothing on the slim chance that we might attract another agent, then get paid work via that new agent with other promoters! While standing there I recognised this guy as someone who had a bad reputation for using bands in this way. Dave, who quickly saw through it all and, before I could even say anything, took offence to the suggestion and briskly told the guy, 'We're professionals, we don't work for nothing.' With that we left with our noses in the air. David was pretty good at taking no nonsense.

Further to my memories of Oxford Street, I also must add the 100 Club, of course, another famous London venue of the day, which first opened its doors in 1942 and is still open today. As well as our weekly stint at the Marquee, we had also picked up a residency here for a promotion called *The Radio Caroline Show*. These non-broadcast shows became occasional Thursday-night engagements for a while. It was around this time – 19 August 1965, in fact – that we first played there.

Having previously lamented the lack of support with Radio Caroline airplay, here we are, I note, playing the first of a series of Radio Caroline-sponsored gigs. I'd forgotten about that, though I should have twigged that we did get at least some support there as Ralph Horton (who I will introduce to you in greater detail in a page or two) worked with them for a while.

We would return to the 100 Club (which took its name from its location at 100 Oxford Street) quite often in the months to come, but on this night we shared billing with The Strollers, The Legends and the excellent Danny Williams. Danny was a smartly tailored, good-looking chap, originally from South Africa. His silky smooth voice had earned him the nickname 'Britain's Johnny Mathis', and there was no doubt that he was headlining this particular gig. His version of 'Moon River' (I'm sure you have heard it many times) was still regularly played on most stations, having been a big-selling UK No.1 single four years earlier.

On reflection, it was still a slightly odd billing; he was more of a cabaret crooner set against our slightly irreverent, full-volume rock shenanigans. Saying that, I don't recall any issues that evening, so I guess it worked well for the audience. But that wasn't always the case at other venues – and it certainly wouldn't be the last time we'd share a mismatched billing (though we were definitely the loudest group on the roster that night). The fact is, we were just happy to be playing anywhere and took our chances. We needed the work.

Talking of being mismatched, two days on from our 100 Club appearance, top jazzer Alex Welsh and his band were headlining at the same venue. Not unusual, as he'd headlined the club dozens of times before, but a handy link here as we would share the billing with Alex and his band later in the year at a forces party, and it was quite a night too (and the term 'mismatched' definitely comes to mind). That particular story is also worth waiting for.

*

Although we were gigging, it really wasn't consistent enough. I was just about keeping up the repayments on my Ludwig kit, but had no extra money for my keep at home. But it was Denis and Graham who had it worst, as they had to find rent, for unlike Dave and me, they couldn't simply go home to their parents' house each night.

As a group, we four were becoming tighter in our sound and getting to know each other very well, both musically and personally. But we clearly needed direction to push what we had going for us. Dave was particularly keen to make a change. To this end, one afternoon at one of our Roebuck rehearsals, two strangers walked in.

Dave, who had been upset about the lack of promotion for the single, decided it was time to move on from Les Conn and had been keeping his ear to the ground for a replacement manager. Arriving at the Roebuck one day, he keenly informed us that he had met someone who he believed could help us and who might be willing to take over the band's management. He had invited the guy along to hear us play and make a judgment. So we met Ralph Horton, who arrived shortly after along with a tall blond German guy called Neil Andersen, who turned out to be another singer, very quietly mannered – and was also, we later discovered, was Ralph's boyfriend.

Ralph was introduced to us as a manager, currently looking after Neil, and no doubt his ex-Moody Blue connections were thrown in at the same time for good measure, as he had worked closely with the band since their days in Birmingham (Ralph had even managed Denny Laine and The Diplomats prior to this). I don't know how much success or work Neil was getting with Ralph, but Dave was clearly very enthusiastic about it all, so the decision on our part had pretty much been made already, really.

And so, after we'd chatted with Ralph, who seemed pleasant enough, he sat and listened to some of our numbers. After an hour, he left with Neil to deliberate. With hindsight, this rather innocuous meeting proved to be a significant turning point in the long-term futures for both The Lower Third and Ralph in the music industry. Neither party seemed to have a clue about its real importance. I can't remember now if we had any misgivings about Ralph taking over as manager either – we were probably so keen to become successful and earn a few quid, we welcomed it.

This deal ultimately turned out to be more of a private agreement between Dave and Ralph. There was no 'Let's sit down and discuss the details, boys,' either from Dave or from Ralph, and that all-important finer detail was kept between them. In fact, the band's naivety about this early arrangement contributed greatly to the major problems we experienced in the long run. When I think about it now, I'm surprised I wasn't a bit more on the ball, and at least tried to find out what was being agreed, but then again I kind of thought Dave was looking out for us collectively, as much for himself. Obviously he had to keep us happy, because we were his backing band.

Soon after that rehearsal-cum-audition, Dave announced that Ralph had thought it through and agreed to manage us. With that decision made, we never saw Les Conn again, and celebrated a new and exciting step forward.

Birmingham-born Ralph Horton had been in the pop business since the early sixties. After managing Denny Laine, he had gone on to work as both roadie, tour manager and booking agent for The Moody Blues, who broke into the big time with the song 'Go Now', and relocated from Birmingham to London. When he came to see us, he had just started working for the pirate radio station Radio Caroline, for which he got the use of an impressive Jaguar Mark X car.

Ralph was quite different to the rest of us. For one thing, he was older. In appearance, he was a bit of a chubby chops, for want of a better description. He could be very aloof – in fact it was very satisfying for me to get a smile out of him, or even see him amused.

Now I think back on it, I feel that he and I were wary of each other. I was soon on his back about our money situation (the lack of) – maybe too much so. But we were often desperate. Despite all of that, I didn't dislike Ralph, though ultimately he was to separate David from The Lower Third. We never knew why he did this at the time, or whether the motivation even came from him. With hindsight again, Bowie history reveals that David never stayed with one particular group of musicians for too long – that's how he operated. Today, I'm just grateful I was involved in one of his outfits.

Ralph definitely wasn't one of the boys, and it didn't take too long for us to realise he was homosexual, though I can't remember how we did so. It made no difference to us, of course. It just wasn't the band's scene – we all liked girls. Dave was particularly prolific in this arena and was easily the most successful at pulling attractive girls. In this way he probably came across as the most heterosexual among us, though our views on his sexuality did change later on.

It has got to be said that Ralph did immediately get on the case and we did get the feeling that we were being both managed and usefully directed for the first time. He seemed to have a genuine belief in what we were doing, and having worked with people like Denny Laine from his Diplomat days, he was already an old hand at helping with transitional styling. And so, first off came our makeover!

At this time both Dave and The Lower Third had no particular look or image. For a start, each of us had a different hairstyle and we looked like a group of individuals, rather than a styled, professional band. Dave's hair, as previously mentioned, was quite long and grown-out blond and he tended to wear on stage what he wore off it. We all generally appeared on stage in whatever we thought appropriate (I sometimes wore my Swedish girlfriend's fur Eskimo boots at the Marquee, just to be different). Again, there was no unity of style in our presentation, we each did what we wanted and styled our hair individually. Brian Epstein, who had championed the famous Beatles makeover, would not have been impressed.

So, just days after meeting him, Ralph announced that he would soon be taking us all to Carnaby Street to get kitted out – seemingly at his own expense. But the first thing we had to sort out was the hair. For this, we were taken to 'Ivan's' in Queensway, his salon just off the Bayswater Road, for a 'wash and cut'. I quickly figured out Ralph's connection with this hairdresser when I noticed a postcard on the wall sent by The Moody Blues.

Now, I had completely forgotten about this until my partner, Christine, discovered it. While helping me research this book at Bromley Public Library, of all places, she found an interesting old early 1966 newspaper cutting. Titled 'Pop Singer Changes His Image', the article was primarily made to promote what turned out to be our final single with Dave, 'Can't Help Thinking About Me'. In the feature, Dave explained how I had inspired (of all things) the whole band's hairstyle.

According to the handouts, David, who once formed a society for long-haired people, has become a quiet, talented vocalist and songwriter. The group changed their style six months ago, when drummer Phil Lancaster joined the group. 'We thought his shorter hair style looked nice and we all copied it,' said David. 'Now we try to project an image of four nice, not moody, people. And we use ballet steps in our performance.

While Ivan's gave David and the boys the latest Phil Lancaster cut, Dave made himself right at home in the chair-swapping gossip with Ivan about Jagger and Bailey, while his long hair was sculpted into a tidy bouffant. Ralph closely watched over the proceedings, of course.

Graham and Denis got the same treatment, their hair being at least as long as Dave's by then. My turn was more of a tidy-up and slight restyling by Ivan, as my hair was nowhere near the length of the others. Nonetheless he did puff it up as much as possible and we all left his salon with trendy 'mod' cuts, united in our looks.

The shopping trip Ralph had planned for us was actually arranged to tie in with an EMI photo session booked for later the same day (the record deal already in place, of course, before Horton's arrival).

At different shops we acquired blue herringbone shirts, dark blue trousers and brown corduroy shoes with rope soles (see accompanying photos). David also had a herringbone sports jacket to replace the one I regularly borrowed to use on my bass drum.

Our fashionable slim ties were a gift from my mother, who made them on her sewing machine at home a week or so earlier. Each sported its own unique floral design and all were brightly coloured, though naturally this doesn't come across in the black-and-white photo shoots in which we wore them. I think it was Dave who had picked up on a developing trend for this kind of tie. When he mentioned that we should get some cool ties properly made to order, to round off the new outfits we were about to acquire, I no doubt put my mum forward as just the seamstress we needed.

Dave came to my home in Chingford Road to check them out. I wasn't there for some reason, but my mate Roger Seamark was and remembers him turning up and loving what my mother had made for him.

'David sat in the corner,' Roger recalls, 'and I sat on your dad's chair. God knows why, but something about Wales came up, so David and I were suddenly speaking a bit of proper Welsh together. We laughed about it being such a different language. He must have mentioned his origins to me, or something like that to trigger this off. I clearly remember Norah showing the floral ties she'd made you all.'

The Welsh connection is interesting. I've been told that David once told a reporter he was going to visit Wales soon (this during the 1990s) to look into some of his family history. I wonder what the connection was? I'm sure that his father was from Yorkshire and his mother from Kent, so presumably he'd checked back further in his family tree at some point.

To Ralph's credit, at the eleventh hour he ensured we looked the part for this EMI photo session, which took place in a small photographic studio in their Manchester Square offices – and outside in Manchester Square itself (this also the venue for many of the early Beatles publicity photos). If you look closely at some of our photos today you can see that we had literally walked out of the clothes shop with our new togs on and straight to the session. We hadn't even had a chance to iron any of our shirts – you can see where they were folded, pre-sale.

One of these studio shots was eventually used on the cover of a 10" EP and has been the most widely used photo of the Third ever since. Some of the photos taken outside in the square emerged in the *Sunday Times* in 1997, taken from a newly published book of EMI archive photographs called *The End Of Innocence*. I don't believe the Manchester Square photos had ever been seen before – certainly not by me, anyway. More were published in 2010 by Kevin Cann in his comprehensive early days Bowie book, *Any Day Now: The London Years 1947–1974*.

It wouldn't be hard for you to picture the music scene in and around EMI headquarters in 1965. The Beatles were pretty much everywhere you looked and were probably the most played act on the radio at the time. During August, when our photo shoot took place, The Beatles' fifth studio album, *Help!*, had just been released and had immediately entered the charts at No.1. It felt quite good climbing the staircase they had made famous two years earlier on the cover of the equally successful *Please Please Me* LP. They would return again for a similarly posed shot in 1969 (this time with beards and much longer hair). Incidentally, the legendary snapper Angus McBean conducted both of these memorable and historic Beatles photo sessions.

Our photographer that afternoon – EMI's busy in-house man – wasn't quite as celebrated as McBean, not then anyway. He was efficient and quite fast, though on reflection it would have been great if one of us had had the idea to pose like The Beatles had done on that staircase, particularly as we used it to walk down on the way outside with the photographer. Mind you, that idea's only just occurred to me now.

*

Even though we had featured on a couple of slightly unbalanced Radio Caroline evenings at the 100 Club, the powers that be obviously learnt their lesson and decided to match us up a little more evenly at our next appearance there with The Artwoods. They were a quality band who never really registered any hit records but were widely respected on the scene, their organ-driven sound very much based in the R&B mould, though they experimented further too. They also had a line-up to die for.

They were named after the band's leader, Art Wood, whose younger brother, Ronnie, would shortly go on to have a hit or two of his own (and in time also become one of David's closest music-business friends). Other Artwood members included future Deep Purple founder Jon Lord on keyboards, future John Mayall's Bluesbreaker Keith 'Keef' Hartley on drums (also formerly of Rory Storm and The Hurricanes) and ex-Roadrunner Malcolm Pool on bass (later to work with Gordon Giltrap and

Colosseum). It's no wonder they sounded pretty good. Not only that, they were great fun to gig with and the dressing-room banter between the bands made these particular 100 Club appearances another highlight for me. It was no surprise that most of the Artwoods went on to have a lot of success in the business and I think Art himself would have had a hit or two if he'd stuck at it. As it was, the band broke up in the late sixties and he became a successful graphic designer.

CHAPTER FIVE

MANDY RICE-DAVIES MEETS MARY POPPINS

Ralph set about getting us work, which also meant auditions, one of which was for shows on the continent, entertaining American GIs. Well, this was where I came in a couple of years previously and it hadn't gone that well, but it was work all the same so I went along with it. Dave said to Ralph, 'Phil knows all about this type of gig, he's done it.' So we duly turned up for the audition.

As I have already mentioned regarding my earlier experiences performing in France and Germany, entertainment in 'the camps' not only centred on pop bands but also fifties crooners too. What I didn't say was that all sorts of acts were booked to appear at these camps in general cabaret form as well, from women dancing with boa constrictors to random dog routines, much as you might see in a variety show of the time in the UK.

Our audition, organised by Ralph, was to put us in good

company as far as 'variety' was concerned. Among our fellow auditionees was an act that required volunteers to run down a sloping structure with squares on it that played notes as you descended. Another act included some ballet dancers. So, being good sports, David Bowie and The Lower Third became volunteers for the novelty act. But when Dave emerged to take his turn running down the musical slope, he magically appeared wearing a tutu. This unexpected sight sent the rest of us into fits of laughter. Dave really milked it for comedic effect. He had a great sense of fun, was always up for laugh and was quite happy to send himself up when the mood took him. Ralph, however, wasn't amused at all, but this somehow made it even funnier. When it came to my turn on the slope of notes, Ralph seemed to cheer up a bit and even had a smile on his face, commenting, 'He looked so camp.'

I quietly asked Graham why Ralph objected to Dave's donning the tutu, and he replied, 'It's 'cos he's dressed as a girl.' We didn't pass the audition, and we weren't invited to join the sloping notes act either. Double bummer!

Stopping off for fish and chips on the way back, Dave and I returned to Ralph's Jag with our nosh and spontaneously pretended to be two stooped old men, making up old cronies banter as we got into the car like, 'I've got a lovely bit of fish for my tea...' and nonsense like that. 'Why am I surrounded by idiots?' was Ralph's response.

Humour was and remained to be, as far as I could tell, a big part of Dave's make-up. It certainly is that way for me. A sense of humour, especially if you are like-minded, is a great way of getting on with people. Dave was always quick to laugh and that could be infectious.

Travelling as we did, mile after mile in the back of the

ambulance, we would fight the boredom by amusing ourselves in whatever way we could. In the way we mimicked the two old men, we also became kids; a bit like comedian Terry Scott used to do in his act. We would ad-lib all of this, just to amuse ourselves of course. With Denis and Graham up front, Dave and I had to make do with our own company for most journeys.

Once, Dave and I made up a language – one with absolutely no rules, just complete gibberish, and pretended to hold a conversation in which each of us understood the other. A bit *Bill and Ben*-like, I suppose (for those of you old enough to know all about the *Flower Pot Men* on children's TV). We would revert to this little game from time to time thereafter.

'I went down the dell' (spoken in a silly, warbly voice) was one of David's favourite recurring lines when we were acting out as kids. Long journeys could take on daft themes like this to pass the time. And we did a lot of travelling.

On reflection, I'm pretty sure some of this daft made-up language came from Tony Newley's Gurney Slade, a rather surreal TV character that Newley himself devised. *The Strange World Of Gurney Slade*, as it was called, was a terrific series broadcast around 1960. It made a big impression on me, mainly because it was so unusual, so out there. It was actually a bit too advanced for its time, as it confused most who watched it, but I loved it and I know David did too. It's sad that it's kind of forgotten in TV history now, but you can be sure that most of the Pythons, for example, were in part inspired by this series.

In one of the early episodes, Newley starts talking to people in this gibberish language, and conversations flow between characters as though each knows what the other is saying. Dave and I did something similar, trying to talk seriously with a straight expression on our faces, then added in real words and daft phrases to try and make each other crack up and laugh. It became a competition between us to see who would lose it first.

There was undoubtedly also a lot of Pete and Dud in this scenario too. They were our heroes at the time and had only just come on the scene. Peter Cook and Dudley Moore's series *Not Only… But Also* had started its first run that year and very quickly turned into a must-see for me, Dave and the rest of the band. We hated it if a gig got in the way and we missed a show. There were no digital recorders or VCRs in our day; if you missed your favourite TV show, that was it.

The brilliant and now famous sketches, when the duo faced each other off as know-it-all East End characters Pete and Dud, complete with flat caps and working-men's clobber, often saw Cook make Moore corpse at a silly phrase or line he no doubt made up on the spot precisely to throw his partner off. There was a fabulous, impish look of glee in Peter Cook's eyes when he saw Dudley Moore start to laugh; it was priceless viewing and still is to this day.

Dave and I certainly did our best to create the same vibe in our own little world, as we flitted from town to town in the night. We often had adrenalin to spare while returning home from our latest ballroom engagement, and acting like Bill and Ben or Pete and Dud helped us to wind down. We should have called it *The Strange World of Phil and Dave* (Phil and Dave sounding a bit like Pete and Dud – I'm not trying to grab star billing here.) I wish we had recorded some of these comedy moments. When Dave started to laugh it was totally infectious. He could set the whole ambulance off when he got going, and there were times when our uncontrolled laughter would physically hurt too. They were some of the best times we had.

So, amusing ourselves during these long journeys was high on our agenda, though often if we'd really had a long day and busy evening, we would be so tired we'd just curl up and sleep. Graham was quite amazing in this way. His stamina far exceeded the rest of us. God knows what we would have done without him, as he was really doing two jobs for the band.

Thinking about this now, the amount of time it would take to cover the same distances today would be significantly less. Motorways were in their infancy in 1965, so most of our treks were made on the main A-roads of the day. The ambulance maxed at a giddy 35mph, probably less than half of what we would safely average in a modern vehicle on a motorway these days. Allowing for today's extra traffic (though at least half of our journeys were made through the night), we probably spent three or four times longer back then covering the same distances we could achieve today.

I should quickly point out that when we weren't being daft and trying to make each other laugh, we could equally fall into some pretty deep conversations. Kerouac was a favourite topic, and this could lead us in all kinds of directions as we analysed the things he had written. I'm pretty sure it was Kerouac's interest in Buddhism that encouraged Dave to look into this particular religion in more depth.

Infinity, astral travel, Tibet and what you might be able to see if you entered the fourth dimension were all subjects we picked over at one time or another. It was very unlikely he would want to talk about what you or he watched on TV the night before (perhaps allowing for Pete and Dud, that is). Just a few more reasons why hanging out with Dave was different to hanging out with any other person I would meet just about anywhere, certainly in my younger days.

We both shared a hunger for knowledge, though he was clearly a more voracious reader than I was at the time, and the latest book he was into often provided an interesting topic of conversation.

Sometimes our debates also took on a more profound shape and one in particular remained with me (I even remember that we discussed this as we stood at the dividing window, looking out through the front of the cab as we drove along). This conversation had taken on a more serious tone, possibly inspired by something we had heard on the radio, and was centred on how people generally saw or were accepting of other people, particularly strangers and/or people in general. The actual detail of this I've now forgotten, but I must have said something along the lines of 'I put people in boxes,' meaning that I generally pigeonholed people into certain categories and stereotypes, which I now see revealed an element of youthful naivety on my part.

David's response was emphatic. 'That's terrible,' he replied, 'you can't put people in boxes like that,' and the discussion continued from there, though I'm pretty sure I didn't particularly agree with Dave's views at the time. But it was something that stayed with me and, I'm pleased to say, eventually sunk in. It still rings in my ears now, and not without some shame I might add. It taught me (the older guy) a useful lesson in acceptance.

That was Dave. Someone, who at times in his life had fought for acceptance but never lost his capacity to accept, or doubted his overall faith in the human spirit. I guess when you are as different and unique as he was, you don't have preconceived ideas about folk or see them through any kind of lens.

*

This is also a good time to share some memories my ex-wife Helene has of David, relating to his interest in the Beat writers and their methods.

'I was sitting opposite David in a coffee bar,' she recalled to me recently. 'David was carefully cutting up words from a newspaper on the Formica table top where we were sat. I asked him what he was doing and he said, "This is how I write songs." He then explained it to me and started to quickly shift the cut-out words in what seemed to me to be quite random moves.

'David then asked me for some words and wrote them down, saying, "Now, these will be Helene's words in the song." It was very interesting to see him working on this, though I've no idea if he did use them in a song. That would be lovely, though, some of my words locked away in one of his songs.

'On another occasion, I remember David sitting in the ambulance, a grey ambulance. The door open and he was doing the same thing again using a glossy magazine this time, cutting up words for a new song.

'There is no doubt he was going places. He was always

interesting company and always very nice to me. I thought David was a lovely chap.'

'Cut-ups' are when a writer snips out existing printed text from a magazine, newspaper or something he has written himself and then rearranges the groups of words to form something new. The writer William S. Burroughs often used cut-ups as a method of experimental writing in the early sixties. Burroughs was a compadre of Jack Kerouac of whom, as you'll know by now, David and I were huge fans. He turns up as 'Old Bull Lee' in Kerouac's age-defining semibiographical novel *On The Road*, and as 'Bull Hubbard' in *Desolation Angels*.

It's funny that Helene clearly remembers David using this technique. I was undoubtedly there at the time too, certainly in the ambulance that day, but I have no memory of him doing cut-ups at all. It doesn't surprise me that he did this, though – it's very much the kind of thing he would do, as there were odd studio experiments and rehearsals where he either wrote down or expressed a feel or sound he was looking for in an unusual way (like that chanting-monk vocal effect he mentioned before our IBC recording session).

As he slowly got to grips with song construction – which, by his later standards, was pretty formulaic to start with – he was starting to flex his wings creatively, looking for a sound or style that was unique to him. In time he became a terrific lyric writer, partly due to all these experiments. What's so impressive, though, is that he was using this method much earlier than was previously known. I have read that David started using cut-ups in the seventies, but I can reveal here that he started as early as 1965, while he was with The Lower Third, yet another

Jones/Bowie 'first' to add to this interesting period of his development.

*

One early attempt to get more national radio coverage was our now infamous audition at the BBC, which I referred to in a previous chapter. On 10 November 1965, we turned up at Broadcasting House, just off Oxford and Regent streets, unloading our gear into the side entrance and from there into a smallish studio. This was all very exciting stuff, but not destined for a happy ending.

The three songs we chose included a new one from Dave called 'Baby That's A Promise' (a song we had recently recorded at the RG Jones studio in Morden) and two covers: James Brown's 'Out Of Sight' and our rather unusual, rocked-up version of the *Mary Poppins* song 'Chim Chim Cher-ee'. This was how it was done back then. A successful audition would provide a positive thumbs-up to allow BBC producers to invite us to perform on their particular Beeb programmes (radio that is). Sadly, we failed the audition, and that was that. A later publication of our audition report revealed comments that were far from complimentary, especially about Dave himself. Among various derogatory remarks, one panellist commented that he 'Sings out of tune.' Our unusual repertoire particularly confused them too. For example, the BBC audition panel – just like Rikki Farr before them – simply couldn't grasp why we had chosen a song like 'Chim Chim Cher-ee' to perform. Irony obviously wasn't their thing, man – though maybe it just sounded awful?

Wouldn't it be great to hear that recording now? Unfortunately they had so many acts auditioning every week, they just reused the same tape over and over. The same was true for a lot of legendary sixties and seventies television shows, which again used the same tape from project to project. The valuable gems that were taped over during these years don't bear thinking about!

Of course, David would later pass another audition as a solo performer and went onto record many great sessions for the Beeb, the cream of these recordings going on to earn a gold record for the sales of his *Bowie At The Beeb* EMI release in 2000.

Maybe later on there were a few red faces at the BBC at their initial dismissal of his talent, who knows? Mind you, we didn't exactly have a slew of BBC radio pop shows to perform on at the time. Radio One had yet to launch, so opportunities for younger bands and artists were pretty limited to say the least.

All I can say is that, certainly visually, David's stage persona in the way he moved and expressed himself at the height of his fame was no different, in my eyes, to that of our performances in '65 and '66. But his voice did definitely improve with experience and maturity, as you would expect.

On stage, Dave was often quite playful, sometimes with a sense of mischief, but could also turn serious and even aloof if the mood took him. He could also be affected if things were not going his way, and sometimes reflect it in his performance. But saying that, he always remained in complete control and oozed confidence. Dave knew what he was doing at all times while on stage, which I couldn't help but be impressed by. I've read that he later got fed up playing the ballrooms, but I think this was as much to do with the endless amount of time spent travelling in a van, the waiting around and general grief that goes with it all. When he was up on the stage he seemed to be in the space he was made for, and he really did get a thrill from it.

Dave immersed himself in his performance, particularly when he was doing his own material. He had a wide range of impressive hand gestures too – not of the rude variety I may add (not for the audience, anyway), just theatrically expressive. It was all part of the package, it was all carefully considered; nothing was wasted.

As a band, during gigs we bounced off each other. I tended to work with Graham but also take cues from 'T-cup', and obviously Dave's main lead. This often created an unspoken, mutual musical inspiration.

Significantly, there was never a pre-prepared play list for each set. Dave was in complete charge of this for every performance (and remember, we often did two sets at each venue during an afternoon and/or evening). He just turned and called out what our next number would be and we instantly reacted. Alternatively, we just got our cue from the story he told that we knew was leading into 'Silly Boy Blue', or 'That's A Promise', or even a band he was currently into whose song we were about to cover, like The Kinks' 'You Really Got Me' or The Pretty Things' 'Rosalyn'. It kept things fresh too, as performing the same numbers, night after night, can really get to you. That negative thought takes me back to my nights at the Van Gogh bar in Rupert Street. With Dave, however, there was a lot of spontaneity.

I have to admit I can't recall all the numbers we ever performed live, sadly none of us can. But the following (though not all in one set) will give you a good idea of what you may have heard if you came across an old recording of one of our shows:

'That's A Promise'
'Baby Loves That Way'
'I'll Follow You'
'Out Of Sight'
'Silly Boy Blue'
'Born Of The Night'
'Bars Of The County Jail'
'You Really Got Me'
'Mars: Bringer Of War'
'You've Got A Habit Of Leaving'
'That's Where My Heart Is'
'Don't Bring Me Down'
'Chim Chim Cher-ee'
'Glad I've Got Nobody'
'Can't Help Thinking About Me'
'The London Boys'

I've a feeling that Dave did 'Bars Of The County Jail' live on just his acoustic guitar once or twice, with us on backing vocals, and 'Don't Bring Me Down' we threw in to our set from time to time too (full band, of course). It was a track he could really attack a tambourine on, an instrument he often used on stage with us, along with a harmonica.

It would have been nice to have some original, hand-written old Lower Third set lists though, if we had made them. I've got some from other bands I was with and they provide some nice snapshots of exactly what was going on at the time. I wish I could remember all the songs we actually did in our time together – there were certainly a few of Dave's own compositions that we never recorded ourselves. Sometimes we would try these out to see what the reaction was like and possibly for Dave to develop further. 'Silly Boy Blue' is one example of a song that changed shape, which I will get to shortly.

As far as our individual popularity went, it was always the singer who got the attention, it seemed. However, at one performance at the Marquee my girlfriend, Helene, sat next to two girls and overheard one say to the other, 'Who do you like, the drummer or the singer?' I'm pretty sure I actually got the vote (my ego wouldn't allow me to forget that one). On the balance of things, though, I would have to admit that was the exception rather than the rule. Still, coming as it did from my girlfriend at the time, it did my self-esteem no end of good.

*

One day when I was due to meet Denis at the Gioconda, I walked in to find him sitting with an attractive young blonde woman. 'Phil,' he said, 'this is my friend Mandy.' And that's how I met Mandy Rice-Davies (of the infamous John Profumo and Stephen Ward scandal that had nearly brought down the British government three years earlier). I don't think I knew who she was at first; Denis probably clued me in a bit later. Evidently when she first arrived in London she had been a dancer at Murray's Cabaret Club in Soho, and this is where she first met Christine Keeler. Mandy was very open about her life and quite happy to talk about 'the scandal', turning out to be a genuinely nice person. She was also very witty too, I remember, and from then on she often came to see us at our Roebuck rehearsals. I remember she was also amused when we ran through

'Chim Chim Cher-ee' one time – Dave hamming it up, proper cockney style, especially for her: *'Good luck will rub off when I shakes hands with you…'*

At first I thought she was spending time with us because she was trying to break into showbiz as a singer, and I remember there was talk that she had connections with a nightclub in Tel Aviv. However, like most of the girls who came into contact with the band at the time, she actually had the hots for David. Mind you, it took me twenty years or so to work that out, following a conversation with Denis Taylor one afternoon. Anyhow, whatever her motives were for hanging out with us back then, she brightened up the room no end. In fact, when she came to our rehearsals I found it quite distracting – but in a nice way.

*

One of the few things EMI records did in promoting our first record was to book us on a radio show. This was actually recorded at EMI's main building in Manchester Square and was a weekly promotional show that the label sponsored and went out on Radio Luxembourg. This radio station was really the main (and at one time the only) broadcaster of pop and/or rock music.

Pop music, of whatever type, had to fit into the existing format of a show, whether at the theatre, on television or on the radio. This format hadn't changed much from the fifties; so, for example, you had The Beatles appearing at the London Palladium in a 'variety' show, alongside comedians, magicians and quite likely acrobats as well. All unthinkable today and laughable, unless maybe on the Royal Variety Show. In the mid-sixties, this new, younger music was still finding its niche in the entertainment business and had yet to establish itself as the major force it became.

So, even though the BBC didn't like us, we did find an outlet, and David Jones and The Lower Third were to perform on a radio show after all. This one on Radio Luxembourg was presented by Shaw Taylor and produced by Muriel Young. Presenters of that time did not emerge from or because of the music, they were already established personalities before this new racket came along. In this tradition we had curious television programmes such as *Juke Box Jury*, hosted by dapper 'man about town' David Jacobs (with his plummy, public-school accent), together with a group of equally out-of-place panellists, all lauding over new records by scruffy herberts trying to get a hit.

Our presenter, Shaw Taylor, was much more in his element when he presented a popular TV show called *Police 5*, a programme that set out to help the police catch criminals with the help of the viewing public. At the end of every show he would famously point a finger at one of his eyes and say, 'Keep 'em peeled.'

The producer, Muriel Young, was also famous and could often be seen presenting children's television at this time. Both of these professionals were excellent at what they did but were simply miscast in trying to present rock and roll. It was not their fault that it was a bit alien to them as the business, as I've said, was still evolving. John Peel had yet to return from America and the likes of Tony Blackburn and co. were yet to come.

Muriel Young would later develop many TV drama shows and also go on to produce a number of TV pop series in the seventies, including *Marc*, Marc Bolan's show and swansong in 1977.

Our base since Ralph came on the scene had become his basement flat at 79a Warwick Square, a short walk from Victoria Station. It was a typical bachelor pad, which he shared with a chap we would also see often, Kenny Bell, another booker/agent and also a trumpet player. It wasn't anything glamorous, but Ralph did his bit to make it as homely as possible. For all that, though, it was a bit dank, with a bathroom reeking of deodorants and aftershave.

On the afternoon of the show we gathered at Warwick Square to decide how we would perform that evening. The show was mimed, which sounds a bit odd as there was a live audience, but acts pretended to play along to their record so that the audience reaction could be recorded. Unbelievably, we decided not to take our instruments but simply to dance instead. Well, we were working with a future superstar, after all.

To show off our hair, as Ivan had intended it, our barnets needed some urgent attention. With this in mind, Ralph asked, or rather told me, to go out and get some hair lacquer. Remember, in 1965 the only hair lacquer retailed anywhere was for women.

'No,' I said, 'I'm not going.'

'Why?' replied Ralph.

'Because it's for women. I'm not going into a shop to ask for something women use!'

'Well, say it's for your sister then,' said Ralph.

'I haven't got a sister,' I said.

I don't remember how this was resolved, but I know I didn't go. Ridiculous now to think I would react like that back then, especially since I had been buying hair lacquer from the age of fourteen from my local barber who sold it to me in a brown earthenware pot for nine pence to hold my 'trunk cut' in place. Thankfully these inhibitions were eventually knocked out of me and I can thank my time with David and the band for that.

Our dance routine was completely made up by us on the spot that afternoon at Warwick Square. I remember feeling very awkward prancing about, particularly when we had to strike a particular pose with a couple of us kneeling while the other two held their hands on our shoulders. I felt like a right chump. But we did eventually take it seriously so that we could do as professional a turn as possible.

Thankfully on the night the teenage audience were hungry, probably for anyone vaguely famous, and by the time we were introduced had been whipped into excitement and applause by the studio warm-up guy and Shaw Taylor's enthusiasm. Our routine went off OK, I think, mainly because it probably looked as though it was a spoof.

Afterwards, Shaw interviewed Dave about the group and Dave told him about me recently joining and what the group's aims were. I heard it broadcast some time later and was pleased to get an individual mention. Shame I didn't record it for posterity.

Before I move on from my memories of Warwick Square, it was at this place that the penny dropped about Dave's probable bisexuality. It was Denis who worked it out first later in the year, as winter set in and he and Graham found themselves freezing cold in the back of the ambulance, which was parked in the square.

Den recalled the moment in an interview with ex-Capital Radio DJ and writer Kerry Juby in the 1980s. 'We were parked about fifty yards from his flat and I was really cold. It was horrible,' Den remembered. 'I was trying to get myself comfortable on these padded seat things and had a blanket over me. I thought, "What the hell am I doing here when Ralph's flat is over there?" So I went over to knock on the door. There was another fellow living at Ralph's at that time called Kenny Bell who said, "I'm sorry, you can't come in." I then realised what David was doing. To me, he was bettering his career.

'My whole opinion of him changed after that, but I got used to the idea. I know Graham wasn't too happy [either]. I remember I went back to the ambulance feeling quite horrified. I thought, "Good God, it's the end of the group," which it wasn't until a few months later.'

A day or two after, when I met up with the boys again, I was brought up to speed on the events of that evening. It was actually a party that Den had chanced upon, a gay party as it turned out. What apparently made it more of an eye-opener was that Ralph had Sellotaped cardboard over the downstairs front window. Bearing in mind that homosexuality was still illegal at this time, it was something he and his friends obviously had to do for their own safety. It sounds crazy by today's standards, I know, but you could, until 1967, be criminally charged just for being gay.

That night, when Kenny Bell answered the door, he actually said to Den, 'You can't come in because Ralph is in bed with David.' That was why Den was so shocked, mainly because Dave was such a red-blooded ladies man in our eyes. We hadn't had the slightest clue that he liked men too. None of us were shocked or concerned that Ralph was gay, that wasn't the issue.

I'm not sure we even knew much about bisexuality,

as none of us had known anyone bisexual before. In my earlier days you were either straight or 'queer' (the word 'gay' had yet to be widely associated with the homosexual community back then). There was no sexual middle ground, so to speak, that I was then aware of anyway, which may help you understand our staid and somewhat archaic reactions.

To be honest, it may have shocked me for a week or two but it never changed my attitude to either Dave or Ralph. Dave was still one of my best mates and what he did privately was his own business.

I would never have guessed then that his sexual preferences would provide one of the music industry's defining moments in the seventies. Incredible really. There is no doubt that David's bravery in revealing that he was gay in 1972 went on to help so many people in the gay community (four years later, he told *Playboy* magazine that he was bisexual). Society has moved on massively since those blinkered days in the mid-sixties and I've no doubt at all that David's contributions to issues like this was not only hugely important, but still greatly appreciated by many, many people to this day.

*

None of the band was particularly domesticated, so we tended to grab our meals from wherever was most convenient, quick and cheap. Food on the road just wasn't a priority. I wonder if being on the fags stemmed our hunger? Who knows? But I know drinking tea and coffee helps keep the hunger pangs away, so I guess that may be why Denis loved his cuppa tea so much. (If you look carefully at some of the photos of The Lower Third on stage, you can just about make out a teapot logo on Denis's guitar strap. That's how much he loved his tea.)

I remember my mum making me sandwiches a few times, concerned that I wasn't eating properly. And I recall once when we were at Graham's girlfriend's flat and about to set off to drive to a gig. She had made him a huge pile of doorstep cheese-and-pickle sandwiches to see him through. My stomach rumbled seeing them.

We were all slight of build, but none more so than Dave. In fact, I always thought he had a calcium deficiency as he had white spots on his fingernails. At the time I thought that this partly signified a dodgy diet and that he couldn't have been that healthy, but I have since learnt that the calcium thing is a myth and white patches on nails are due to an injury to the base of your nail. God knows what he'd been doing to his hands, because he had loads of these spots.

Anyway, Dave and I were generally getting well fed at home, unlike Denis and Graham. Though I think Graham probably got a bit more nosh from girlfriends, Denis tended to rely on the Gio and one or two similar favourite establishments. He was much liked and he befriended many, did our Denis.

I do remember with some affection there was a special pie stall outside Victoria station that was open really late at night. We would often make for that stall whenever we were in the vicinity late after a gig. You couldn't beat a steak pie with HP sauce, particularly as we were often coming down (adrenalin wise) following a good show, especially when those urgent hunger pangs suddenly hit. And they were bloody good pies too – I'm genuinely getting hungry thinking about them now.

One nice memory of that stall was catching up with the

guitarist and composer Graham Dee, who stopped by while the four of us were filling our faces late one night. Funny, but there are lots of stories of bands meeting up by chance at the Blue Boar motorway services on the M1 (which I will expand on shortly), but not so many about that Victoria station pie stall, which many a band would head to for sustenance.

It was good to catch up with Graham. I asked him what he was up to and he said he was with The Walker Brothers, which certainly impressed me as the Walkers were at their height at the time. He had some pretty hair-raising stories of their gigs too, many of which they had to abandon after the first two or three songs because the audience stormed the stage. He said it often got very dangerous, particularly for the Brothers (who, I'm sure you know, weren't brothers at all). At a couple of their shows they had most of their clothes ripped off before they could be rescued, and were also nearly seriously crushed at the same time. Vivid stuff.

Notably, Graham also joined the band Them (twice), at the request of Van Morrison, and was generally a much sought-after session musician. He has quite a resumé, and of course was very friendly with our Dave too, often spending hours chatting with him at the Gio. David seemed to know everyone. In fact, Graham Dee evidently used to wake up Denis and Graham in the ambulance during early mornings in Denmark Street so they could move it and not get a parking ticket.

Another nice thing about Graham is that he has always asked after me whenever he has bumped into my mate John Urquhart. He obviously has fond memories of those amazing days too.

*

Ralph came up with some timely work in Birmingham – his hometown, of course. He had leaned on an agent contact there and we got bookings for a week. We set off one morning in the ambulance, Ralph and all, and drove up to Birmingham on the brand-new M1 motorway. We would get to see a lot of that motorway in our time, and get to know the infamous, aforementioned Blue Boar services of course, the only early hours motorway services watering-hole available for desperate, half-starved musicians on their way home from a gig – and used by the odd lorry driver too.

The Blue Boar wasn't known for its quality cuisine. You got what was available at that time, and quite often it had partly dried to the plate by the time scruffs like us started to wander in. Generally we stuck to tea and coffee and a bun. We knew how to live.

It wasn't unusual to see a number of groups around the restaurant at different tables, generally looking the worse for wear. By this time of the night the four of us would just sit around a table in complete silence, enjoying our brew, half asleep.

The bookings on this particular Midlands run were a mixed bunch, with a big question mark as to our suitability for some of the venues. We were booked to play in schools (school social clubs, I suppose) and also nightclubs.

Ralph took us to meet his mum, sister and their pet dog called 'Moody'. Typical of our circumstances, we had nowhere to stay. One night we went as visitors to a club where, lo and behold, Mandy Rice-Davies came to the door and got us in as her guests. Someone, probably Dave, must have known she would be there. This particular nightclub was more a casino with live music, and the band graciously invited us to get up on stage and do a

David, c. early 1966. © *Pictoral Press Ltd / Alamy*

Above: Davie Jones and The Lower Third, EMI Manchester Square, August 1965. Myself at the back, with Graham Rivens (left), Davie Jones, Denis Taylor. © *EMI*

Below: The Lower Third lined up in all our glory. © *Phil Lancaster Collection*

Above: School pals Denis Payton, Les Heath and myself. Walthamstow, c.1960. © *Jack White*

Below: The Who, pictured in 1965. The band that most influenced David Bowie and the Lower Third. © *The Visualeyes Archive / Getty*

The Lower Third rock the Marquee Club in London. © *Helene Lancaster*

Above: Modernists Patrick Kerr, Dave Jones and yours truly enjoy the high seas in the summer of 1965.

Below right: Dave and Pretty Things drummer, Viv Prince, on the Isle of Wight ferry. *All photos © Denis Taylor*

New record by local group could put them among the charts

THEY USED TO BE KNOWN as Oliver Twist and the Lower Third, and were very popular with Thanet teenagers at their weekly dance dates in the Orchid Ballroom, Margate . . . now Oliver Twist has left the group, and a 19-year-old Londoner, David Bowie, has joined them to record a disc released on the Pye label this week, entitled "Can't Help Thinking About Me" — and it's one which, I think, can't help getting into the charts.

"Can't Help Thinking About Me" moves along with a great beat, has a good vocal sound and a tremendous backing provided by the group — Denis Taylor (22), lead guitarist, Graham Rivens (20), bass guitarist, and Phil Lancaster (22), drums.

On the flipside, David sings, And I Say To Myself."

In the last few years both David and the Lower Third have played at clubs, theatres and ballrooms all over the country and have appeared often on television and radio.

At one time David was banned from television because of his exceptionally long hair. Now it has been shortened.

He is hoping that through his new record, his new name will become known. For he was once

known as Davie Jones and recorded under that name in the past.

"If this record is a hit — that's all right — but we really want to become established," he says.

During the last six months, David and his group have been concentrating on improving their stage act. They have changed their manager and their agent, and are now appearing every two weeks at London's Marquee Club. Local fans of theirs can hear their new record on the pirate radio ship, Radio London.

Page 2

CHART PARADE Two

In TOP 50 Britain

This Wk	Last Wk	No. of Wks in charts		
1	1	5	NANCY SINATRA	These Boots Are Made For Walking
2	2	3	ROLLING STONES	19th Nervous Breakdown
3	12	2	PETULA CLARK	My Love
4	6	7	HERB ALPERT	Spanish Flea
5	4	7	MINDBENDERS	A Groovy Kind Of Love
6	3	7	CRISPIAN ST. PETERS	You Were On My Mind
7	5	5	SANDIE SHAW	Tomorrow
8	14	4	SMALL FACES	Sha La La La Lee
9	5	6	CILLA BLACK	Love's Just A Broken Heart
10	13	4	DUSTY SPRINGFIELD	Little By Little
11	24	4	FORTUNES	This Golden Ring
12	7	7	OVERLANDERS	Michelle
13	9	9	PINKERTON'S ASSORTED COLOURS	Mirror Mirror
14	20	3	BARBRA STREISAND	Secondhand Rose
15	44	2	THE ANIMALS	Inside Looking Out
16	18	5	LEN BARRY	Like A Baby
17	27	2	BEACHBOYS	Barbara Ann
18	17	4	THE TRUTH	Girl
19	19	4	STEVIE WONDER	Up Tight
20	45	2	GENE PITNEY	Backstage
21	10	17	ST. LOUIS UNION	Girl
22	39	3	EDDIE ARNOLD	Make The World Go Away
23	48	2	P. J. PROBY	You've Come Back
24	11	13	SPENCER DAVIS GROUP	Keep On Running
25	16	12	HERMAN'S HERMITS	A Must To Avoid
26	15	5	PAUL & BARRY RYAN	Have Pity On The Boy
27	23	3	LEE DORSEY	Get Out Of My Life Woman
28	—	—	LOU CHRISTIE	Lightnin' Strikes
29	22	15	OTIS REDDING	My Girl
30	21	19	FOUR SEASONS	Let's Hang On
31	—	1	SONNY AND CHER	What Now My Love
32	42	2	MITCH RYDER & DETROIT WHEELS	Jenny Take A Ride
33	38	5	SWINGING BLUE JEANS	Don't Make Me Over
34	—	1	ELVIS PRESLEY	Blue River
35	32	3	ROGER MILLER	England Swings
36	—	1	BILLY FURY	I'll Never Quite Get Over You
37	26	4	NASHVILLE TEENS	Hard Way
38	28	5	DYLAN	Please Crawl Out Of Your Window
39	—	1	DAVID BOWIE	Can't Help Thinking About Me
40	25	13	BEATLES	We Can Work It Out/Day Tripper
41	31	4	CHRIS FARLOWE	Think
42	—	1	JAMES BROWN	I Got You
43	37	7	BERT KAEMPFERT	Bye Bye Blues
44	23	4	SECOND CITY SOUND	Tchaikovsky 1
45	34	4	ROY ORBISON	Breaking Up Is Breaking My Heart
46	—	1	FOUR PENNIES	Trouble Is My Middle Name
47	—	1	PETER AND GORDON	Woman
48	—	1	RAY CHARLES	Crying Time
49	—	1	CRYIN' SHAMES	Please Stay
50	—	1	HOLLIES	I Can't Let Go

Left: The Kent press back their local musicians recording plus a *Record Retailer* press advertising for David's first single release as 'David Bowie'.

Right: Number 39 with a bullet! David's first sniff at a record chart he would later dominate.

All photos © Phil Lancaster Collection

Above: Promotional photo session for EMI's Parlophone and the release of 'You've Got A Habit Of Leaving', outside Hertford House and the home of the Wallace Collection museum, Manchester Square. © *EMI*

Below left: Title of Gaby Sturmer's David Bowie promotional flyer, as referenced later in the book. The lettering was by David himself. © *Kevin Cann Collection*

Below right: Promotional copy of David and the Lower Third's first single.

© *Kevin Cann Collection*

Above: Once a poser… Cliff Bennett, Dave and I bust some shapes. ©*Denis Taylor*

Below left: Rejected promo photo, EMI House. © *EMI*

Below right: My sixties address book.

couple of numbers. This we did and thoroughly enjoyed our 'guest appearance'.

Afterwards I sat at a table with Mandy and Denis and started bemoaning the fact that we had nowhere to stay. Mandy (a Birmingham-bred lass herself) said we could have slept on her parents' floor if it wasn't for the fact that her guitarist was already crashing there.

On a nearby table were some of the actors from a popular TV soap of the time called *Crossroads*, a big hit with my mum. I recognised Anthony Morton, who played the slightly comical Carlos the chef. When I pointed him out to Mandy she said, 'He probably couldn't open a tin of baked beans.' Morton later went on to play a greasy gangster in the influential Mick Jagger/James Fox film *Performance*, which was slightly cooler than *Crossroads*.

During the evening, I asked Mandy how things were with Christine Keeler, her famous friend in the Profumo affair. She told me that it wasn't good, as Christine was still being hounded mercilessly by the press and having to hide away most days. Bearing in mind this was a good couple of years since the scandal had hit the headlines, it was an indication of just how big the whole event had been. It can't have been easy for either of them. They were both well fed up with it by then, though I think Mandy didn't let it get to her and just got on with life.

I was sorry to hear of her death in 2014 at the age of seventy – yet another of our little gang who has slipped away. Reading her obituary, I could only imagine her as she was back at that club in 1965, youthful, vivacious and a lot of fun. In 1986, she appeared in the film *Absolute Beginners*, playing the mother of the lead male character, Colin. David wrote the excellent theme tune and also starred in the film, and I've since wondered whether he and Mandy met again during production. Someone out there may know – I'd be interested to find out.

Mandy was a really nice girl, though, in my estimation, and certainly knew how to live. She will always be remembered for something she said in court during the Stephen Ward trial. For any younger readers out there, Ward was being tried for living off the immoral earnings made by Mandy, Christine Keeler and other girls. One of his many high-powered party guests turned out to be none other than the Secretary of State for War, John Profumo – hence the huge press interest.

When the defence council for Lord Astor, another man caught up in the affair, pointed out that Astor denied even meeting her, Mandy replied with a giggle, 'Well he would, wouldn't he?' But I think my favourite Mandy Rice-Davies quote came much later when she described her life as 'One slow descent into respectability.'

Back to our evening in that nightclub in 1965. Later in the evening, on the busy dance floor, Mandy nearly brought another drama right to our doorstep. A slight panic set in when Denis or Graham said to me, 'Quick, we must find Dave.'

'Why?' I asked.

'Because Mandy's fiancé has just walked in and Dave was dancing with her.'

Her fiancé, who I then spotted, not only looked like a current champion boxer, he actually was one, and he clearly seemed like a guy you wouldn't want to mess with. As I said earlier, it wasn't until quite a few years later, while reminiscing with Denis, that I found out that Mandy wasn't just hanging around with us because she enjoyed our music. Luckily, one of the boys spotted the pair, dancing much closer together than would have been advisable for Dave's long-term survival, and this allowed him just enough time to quickly scamper off into the shadows for safety. But it was a close-run thing.

Sometime after the demise of the Third, Denis went to Tel Aviv with Mandy to accompany her in her cabaret act, and still has a few nice photos taken with her there in his scrapbook. Denis also recently told me that Mandy had invited Dave to accompany her to play at her club in Israel the night we met her in Birmingham, but he had turned her down.

We must have ended up sleeping uncomfortably in the ambulance after we left the club that night. It's a bit hazy now, but I know we never had anywhere else to lay our heads. It was just the start of what turned out to be quite a memorable week in the city, particularly as all of us had a sweet tooth.

Graham had a brother who just happened to work at Cadbury's in Bournville, south Birmingham. I guess it was a rare opportunity for Graham and his brother to get together, but he also invited the whole band to tour the factory. We accepted the invite, but for some reason Dave didn't come with us that afternoon. He certainly had a sweet tooth, so I can only assume that Ralph had prearranged something important for him to do – or maybe an affair of the heart with another young Brum beauty had proved more tempting?

So we turned up at Cadbury's, looking, as you would expect a mid-sixties rock band to look, with our neatly coiffured mod barnets, trendy clobber and a bit of a swagger. In those days there were no set Cadbury World organised tours and the factory wasn't open to the public as such. This was just an employee giving us a private tour around the workplace, explaining the various processes involved in chocolate production, packaging, distribution and so on.

All went well until we got to a group of male operatives. From then on we got embarrassing wolf whistles all the way. It was probably due to similar experiences in the past that Dave had felt compelled to start his 'Society For The Prevention Of Cruelty To Long-Haired Men' the year before. He was deadly serious when he set it up, too, earnestly wanting to highlight the plights that he, and other guys with lengthy tresses, faced.

But as heartfelt as it no doubt was to start with, it also turned out to be a particularly handy promotional story. Les Conn picked up on it immediately and, together with a BBC TV producer friend called Barry Langford, spun it mercilessly into a clever and very successful media promotion. Before long it was all over the national press too, and Dave Jones received his first taste of notoriety.

He even managed to get his message broadcast on national television, explaining the background to the whole campaign during an early evening BBC *Tonight* interview with TV stalwart Cliff Michelmore (*Tonight* was roughly the equivalent of today's *One Show*, I suppose). The light-hearted interview (though clearly treated seriously by Dave) concerned the incessant public teasing and bad treatment Dave and his male friends received because of their hair. This, his first-ever TV interview, which is quite well known now having somehow been saved for posterity, was only broadcast seven or eight months before our Bournville visit, and was probably well remembered even by some of the guys teasing us at Cadbury's that day.

David said to Michelmore on *Tonight*: 'We've had comments like, "Darling!" and "Can I carry your handbag?" thrown at us and I think it's just had to stop now…' Eight months on, Dave's hair was now mod short, like the rest of us, but for all that he always looked different from the regular guy in the street. That was our job, of course, to be different, but different sometimes attracted unpleasant attention as well.

Dave later said that he used to stop traffic just walking down the street due to his long hair. That really happened. He also had some nasty encounters with people, too. He had actually been attacked in the street a few months before I met him when some thug, who simply didn't like the way he looked, landed a few punches on him until he hit the ground.

The Pretty Things' Phil May, whom we would encounter on our travels and who would also famously wear his hair down to his shoulders, later revealed his own experiences during this period: 'We were looked down upon because of our long hair, the way we dressed. People on the street would look at you and you saw hate in their faces – they hated you solely for the way you looked, nothing more.'

It's worth remembering that the early to mid-sixties really was an incredibly staid time. I'm sure it's hard to truly appreciate today. The country was only just starting to move on following post-war hardships; conscription had only come to an end in late 1960, and every young man who was fit to serve up until then (from the ages of seventeen to twenty-one), had to have short hair – with no exceptions. That was the society we lived in then, and men were still expected to keep their hair respectably short.

But, back to our Cadbury's adventure, overall it was an impressive visit and the whole set-up (a very large operation) was brilliantly organised, as you would expect. If the *Willy Wonka* films ever turn up on TV, they take me back to that afternoon in Bournville (which, thinking about it now, could easily be a made-up Roald Dahl place name).

I know what you're wondering. Yes, we did come away with quite a few bars of chocolate, which I'm sure lasted for at least the rest of our Midlands trip. So Dave didn't miss out on his favourite bar of Fruit & Nut in the end.

Another regular Birmingham club we were booked to play during this particular Birmingham trip was the trendy Elbow Room at 146 High Street, Aston, just north-east of the city centre. This place had a long history and evidently only closed in 2012 after a firearms incident.

In 1967, Steve Winwood (whom I met, with Dave, when he was part of The Spencer Davis Group), Jim Capaldi, Chris Wood and Dave Mason founded Traffic at this very club – which also counted big-time footballer George Best as an occasional guest.

Luckily for us, the Elbow Room also produced one night's lodging – a rarity when we travelled away. During the set and between songs, Dave looked at me and said in a warning tone, 'She's mine,' nodding in the direction of a waitress he'd been talking to. I should have been flattered that he thought I posed a threat, but I was actually dumbfounded and slightly put out that he even said it.

Anyway, Dave said she was studying to become an actress (yes, working as a waitress in a cocktail bar, and all that...) but, more importantly, would put us up for the night. With the prospect of a night at her gaff, I suppose he was staking his claim early. Graham decided to take up an alternative offer elsewhere, so after the gig Denis, Dave and I set off back to the waitress's flat – which was nothing more than a bedsit, but pleasantly homely all the same.

Denis settled himself in an armchair beside a hearth that contained an electric bar fire and made himself comfortable. I can see him now, starting to dose off with his legs sprawled out awkwardly. Our kind waitress/actress said I could sleep in her flatmate's bed as she wouldn't be back. 'But I don't know if there are any fleas,' she joked (I think).

Eventually we all settled down. Denis snoring by the fire, me rigid for fear of stirring up the fleas in the flatmate's bed, and Dave in the bed next to mine getting very cosy with our friendly hostess. The lights may have been out but there was not much sleep to be had for me (or Dave, as it happened).

I could only try and describe what went on that night by the use of a simile: it sounded a bit like someone stropping a razor all night – and I do mean all night. You will have to be male and of a certain age to know this sound, very common in barbers' shops once upon a time. Just one of the many highlights of life travelling with David Jones. He did give me all the gory details later that day, but that will remain between us. Some things are definitely meant to remain on the road.

In the end, it was probably only Denis who got any proper sleep that night; he seemed oblivious to it all and happily snoozed away. I think Graham had a half-decent place to sleep too and had a good night. He actually stayed at the home of two of Ralph's gay friends. This friendly couple of guys, who had earlier attended the gig, kindly offered to wash our sweaty stage shirts after the show, so Graham bundled them all up and took them with him.

Keeping our stage gear fresh was a problem when we were away. While Dave generally came prepared with enough changes of clothes to cover the gigs required (being the front man, he had more freedom with his costume), the three of us just had the one stage outfit each. It wasn't unusual for us to use the same sweaty gear we had on stage the previous night again before we could get them cleaned back at home.

When we met up with Graham the next day and retrieved our freshly laundered shirts, I complained that my cuffs were still wet. Graham quite rightly had a go at me saying, 'You should be grateful for small mercies.' I was well rebuked and did feel bad about it when I realised that these guys had washed all four shirts in the early hours before bed, hung them up then ironed them later in the morning.

Nothing should be surmised from Graham's choice of place to kip, it just so happened that many of Ralph's friends were gay men. We didn't mind. It was any port in a storm for a place to kip as far as DB and The Lower Third were concerned. I just chose a busy barber's shop!

CHAPTER SIX

THOSE MARQUEE NIGHTS

One major thing Ralph did was to get us signed up with Marquee Artists. This was a booking agency directly associated with the Marquee Club, but also booked bands into many other venues. From this agency we got work throughout the UK and abroad, but most importantly it got us a residency at the world-famous Marquee.

We took up a Friday night residency at the club. This brought us a following of fans that cottoned onto the type of music we were putting out and proved quite a contrast to the audiences we attracted throughout the rest of the country, who often hadn't a clue what to make of us.

I guess the Marquee audience was that much more sophisticated in many ways, it being one of London's hippest venues, and playing there week after week the audiences were able to get to know us, many learning our songs and singing along with us. This was very welcome exposure and at a prestigious venue too, even though we were only paid £12 a night, which we had to split between the four of us. At least that's the amount I remember, but I've since come across a contract that shows we were paid £20. I can't tell you how tight money was for us back then. Every shilling mattered.

It was at the Marquee that we felt confident enough to experiment and probably where we gave our best shows. We certainly had some amazing nights there, I'm sure some of the best of my career when I think about it, and Dave was in his element when he received a positive audience response. He could work them as well as anyone on the scene at the time, he was just a natural. I had one of the best vantage points to see him in action and even today can clearly picture what he was like; his unique showmanship, the way he could engage people, even the way he would hold the microphone.

In 1983, David reflected on his early years as a mod, and how central the Marquee and modernist lifestyle was to him back then:

> *I got friendly with the [Marquee] owners; for me there were no rules at the door so I used to creep in and watch what was happening. The Marquee, the Scene, Eel Pie Island in Twickenham, they were all a circuit. At the time, sixteen years old for me when I was frequently in those places, it was during the era of the first batch of mods. There were two batches of mods in England, the first lot being in 1962–63. The initial crop called themselves modernists, which reduced itself down to the mods. That was excessively peacocky. These weren't the anorak-quilted, gabardine raincoated mods that turned up later on motor scooters.*

The scooter thing wasn't quite as big with the early mods at that time; it was still trains.

You weren't supposed to like bands like The Rolling Stones, and especially The Action, The Who and all that crowd who came along later, these were the anorak boys in the later sixties because they weren't real mods. I did secretly [like them]. But I felt sad the former fashion had died out.

I dressed the archetype: mohair suits, two-tone suits; the shoes were high pointers; Billy Eckstine shirts with big roll collars. You either had a pinned collar or button-down or roll collar.

To try and give Ralph a hand on the bookings front, Den managed to blag us a gig at the Bata Clan Club, which was just off Regent Street. It wasn't a particularly special venue, although it was certainly no more unacceptable than most of the other places we were playing at the time, but Ralph was having none of it. He didn't consider it a suitable venue for Dave to appear at and basically forbade him playing there. So it ended up just the three of us, minus David, performing at the club with Den filling in on lead vocals. This was all well and good – well sort of. Den was no Bowie on vocals, of course. The trouble was, Denis could only remember the words to about four of our songs, so that's basically all we did, repeating them all at least twice. No one seemed to notice or worry about it and we got paid OK, so it was job done.

The sad thing about this particular appearance, though, is that there was a professional photographer working there that night, snapping away. Den still has a nice photograph of him singing at that gig. Luckily, my future wife Helene took a few basic shots of us at work at the Marquee (which are the best-known photos of David live with The Lower Third), but I've never seen any professional photos taken of us on stage anywhere. So Ralph's silly huff that the Bata Clan wasn't suitable for Dave (which we all thought was actually more about Ralph himself not making the booking) no doubt denied us all of some great live photos of Dave and the Third live on stage. Thanks, Ralph.

*

Riding in the back of the ambulance one day, Dave and I were discussing what we could do to improve the show, something that would make us different from the rest. It had to be something spectacular.

Dave always liked Gustav Holst's suite *The Planets*, and particularly the 'Mars' movement, which opens the piece. It had been the theme from *Quatermass*, Dave's favourite television show when he was a boy. I knew this piece well, having long been a lover of the whole suite.

As 'Mars' was the bringer of war, Dave said, 'What about bombs and effects going off on stage while we are playing it?' That sounded great and we both quickly started to get excited about the whole idea.

'How about fireworks and smoke effects?' someone said. That would really dramatise the whole production, we thought, as we continued to dream up ever-more spectacular scenarios for this unparalleled, highly charged crescendo. If nothing else, loud bangs and dramatic flashes would wow our audiences into submission. They wouldn't know what hit them.

What we hadn't properly considered was how we, a four-piece rock group, would be able to replicate something that really required a full orchestra and at least one or two stage crew. But that didn't stop us.

We learnt the main theme quite quickly, which (incredibly) worked very well in rehearsal, particularly employing Denis's guitar feedback (everything was feedback à la Pete Townshend then). I played the triplet drum signature, Graham gave it some extra welly on bass, 'T-cup' bent his guitar strings and slid the neck against his amplifier while Dave added a wailing mouth organ over the top of it all. With that we were rocking and in a way, I suppose, we became the first Bowie band to go to Mars.

We tried it at the Marquee first and it worked well, so we decided that it should definitely become part of our repertoire. It was murder for me to keep those triplets going on the snare and floor tom at the same time, but it was worth it. We stopped short of all the pyrotechnics in the end, no doubt due to lack of funds, and just relied on the club's 'lighting man' to go as mad as he could with the lights available to him – which basically meant switching the stage lamps on and off quickly at the right time. It was early rock theatre of the basic kind for sure, but still an eye-opener.

Denis Taylor also recalls working with Dave live at the time:

Well, we used to do what David liked… start off with an ordinary number and work up to a crescendo. It used to be planned out quite consciously but sometimes he would stick in other numbers right there on the stage, which I didn't really like as they were generally technically hard. The more involved ballads Davie used to do by himself on his acoustic. We were always loud and our sound did get louder as we progressed, which I know Dave moved away from with his next band.

Replicating Holst's 'Mars' live was typical of David's desire to experiment, as was the case at a private recording session on the last day of August 1965, at the RG Jones studio in Morden, where we were paying by the hour to try out new songs. David had come up with a system of writing down vocal sounds using a sort of hieroglyphics; meant for backing singers who couldn't read music, except it was more to do with the overall sound he wanted. He persuaded Ralph to let him take extra time to record using this new method. Kenny Bell, who was with us that day and was not particularly taken with David's experimental approach, said to Ralph, 'I don't know why you let him get away with this.'

I can't be sure, but the song we were working on that afternoon could have been 'Silly Boy Blue'. I certainly remember we recorded a demo of it at RG Jones, which I've heard since and can tell was never properly polished by us in the end (the demo is very basic, as Dave was still developing the melody and lyric before the tape rolled). That track reminds me of the way he would sometimes make words up on the flow as a new song developed – ensuring that the general feel of it was captured so that he could firm up a more thought-out lyric later on. I suppose in this way he was doing more than just 'la la-ing' through it; he was trying to convey more structure. Even at this time he was more experimental than any other musician I would record with at any time.

'Silly Boy Blue' later became a completely different type of song, about Buddhism mainly, rather than a play on the actual nursery rhyme that had inspired his original lyric (Dave had a Wally Whyton children's song book that he sometimes thumbed through for inspiration). But the essence of the work we did on his original 'Silly Boy Blue', given that it was a basic first-take demo, certainly gave Dave a firm starting point to develop the track properly, and I think John Eager made a great improvement to the drum track. It became a special song I think, and the opening line David eventually settled on is lovely:

> *Mountains of Lhasa are feeling the rain,*
> *People are walking the Potela Lanes,*
> *Preacher takes the school,*
> *One boy breaks a rule,*
> *Silly boy blue...*

David also made a very upbeat recording of this song for an early BBC session (they did eventually let him loose as a fully accredited session artist, discovering at the same time that he didn't sing out of tune after all). That track is also included on the *Bowie At The Beeb* compilation, by the way. Actually, if David's first 1967 album has somehow passed you by, I do recommend you check it out. It's very quirky, of course, but there are some lovely songs to be discovered on it, and all so different from anything he released with The Lower Third (I'm sure many people back then wouldn't have thought it was even by the same artist).

Another track we demoed at RG Jones (but which didn't make any of David's albums in the end) was 'Baby That's A Promise'. Both of these demos have since been bootlegged, so are fairly easy to find today.

David's burgeoning experimental streak also revealed itself during one of our ambulance journeys while we were chatting together, testing out new promotional ideas. While discussing our visual presentation and what we could do to improve it, he said, 'What about putting make-up on for the stage?' I immediately thought he meant clown's make-up and said something like, 'Yeah, why not?' thinking it might be a gimmick we could test.

I then called through the partition to Graham, who was driving of course, and asked what he thought of the idea. 'Not fuckin' likely,' was his curt reply, and with that nothing more was said on the matter. Graham had obviously got the drift of Dave's 'artistic' suggestion better than I had: that he meant we doll ourselves up a bit. I wonder now what he would have suggested and how far he would have pushed it had we gone along with it?

But it was coldly rejected by a unanimous decision of one – only to surface a few years later and become one of David's trademarks as a performer. There is no better example of this than the incredible *Aladdin Sane* album sleeve. Something like that would have been light years away from what he would have been considering then, and what was generally happening in the music scene in our day. And even in 1973, when *Aladdin Sane* first appeared, Dave was drastically pushing the boundaries further than anyone had dared. Just as he always did – when he was allowed to.

*

As our reputation at the Marquee grew we knew we must have something going for us, particularly if we could make it work at this important venue. We were even signing autographs now, which was marvellous for our egos and general confidence. As I've said previously, I loved these Marquee gigs and really felt at home there.

Midway through our set, Dave suggested we feature a drum solo as part of our routine while he, Denis and Graham buggered offstage to have a rest and leave me to it. That was fine by me, I could really let loose and enjoy myself, particularly because of the attention I got. Drum solos for this dual purpose were quite usual in those days. I loved it because the audience would come right up to the stage to watch and wildly applaud at the end. The stage was all mine. What more could you want? I think David did something very similar on his 1976 world tour, which I didn't see but have heard about.

The room at the side of the Marquee stage, where you waited to go on, was a place for high spirits and much pre-show banter. It was about the same size as a small sports changing room, with an adjacent bathroom with just enough space for a toilet and a small sink.

A lot has been made of David's unusual eye; he had told me he'd got it in a punch-up at school with his best mate, George Underwood. Anyway I had a habit of blinking my eyes a lot in those days, a bit like a tick I suppose, and while we were waiting beside the dressing room to go on stage one night Dave started mimicking my habit, blinking his eyes and taking the piss. It was a strange scenario really, as we were in a small space beside the stage, directly facing one another, a bit like a very close up comedic duel.

I retaliated by calling him 'wonky eye', just as part of our banter but I sort of wished I hadn't said it. Typically, he took it well though. But we were all conscious that he had a very sensitive side and aware that the occasional tear was not unusual. I often wonder how he managed to put up with some of the controversial press he later courted – though I imagine this is where the famous characters he created helped a lot. If anyone didn't like Ziggy Stardust, for example, as it was just a character and not actually David himself they were having a go at, maybe it reduced the impact? It was a really clever move on his part. He really was the textbook rock star. What he didn't learn from others he invented.

He could be a thoughtful bloke too. One time at an afternoon Marquee rehearsal (for an evening gig) there seemed to be a lot of people hanging about and the manager, John Gee, took exception. He raised his voice telling anyone who shouldn't be there to go, and started rounding people up. Just as Gee headed for my girlfriend, Helene, Dave – quick as a flash – called out loudly, 'She's our drummer's fiancée, John,' warding him off. My reaction to that was slightly mixed, being one of gratitude to Dave but also one of deep discomfort as we had no marriage plans at that time and with this statement Dave was sending me down the aisle! Dave then, walking past Helene, gave her a cheeky kiss on the cheek and a smile before jumping up on stage.

Another example of thoughtfulness came when we were out and about one day on the way to a gig. During the journey we drove up Putney Hill and Dave asked if we were going to stop and pick up Helene. She lived and worked as an au pair in a building on the hill and he knew we were going to pass her place. Travelling with us in the ambulance that afternoon were two Swedish girls who Dave had invited along.

I told him that Helene would have joined us if she could but was working that night. David replied, 'Oh, that's a shame. I invited these Swedish girls along especially as company for her.' Helene, if I haven't already said so, is Swedish herself. It meant a lot to me that Dave had considered her in this way.

Helene was an au pair to Valerie Hanson and family. Valerie was an impressive lady. Not only a successful actress and television director, she was also very philanthropic (though I only learnt about her humanitarianism in recent times; we didn't have a clue back then).

Valerie was notably the first female to direct BBC television programmes, although when I met her for the first time she was directing *Emergency-Ward 10* (for ITV), which was like an early version of BBC TV's *Casualty*. She worked on many TV dramas over the years and I would often see her name pop up in the titles.

I did much of my courting at Mrs Rilla's, for that was Valerie's married name. She had wed, but parted from, the film director Wolf Rilla. Wolf made many films, but is most remembered today for his classic sci-fi horror *Village Of The Damned*, which starred George Saunders. A few years later another director made a less popular sequel called *Children Of The Damned*, but it's Wolf's original that most people know.

Even though Wolf and Valerie were estranged, they still remained on friendly terms and I would sometimes meet Wolf at the flat, or when I was collecting his daughter Madeleine from him after a visit.

That was Helene's main job for the couple, taking care of their daughter Maddy, as we knew her. I was almost a permanent fixture at their comfortable flat, which was just off Marble Arch, or at the home they had later on by Putney Bridge. When I wasn't gigging I would collect Maddy from school and babysit her with Helene.

As well as trying to make it in music I was also hoping to branch out in other creative ways, like writing, and also a bit of acting if the opportunity arose. Well, I had the obvious connection in Mrs Rilla, so I told her my dreams. She was very responsive, but initially got the wrong end of the stick, believing that I wanted to get 'behind' the camera. When I got that straightened out Valerie kindly wrote me an introductory note, on ATV notepaper, and sent me off to a casting agency for TV and film extras. I duly turned up at the address but was quickly given the heave-ho, so that did my confidence no good and pretty much put me off for good. At least the band was looking positive, and week-on-week we seemed to be progressing. Things could easily have been worse.

Years later, when Helene and I had our first child, Stefan, we visited Valerie to show her our new boy. She was delighted and wanted to get involved in his education, which was typical of Valerie, who is a very caring person. I didn't know this at the time, but she spent many years previously setting up a soup kitchen for the homeless in Northampton. From the age of about twenty to thirty, Valerie worked every day from 8am to 8pm, unpaid, helping people at what soon became a shelter. It is still going strong and is known today as Valerie Hanson House. What an amazing thing to do.

By the time we met up with Valerie again, I had amassed a number of fledgling plays that I was unsure how to progress, so I asked her to look the latest one over. This she did and when we caught up with her a short time later she said to me: 'I have a lot to say about your play, Phil. Do you know you have written three plays in one?'

Well, she should know. But quite how I was going to sort that out – that is, identify the three and then develop the best of them – was a bit beyond me back then. So the plays returned to the drawer and it was back to the day job. Seeing Valerie again like that brought back all the Lower Third memories again, though, and I wondered how the boys were getting on, as we had by then lost touch.

On a final note about Valerie Hanson, she also taught at the Royal Academy of Dramatic Art (I told you she was an impressive lady) and her first pupil just happened to be Anthony Hopkins.

She also worked with another young actor called Anthony Newley (she clearly liked her Tonys!). In fact, she was seriously impressed with him, crediting him as the 'greatest actor in England' at the time. When you think of the incredible names who were at the top of their game back then – including John Gielgud, Laurence Olivier, John Mills, Peter Ustinov and Ralph Richardson – this was an incredible endorsement from a lady who really knew business well. I wonder if Anthony Newley ever knew?

I wish I'd known about Valerie's Anthony Newley connection at the time, as Dave was a big admirer, and of course often mimicked Newley when he felt like it. In fact, it was a bit unnerving, drumming behind Dave at times, when suddenly you'd hear Newley through our speakers during the set. It was interesting to hear him switch between styles, often just to surprise the audience as much as anything.

Of course, Newley certainly wasn't a bad guy to emulate in the business. He could literally do anything, including mime, creating successful musicals and writing many hit songs, he was that talented. *The Guinness Book of British Hit Singles & Albums* graciously points out that Newley was 'among the most innovative UK acts of the early rock years...' Not a surprise: Dave always knew that.

I was a big fan too, though to be honest Dave and I never spoke much about him; there was a kind of mutual understanding that we both knew he was a significant talent. I saw him in the flesh once when Roger Seamark, myself and some other mates went on the Jazz Boat. That was a cruise from, I think, Southend to Margate, where all the top trad jazz bands played on board, mostly on deck. Anyway, we were waiting to get on board when we spotted Newley, already on the boat and climbing some stairs. We found out that he was there to check it out before he started filming his Ken Hughes movie *Jazz Boat*, which would date this trip, and this Newley encounter, to about 1959.

Like Dave I also loved Newley's recordings and thought he was a great singer. I was especially pleased when Sammy Davis Jr became besotted with him, as I'd always loved Sammy Davis. Because Anthony Newley spent so much of his later years in the USA, he kind of lost touch with his British audience in the end, but he also made some great films along the way and I'm sure will not be forgotten.

Just looking back at Newley's *Jazz Boat*, and those involved with the film, I see that Nicolas Roeg was one of the main cinematographers. He, of course, was the famed director of many great films, such as *Walkabout, Don't Look Now* and Dave's very own *The Man Who Fell To Earth*. Now, that was a film and a half. I pretty much expected Dave to go on to great things, but I'm not sure I ever thought he would make the silver screen. I thought he was terrific in that film too, though I did struggle with the storyline at the time.

I'd forgotten that bandleader Ted Heath also made a rare on-screen appearance in *Jazz Boat*. Heath was one of the biggest names on the scene back in the day, and I'm told was a good friend of Dave's future manager, Kenneth Pitt, who shared offices with Heath around this time.

I've digressed a lot since I mentioned Valerie Hanson, but there is a sad postscript. In 1985 we learned that her beautiful daughter, Maddy, had died in a car accident. Valerie actually called to tell us herself shortly after the tragedy. It must have been awful to lose her daughter like that.

Wolf passed away in 2005, while Valerie turned ninety in 2017, and – I'm delighted to say – is still going strong.

CHAPTER SEVEN

THE BIRTH
OF BOWIE

In the summer of 1965, Ralph secured us a new residency. In fact, he was running the gig himself along with his friend Kenny Bell, so we certainly should have been given it. We were to play a summer season of Friday nights at the Pavilion in Bournemouth and then Saturday nights at the Winter Gardens in Ventnor, on the Isle of Wight. We would round off the weekend back at the Pavilion on the Sunday. Each week we were to support a 'name' band or artist who usually travelled to the Isle of Wight gig with us (we would park our ambulance at Southampton docks and load our gear into a removal van with the other band on the bill).

To add to the prestige of these shows, Ralph also booked Patrick Kerr, presenter of the popular TV music show, *Ready, Steady, Go!* Patrick was engaged as the evening's host and general master of ceremonies and was perfect at that; his pleasant manner made him a popular addition.

He was to become a good mate of the group over these trips and was always a lot of fun. Being a trained dancer, Patrick would often introduce new dance styles on *RSG!* He also introduced popular dance competitions while compeering our gigs. It was good to be around someone who was already an established TV personality.

Patrick was a good-looking guy who, I think, was half Spanish. As we got into these south coast shows I would pal up with him and we would often knock about the local towns together.

I had been buying little furry animals in a gift shop each week for Helene, who had to remain back in London. Patrick was with me one day and said, 'I'll buy one for Brian's flat,' Brian being Brian Jones of The Rolling Stones, and chose one he thought his friend would like.

I got on well enough with Patrick for him to ask me once, 'Do you want a girlfriend?' Sitting quietly nearby was a very pretty little blonde.

'No thanks, I'm courting,' said I (and I did use the word 'courting', which just illustrates how long ago this was).

'Oh well,' said Patrick. 'Only, I'm trying to move on a girlfriend for Brian [Jones, again].' Patrick was good friends with the top guys in the rock and pop world and had some great stories.

He once told me how he and George Harrison had been smoking pot together at George's home. It must have been quite strong weed, as George said to Patrick, 'Can you dig those choir boys singing at the end of the mantelpiece?'

There was also absolutely no side to Patrick at all. As I've already mentioned, during our travels the group rarely had a proper bed for the night. On one memorable night we all bunked down on a floor at a guesthouse on the Isle of Wight, Patrick included (I presume either Dave or Ralph bagged the bed). As various bods in the room came to life in the morning, including our Dave, I noticed Patrick getting up off the floor with his underpants inside out and the label showing. That both amused and impressed me. Here was a TV star happy to simply muck in with the rest of us. I was very sorry to hear about Patrick's death in 2009. It would have been really good to meet up and shoot the breeze with him one last time.

These regular dates also gave us a chance to spend time socialising with some of the better-known groups who played with us. For example, the name bands on these Bournemouth/Isle of Wight appearances included, as the season progressed: Van Morrison, then with the group Them; The Who; Johnny Kidd and The Pirates; Cliff Bennett and The Rebel Rousers (including Chas Hodges, later of Chas and Dave); The Pretty Things; and even Jess Conrad. Working in such close quarters with these great bands and front men rubbed off on all of us for sure, and I've no doubt that it gave Dave that extra spur to make it himself. In many ways these summer months, more than any other in our band's short history, marked the birth of Bowie.

*

The routine at the weekend was for us all to drive down to Bournemouth on the Friday afternoon, set up our gear and maybe (though rarely) have a quick practice before the weekend's gigs. Before this series of Friday evening Pavilion gigs kicked off, we did a one-off trial night on 10 July, arranged and promoted by Ralph and Kenny Bell. It was a busy night for them as they had managed to book The Who for an appearance at Ventnor Winter Gardens too. That went so well that hundreds were turned away at the door and the idea to book similar top acts for a regular summer promotion was born.

Bournemouth was always a popular and busy resort and although we didn't turn people away at the door that night (a baking hot one, by the way), the hall was full enough and the crowd nicely responsive. This time we obviously did enough to impress the Pavilion's manager, our positive debut proving equally beneficial for Ralph and Kenny (who managed to secure The Who for another gig there the following month).

*

As accommodation was definitely not high on Ralph's list of priorities, any sleeping arrangements made for us there – certainly early on in the season – were purely left to pot luck, a fair wind, and the rare aforementioned guesthouse indulgence.

Ralph, of course, always stayed at the hotel by the Pavilion so occasionally we would congregate in his room and kip on the chairs. Sleeping that is, as best we could. He did sometimes have the heart to order up some sandwiches, which we swiftly devoured. Unfortunately this free board ruse didn't go far into the season as the hotel porter caught on to it and complained, of all things, that people were putting their feet up on the furniture. Denied entry there, alternative accommodation was then urgently sought. There was only so much sleeping in the ambulance we could put up with.

When even Dave started to get fed up having to rough it at night, the pressure was suddenly on Ralph to get it sorted. This he did, at least for the Friday night accommodation, in a semi-formal arrangement with the Bournemouth Ballroom manager. This man had a caravan in his back garden and he kindly said we could stay in it while we were in town. This was only a small caravan with two double beds, but it was at least a proper place where we could get our heads down after the gig and grab a few hours' sleep before we needed to set off for the ferry across the Solent.

At times it even felt like we were away on our holidays during those short stopovers. That caravan – as simple as it was – was a brief reprise from all the rushing about we had to do, and regular day-to-day pressures we all felt in a struggling new band. It felt good to pitch up there.

As usual Denis and Graham bunked together, as did Dave and myself. The caravan must have been quite old as in our half we quickly discovered that there was a leak in the roof, precisely above the bed Dave and I had chosen. So whenever it rained it became a race between the two of us to claim the dry side of the bed. From memory, Dave usually won. Oh yes, the glamour of it all!

It was so ironic to see David on TV, back in Bournemouth during the height of his Ziggy Stardust fame in 1973 – on BBC's *Nationwide*, I think – wowing a frenzied audience at the Winter Gardens (which was another large venue in the town, just up the hill, about a quarter of a mile from the Pavilion). During this film David rushes out of the venue's back door and into a waiting Daimler, then the police help his car escape the crowds of eager fans gathered around it. I remember watching this, thinking that it was only eight years earlier that we regularly slept together in a small Bournemouth caravan bed, while water dripped onto our heads.

When someone becomes hugely successful in the

way that Dave did, by sheer perseverance and ability (particularly when they have come from such a humble background and been willing to slum it in the way he did), it certainly gives that success an added feel-good factor. I couldn't think of anyone more deserving and I was so pleased for him, and of course, not a little jealous.

Years later when I recalled our Bournemouth days to Denis he reminded me of the time I exited the caravan one morning following a particularly restless night, exclaiming loudly, 'Bloody hell, it's like sleeping next to a sack of twigs,' such was Dave's 'bag of bones' physique. Bag of bones it may have been, but he certainly looked good in all he wore, and that physique added to his great stage presence. All the same, it was still a physique that wasn't very comfortable to share a little bed with.

Slumming it a bit on these long weekends had its benefits, though. For example, it was great to be regularly working alongside successful artists such as Cliff Bennett and The Rebel Rousers. The previous year, Cliff had successfully made the UK Top 10 with 'One Way Love' and would do similarly well with a cover of The Beatles' 'Got To Get You Into My Life' in 1966. The group weren't just good musicians, they were a friendly bunch too, as were most of the groups we encountered.

I believe that Cliff went on to make his fortune in shipping during the 1970s and beyond. I know he still does a small amount of gigs every year as Cliff Bennett and The Rebel Rousers, even though he must be well into his seventies now.

Two days after our Ventnor Winter Gardens appearance with Cliff Bennett (on 24 July), Queen Elizabeth II visited the same venue, no doubt just a little disappointed that she had missed our show. If she had only known we would be back the following weekend with Johnny Kidd, maybe she would have hung around?

Johnny Kidd and the Pirates did the whole weekend with us in Bournemouth and on the island. All the groups shared the same dressing room, so we had time to get to know them a bit, and we all travelled together across to the island on the White Link Ferry.

Dave had already met Johnny and had previously supported him while playing sax with his first band, The Kon-Rads. In the dressing room we were all impressed when Johnny (real name Freddie Heath) put on his long leather pirate boots – real authentic-looking they were, too. They went well with his black leather jacket and strides, and the eye patch he always wore on stage. He really looked the part, did Johnny, and gave a great show.

That afternoon, as we sat around the dressing room having a general catch-up chat, Johnny said to Dave, 'You should record "Shakin' All Over", you'll do well with that.' He then turned and addressed all of us collectively, in case we hadn't taken the hint: 'You young groups should record my songs.' I can still remember him telling us that like it was yesterday. Although it sounds like he was being arrogant, he wasn't really, and actually he was right. It was a great record and I'm surprised there weren't more covers of it back in the day. I could feel his frustration.

One other funny thing that stayed in my memory of that afternoon with Kidd was when he and a couple of his bandmates were telling us about their groupie success rate, Johnny asking his bass player quite earnestly, 'How many times have we caught crabs now?' Of course, he wasn't referring to the beach variety.

'Shakin' All Over' was Kidd's biggest hit (it stayed at No.1 for quite a while) and by 1965 was already five years old. But it still sounded cool and contemporary and brought the loudest audience response of the evening. The funny thing is, while listening properly to David's 1960s homage album *Pin Ups* – which was recorded and released in 1973 – I realised that he and Mick Ronson gave Kidd a friendly thumbs-up by including the classic 'Shakin' All Over' riff as part of the cover of 'I Can't Explain'. Perhaps the song was just too obvious for Dave to cover on that album, but I would have loved to have heard him sing it, all the same.

Johnny also had an impressive, authentic pirate cutlass, which he ensured was a key part of his act. Alice Cooper did something similar in the early seventies, though Kidd would often stab his sword firmly into the stage for dramatic effect. It was a real sword, no messing about, and the point hadn't been at all blunted for safety reasons. It's very unlikely he could get away with that kind of stunt today, what with 'elf an' safety' and all that nonsense.

A final funny story about Johnny and his cutlass relates to a gig he did with The Pirates at the Cavern Club in Liverpool. While setting up for the performance, Kidd's road crew wisely pointed out to him that the whole of the famous subterranean venue, including the stage itself, was made of brick and concrete, and that it would be dangerous to try and impale the cutlass into the floor during the show.

And they were right to be concerned. Kidd either ignored them or got caught up in the moment and launched the blade into the floor anyway – only to watch in disbelief as it ricocheted dangerously off the ground and out into the tightly packed audience. Apparently no one was injured but the drama, it seemed, had only just begun as an opportunist audience member grabbed the sword and swiftly made his way for the exit.

Kidd's trusty road manager immediately took up the chase and apparently trailed the scally for a mile or so across the city centre before safely retrieving it. That was one brave road manager.

It was awful when Kidd died in a car crash the year after we worked with him. I was very shocked and saddened when I heard the news. I hardly need to point out that he was one of the music scene's real characters. Although he seemed much older and more experienced than us at the time, he was actually only thirty when he died.

Less friendly, though perhaps just shy, were Northern Irish outfit Them. My only memory of their lead singer, Van Morrison, was when he was walking down the stairs while heading towards the stage. He looked quite moody and dramatic, his long red hair touching the shoulders of his black suit. Them were quite a big deal at the time – they had two quality hits that year: 'Baby, Please Don't Go', which made the Top 10, and 'Here Comes The Night', which was only held off the No.1 spot by The Beatles' 'Ticket To Ride'. It's no surprise that these Bournemouth and Isle of Wight package shows were so successful at the time. 'Here Comes The Night' must have registered well with Dave that weekend, as it was one of the songs he later included on *Pin Ups*.

Likewise, David also included another headline band's recordings on *Pin Ups* that he certainly heard live at Bournemouth and the Isle of Wight: The Pretty Things 'Rosalyn' and 'Don't Bring Me Down' – both big hits from a band he particularly admired. He was good mates with Pretty Things' charismatic lead singer, Phil May, while I became quite chummy with their rhythm guitarist, Brian Pendleton. Like myself, Brian was a bit of a jazz freak and we had some long, memorable conversations about our mutual interest.

It was very lucky that one of our band members had an interest in photography, as there are quite a few photos from these special weekend trips that have survived. Denis, who later became a professional photographer for a time, brought a camera with him and some of his photos are featured in this book. At least Denis had some foresight.

The funny thing about the classic photos Denis took of Dave with Phil May was that Dave had only recently cut his really long hair back, so he appears quite respectable next to Phil with his flowing locks. Looking back at some of the photos taken by Denis at the time, we could all be extras in the film *Quadrophenia*.

While I'm on the subject of photography, it's also worth mentioning that Ralph Horton owned an 8mm film camera and had it with him during some of these trips. He shot footage of us on the ferry to the Isle of Wight when we were in the canteen joking around with The Pretty Things, on the island and also with us fooling around on the sea front at Bournemouth. In fact, in Bournemouth we were a bit naughty as Ralph filmed us running in and out of a public toilet, being daft. I doubt any of this footage has survived, it certainly hasn't turned up anywhere over the years. And what did happen to Ralph? No one seems to know.

Shortly after one of these weekend adventures we all enjoyed a film night at Warwick Square, when Ralph played back all the footage he had taken of us – great fun. It wasn't a very long film, probably about five minutes in all, but there were some enjoyable scenes in there. In fact, when I recently saw some 8mm footage of The Beatles, taken on the beach and on the seafront at Weston-super-Mare in 1963, it immediately reminded me of Ralph's film with us.

*

Bookings for bands were never planned according to where we might be in the country. It just never worked like that. Gigs were generally hard to get and you had to grab them where you could. You might be in Leicester one night, Hastings the next, then back up to Leicester the day after that.

All that extra mileage takes extra petrol and that was something we could rarely afford. Our ambulance only used to manage eight miles a gallon, so it often needed a refill. On one occasion, having played somewhere in the far north, or Wales, or maybe even Leicester, on a Thursday night, Graham drove right through the night to get to Bournemouth on the Friday, only to run out of petrol just a few miles short of our caravan.

It was light by this time so Dave and I set off in the sunshine with the intention of hitching a lift to the ballroom manager's home to ask him to lend us some money (we were totally skint, as per usual), hopefully take us to a garage for a can of petrol, then get us back to rescue Graham and Denis in the ambulance. After we had walked along the side of this quiet country road for a while with our thumbs stuck out hopefully, a Land Rover drew to a halt. We immediately ran to the driver, who popped his head out of the window. He was dressed in tweeds and I quickly surmised he was well to do from his clothes and his manner of speech. He asked where we were heading and we told him of our predicament and our plans to knock up the venue manager, and so on. This true English gent said he would help and told us to climb in. Not only that, when we got into his vehicle he offered to lend us the money for the petrol. He said, 'Will a tenner do?' His wife, sitting beside him, then laid a steadying hand on his good will and said, 'Oh, I'm sure five pounds will be enough, won't it?'

The country gent started to chat and tell us about his morning thus far, having had some trouble with another Land Rover, and soon got us to a garage. There we filled a can and he drove us back to the ambulance. What they made of it all I don't know, but their charitable deed I never forgot. I took his address with a promise to repay the debt. This weighed on my mind and as soon as I could I gave Ralph the details and told him to make sure he paid the man back. I never knew if he did.

I was so impressed with this chap's kindness and trust to have picked up two herberts from nowhere, and to have done such a good deed without any hesitation. I wish I could thank him in person today, but I guess he will be long gone now.

*

When it came to the Bournemouth weekly residency that Ralph was personally promoting, he had obviously seen an opportunity not only to promote the band but to make some good money at the same time – though it didn't set his bank account alight in the end. The general idea for this promotion may have come from an earlier unsuccessful gig-cum-audition at a now forgotten seaside venue that we did. After our performance, in either Bournemouth or Brighton, we weren't offered the longer residency we were hoping for, and to add insult to injury were fobbed off by the agent involved with the stupid excuse that we were just 'too good'.

Things like this were always pretty annoying for us all, but this setback particularly upset Dave at the time, enough to write to *Melody Maker* to let off some steam (and get a bit of free publicity at the same time). They printed his letter on 3 July under the heading, 'Bit Much':

After playing a South Coast club we confidently anticipated a week's residency, if we reached the mark. We soared above this mark. Then the promoter unblushingly told us we were 'too good'. As a four piece, we keep our price low. After our week the promoter was afraid that he would have to pay far higher to get a group of our standard. Prestige is all very well, but must we spend hours rehearsing, just to be told to lower our standards?

Davie Jones, The Lower Third, Bromley, Kent.

Although that trial gig came to nothing, at least it planted a seed in Ralph's head, and that led to these regular weekend bookings.

While our Marquee Club appearances were undoubtedly the highlight for the best audience responses, in my memory our Bournemouth and Isle of Wight shows and all the experiences we had around them are probably my fondest memories of my time with Dave and the boys. As I said, although we were hard at work (we gave every gig our all and more), it did feel like a mini holiday by the sea. And well deserved, too.

*

It is no real surprise that most of our gigs during these memorable summer months were located around the coastal resorts. These were still the years before cheap foreign package deals changed the way most Brits holidayed during their well-earned summer breaks; it was only towards the end of the decade that things started to change. But in the summer of '65, the British public still filled our seaside towns and that provided entertainers of all kinds with very valuable seasonal work.

Mixed in with this traditional family group were swelling ranks of rebellious, post-war born teenagers, many in employment and able to make their own lifestyle holiday choices like never before, and also many who would just travel out of London for a weekend of partying by the sea. It would be these young adults who would be our main demographic, and it wasn't unusual to see friendly Marquee or 100 Club audience members out front at one of these shows.

The pirate radio stations had picked up on this trend and by the mid-sixties were promoting their stations by arranging concerts by the sea (it was also a way for them to generate extra cash to help keep their stations afloat). These often took the form of trendy all-nighters, where we would have been one of two or three bands that would play, two or three times, into the very early hours while the kids burnt the candle at both ends on the dance floor.

One of these all-nighter events was alongside The Yardbirds, the band that included the charismatic singer Keith Relf. Dave got on very well with him and they also both looked very similar facially. He loved the band's music too and they again featured prominently on his 1973 *Pin Ups* album, which included covers of The Yardbirds

'I Wish You Would' (which the group performed that night) and 'Shapes Of Things'. I had a long, interesting conversation with their bassist and founder member Paul Samwell-Smith about anything and everything to do with music. Really nice chap and really knew his stuff. Multi-talented too, he became a world-class producer. I can't actually remember Dave and us performing 'I Wish You Would' live, though I've read elsewhere that we did. If so, it's sadly lost from my memory now.

On the *Pin Ups* album sleeve it's easy to see how highly David cherished these years of his life too, pointing out that the album's selection were of his favourite songs from 1964 to 1967. It's a great album, by the way: David's vocals are terrific, and Mick Ronson's string arrangements on tracks like 'See Emily Play' and 'Sorrow' are quite special. I will hold up my hand here, though – it wasn't until I started writing this book that I played it in full. I knew the odd track ('Sorrow' was quite a success for David as a single, I recall) but listening to David's treatment of those tracks collectively, all these years on, and I love what he did with them. He never wandered too far from the source (except maybe the latter part of 'See Emily Play', but even then it suits the mood and manner of classic Pink Floyd in its own way). I think all the bands and writers he covered on it (including Pete Townshend and The Who) must have been pretty happy that he had even included them, and I'm sure they've all benefited handsomely from the extra money he's brought them over the years.

We did a few of these all-nighters in Brighton too and also at least one in Southend-on-Sea. Of course, one gig seems very much like another after a while and today particular highlights are hard to pick out, but I do remember us driving slowly away from Southend that time, Dave sitting opposite me already asleep, his head cushioned by his sweater on a speaker, the boys at the front quietly studying the road while I reflectively watched the town's bright lights fade in the distance as we made our way back towards London. We must have gone down quite well because I remember feeling quite content. I grabbed myself some kip after that and the next thing I knew Graham and Den were shaking both of us awake so we could drop Dave off home.

The previous year had seen the first mods verses rockers seaside conflicts (as portrayed in The Who's fabulous film *Quadrophenia*). These altercations were mainly confined to teenage away days during the various British national bank holidays, and to seaside towns like Brighton and Hastings (the May 1964 disturbances were quickly referred to as 'the second battle of Hastings'), and Margate and Clacton were the scene of some major bust-ups between these intemperate youth groups. Luckily for us, we never saw any trouble at all, and never had to make haste after a show from a bunch of pissed-off, greasy motorcycle riders either. Saying that, we would never have been able to make any kind of getaway in our regulated, snail-paced ambulance. Some emergency vehicle that would have been!

Twelve months on and the police and local authorities were now ready to head off any repetition of the previous year's seaside troubles and largely quelled incidents before they could gain traction. So our summer of '65 by the seaside was thankfully incident free – we four being of the loving kind, not the fighting sort.

*

Although not lucrative, our south-of-England residencies proved a success for us in other ways as we built up loyal followings in both Bournemouth and on the Isle of Wight, much as we had at the Marquee. Again, this was encouraging as we knew we were always welcome, unlike some of the out-of-the-way places we played where we may as well have come from Mars for all the audience knew (though we probably didn't play them 'Mars', being out-of-town folk and all).

*

All the groups travelled with their equipment on the ferry, the gear having been loaded in to a removal van. We then all piled in the back of this removal van at the other end for the ride to the gig (often both bands and crew together). Bouncing about in the back, it was not unusual to see my drum cases used as a makeshift table to roll makeshift joints.

The man whose removal van it was (a company called Mews and based on the island) became our regular Mr Shifter and got to know us quite well in a bemused sort of way, for example calling me 'the vicar' because of the stand up collar on a 'shorty-mac' that I always wore at the time.

Our removal van man was not always so jocular, though, and wasn't averse to creating a bit of drama. Around this time Dave was becoming more aloof and it had become his habit not to join in manhandling the equipment on to the van. On one particular hot Sunday morning it was time to load the van up to catch the ferry back to Bournemouth, and Dave was doing his latest not-doing-anything-to-help type of thing. I took exception to this and decided that, if that was how it was going to be, I wouldn't do anything either. It was a sort of childish protest, but I felt I had to make a stand. As it turned out, I wasn't very good at it.

The bloke whose responsibility it was to get us and his van on to the ferry before it sailed was slogging away, loading amps and shouting at me to get my arse in gear. When I didn't respond, he flew at me, literally picking me up by my shirtfront to shake me into action. That did the trick. I'm pretty sure that Dave still didn't join in, it didn't register with him at all, and I lost half of my shirt buttons.

*

During one of these summer of '65 visits, a memorable incident occurred on our journey back to Southampton. Following a cup of tea below deck, I wandered up to get some air and saw Dave and Ralph together – both looking very unhappy and clearly keeping themselves to themselves. The visit itself had passed off without any drama, and indeed had gone well, so at first I thought they must have had a rare argument. Denis and Graham were not far away, so I asked them what was up.

Apparently, a guy in the general tour party (not in our immediate group, I hasten to add) had tried to get a little too friendly with Dave and made a grab at his privates when he saw him alone somewhere on the boat. Dave never mentioned any of this to me at the time, or ever, which was strange as we talked about most things (including one or two things that will forever remain private to both of us).

There is no doubt, though, whatever happened on the Solent that morning clearly upset him. On arrival at Southampton, Dave travelled back to London with Ralph, so I've no real clue how long it took him to get over the incident.

In 2017, sexual predation became a major and widely

debated news story, one that particularly centred on the entertainment industry. But predation of this nature is unfortunately as old as the hills and if a guy as streetwise and sexually liberated as David Bowie can fall victim then it's no wonder that many similar crimes remain unreported.

*

Such was our following at Bournemouth that one night a local group, who were booked to play with us at the Pavilion, performed a cover of 'You've Got A Habit Of Leaving', just before we were about to do our set. We must have given off the impression that we were doing reasonably well, particularly as we had a single out and because we regularly drew some loyal local followers. However, we were certainly not doing anywhere near as well as some that we were billed to support. We were flattered by their appreciation of the song anyway, and they did a pretty good job of it too.

*

The weekend that The Who came down to play with us in Bournemouth – Friday, 20 August 1965, to be exact – was certainly one of the highlights for me. To get ourselves fully prepared for this important evening gig, we had an extra afternoon rehearsal to ensure we were at the top of our game, while we eagerly awaited their arrival at the Pavilion. Part way through performing one of Dave's original efforts, Pete Townshend walked into the ballroom, which immediately got our attention.

When we finished the number, he approached the stage to say hello and asked whose song it was that we were playing, to which Dave replied 'It's mine'.

'That's a shame,' said Pete, 'sounds like my stuff.' I think he was initially a bit taken aback. That was the first time Pete and Dave properly acquainted themselves, I believe.

After we stopped rehearsing, I sat with Pete to chat and he asked me about earnings. He initially asked what we were on and I dreaded the embarrassment of telling him, but before I could answer he volunteered, 'We're on fifty quid a week, do you think that's alright?'

'Yes' I said, 'sounds alright to me.' Bloody hell, just a bit! It seems that the afternoon was very memorable for David too, as he recalled during an interview in 1993:

We had a thing about The Who. In fact, we used to play second support to them in Bournemouth. That was the first time I met Townshend and got talking to him about songwriting and stuff. I was hugely influenced by him.

We had songs called 'Baby Loves That Way', 'You've Got A Habit Of Leaving' – some really duff things. Townshend came into our soundcheck and listened to a couple of things and said, 'You're trying to write like me!' I said: 'Yeah, what do you think?' He said: 'Mmm, well, there's a lot of bands around like you at the moment.' I don't think he was very impressed.'

Just before the gig in the dressing room, which we were sharing with them, Pete called me over to show me his new Fender Stratocaster, sitting gleaming in its case. 'Are you going to smash it up tonight?' I asked. 'No,' he replied, with a serious look on his face, 'I've got too much on hire purchase.'

I had a friendly chat with Roger Daltrey as well, who initially said to me, 'I know you, don't I?'

I'm not sure who I reminded him of but I replied, 'No, we haven't met before.'

As we were chatting I watched him slide some 'lifts' into his shoes. He looked at me and said with a smile, 'I have to use them, otherwise no one will see me.'

I have no memory of John Entwistle at all, it's like he wasn't there, and contrary to his wild man legend, Keith Moon was as quiet as a mouse. I know he became a close friend of David's in later years but I can't remember him talking with any of us that night.

When The Who did their set, I watched from behind the stage. Roger Daltrey was in full flow, whacking Keith Moon's cymbals with his mic. When he spotted me he smiled and held up his hand to show me it was bleeding.

It was an electric night – The Who were amazing and the audience went wild. It was brilliant to have been part of such a special evening, and I've no doubt that our set, with our band of loyal local followers in support, added greatly to it all. In fact, if you had been near the front towards the end of our set, you would very likely have collected a free single. Ralph had brought a whole box with him and handed them all out to eager hands as he mingled with the audience. When I think about it now, and compare them to their value today, Ralph probably gave away the best part of £15,000 in a few seconds.

Later, Pete came back to the hotel with Ralph and the rest of us for a nightcap. Pete paid for a round of drinks, which we both carried from the bar together, before settling back in the hotel lounge to talk.

Pete asked Ralph if he promoted at any other venues and we also spoke about stage presentation, Pete saying something like 'You can put a Union Jack jacket on John

Entwistle and he'll just stand there and wear it.' By that I think he was describing John Entwistle's taciturn demeanour – that you could dress him up in the latest trendy clobber, but his actual performance would remain exactly the same.

Dave listened on intently as Pete pretty much led the way with the conversation. Pete was obviously aware that we were all in awe of him and The Who in general, and it was really good of him to treat us so well. That night, Pete Townshend came across as a really decent guy and I've since heard a number of people talking similarly of him. He made us all feel like equals.

When it was time to call it a night, Pete asked where we were staying. 'A caravan,' we answered.

'I wish I was,' he replied. Meaning, I guess, that he was fed up with hotels. I'm not sure he would have liked our leaky caravan that much, though.

Of course, both Pete and Roger are still working to this day, I'm delighted to say, and that's quite something, particularly as Pete's hearing was badly damaged by the extreme volume of their earlier gigs. I know that both men are also passionate about their support of the Teenage Cancer Trust and have raised many millions of pounds for that charity and other equally important causes over the years. If you check out The Who's website you'll see they are always helping someone, somewhere. Their annual Royal Albert Hall charity concerts are particularly important, special events well worth supporting.

Bournemouth wouldn't be the only time we shared billing with The Who either, as we would also get to work with them at the Marquee towards the end of the year. And while I think about it, it was also at that Marquee gig that Denis put me forward as a replacement drummer for Keith Moon. I kid you not. I can explain, and will do so in a chapter or two.

All in all, 20 August was a red-letter day for Davie Jones and The Lower Third. Not only were we supporting The Who in concert but it was also the day our first single, 'You've Got A Habit Of Leaving', was officially released. It was great when Dave announced this to the sold-out Pavilion audience, who were mostly there for The Who, of course, but contained a healthy number of our followers too. We definitely performed the song with additional pride that night and it received a great response. I can still hear Dave singing it now, and working his magic on some of the girls pressed up at the front of the stage, all staring up at him doe-eyed. I'm sure many of them were thinking to themselves, 'I would never leave you David, honest!'

We even had a few single reviews too, in fact *Record Mirror* was actually quite positive about it and I still have their review pasted in my Lower Third scrapbook:

Davie Jones is a highly talented singer. It's a curiously pitched vocal sound with powerful percussion and a slightly dirgy approach. Plenty happening: lots of wailing. Very off-beat.

It's definitely a curious business, this, as you could never really work out what would or wouldn't take off in the singles charts. During August '65, comedian Ken Dodd's ballad 'Tears' held the No.1 position for most of the month and was so popular it even outsold The Beatles' biggest singles, becoming the top-selling record of the year. It just shows you, for all our efforts at getting ourselves seen and heard, if we had acted as uncool as Ken Dodd we may have had a hit. I could have even got my own Dickie Mint out! (If you skipped the early chapters of this book, this reference to my very own schoolboy ventriloquist act will mean nothing to you. Shame.)

Actually, I'm not being disrespectful to Sir Ken Dodd here, as I was actually a big fan of his. I saw him live three times and he was one of the most talented comedians I have ever seen. This late detail about Doddy has come to mind due to his recent passing, which came as we were working on the last edit of this book.

*

A final memory of our stint in that Bournemouth caravan includes the caravan owner's wife – the spouse of the guy who managed the Pavilion at the time. One morning, this lady took pity on us and kindly invited us into the house for a full English breakfast. It was a wonderful treat. We were all starving having hardly eaten anything the day before.

I'll never forget seeing Dave at work that morning – shamelessly flirting in the kitchen with this attractive older lady, who was quite a few years his senior. There was no doubt she seemed flattered by the attention and played on it. The rest of us all shared a crafty smile between us while all of this was going on, though to be honest we were more focused on the breakfast itself. Dave really made this lady's day, I think.

One of our more unusual summer Pavilion Bournemouth bookings was as main support to singer and actor Jess Conrad, who was backed by a scratch band called The Puppets. Later on, I read that Dave's first band, The Konrads, had taken their name from Jess Conrad as a kind of homage after an early supporting appearance (this before Dave joined them) – though I suppose they adjusted the Conrad spelling to avoid any possible name infringement issues. Coincidentally, Dave ran into the man in 1964 while making his TV debut appearance at BBC Television Centre in White City (at that point he was the front man of Davy Jones and The King Bees and promoting their first single, 'Liza Jane', on a show called *The Beat Room*). A couple of weeks before that he made his first TV appearance on the BBC's *Juke Box Jury*, in front of a judging panel that included actors Diana Dors and Jessie Matthews, promoter and agent Bunny Lewis and comedian Charlie Drake. Evidently, only Bunny Lewis liked 'Liza Jane' so host David Jacobs dutifully apologised to David, rang his bell and the word 'Miss' was flashed up on screen (you either had a 'Hit' or a 'Miss' on this show – it could be brutal).

Jess was very amiable and, after we put on our new stage outfit – the one we had used for the recent EMI publicity shoot – he was particularly taken with my mum's ties. 'All the young groups are wearing those now,' he said to us collectively. Then, looking a bit closer at one of them when I pointed out my mother had made them, he complimented her work, saying, 'They are very stylish.' She was delighted when I told her.

Curiously, Jess Conrad had also been working with Joe Meek and had recently released a Meek-produced single on Pye called 'It Can Happen To You', which was the main song he was promoting that night. I can't recall Jess having any hits, but he always seemed to draw a reasonable audience and would often pop up on TV and the occasional film.

Towards the end of our Bournemouth residency – and particularly the weekends that Ralph came down to join us – we would all feel a bit miffed when David returned to London with Ralph in his Jaguar, while we slowly slogged our way home in the ambulance. It didn't feel the same when he travelled separately from us. This should have been even more of a warning that the dynamics within the group were beginning to change. Dave was starting to adopt a more aloof presence.

On one of these occasions, while Dave was riding home with Ralph, Patrick Kerr joined us for the journey back to London. That kind of made up for David's absence on that particular night and we had a blast on the way home. We all enjoyed Patrick's company.

A week after our night with The Who we were back at the 100 Club in Oxford Street. Performing here had added interest for me as I had been a regular visitor to this club with my Walthamstow mates to hear Alex Welsh, along with all the other famous traditional jazz bands of the early sixties.

This was our second *Radio Caroline Show* appearance at the club and this time we shared billing with Peter Jay and The Jaywalkers, a seven-piece instrumental outfit, and an attractive Aussie singer and actress called Patsy Ann Noble. She would soon become Trisha Noble and, like Jess, often popped up on TV shows such as *Danger Man* and *Callan*. She went on to become quite a successful film and TV actress in the USA, too.

Dave was friendly with The Jaywalkers, whose line-up included a charismatic young guitarist and front man called Terry Reid. Terry was ridiculously young, about fifteen I believe, but looked the part, played guitar brilliantly and had a fabulous bluesy voice to go with it – even at that tender age. He became much respected on the blues and progressive rock scene, and still is today. He even helped introduce Robert Plant and John Bonham to Jimmy Page and John Paul Jones – and that turned out rather well. I know that Dave remained friends with Terry and I'm surprised they never, to my knowledge, worked together at any time. That would have been interesting, for sure.

Later in the evening, following on from our gig with The Jaywalkers, The Honeycombs had arrived at the club and were setting up their gear, as we were getting ready to leave. 'Have I The Right?' had been a chart-topper for them the previous year, recorded at Joe Meek's Holloway Road studio (i.e. his flat – famously a partly converted recording facility). Two No.1 singles had also been made at Meek's, which was definitely one of London's more eccentric recording facilities: 'Telstar', by The Tornados, and 'Johnny Remember Me', by John Leyton.

My counterpart in The Honeycombs was Honey Lantree, a rare lady musician in a very male-dominated world. Although she would mime playing drums for the many TV appearances they did promoting 'Have I The Right?', it's well known that the single didn't feature any drums at all, just the band stamping a beat on the stairs in Meek's hallway. It was no wonder Meek later fell out with his landlady.

Although I can't recall any major interchange between The Honeycombs and us, it's fair to say we rubbed shoulders. If pressed, however, David might have said, 'We passed upon the stairs...'

My cousin Carole came to see us at the 100 Club one evening, and recalls seeing me in the doorway with Sonny and Cher. I have no recollection of this but, as I've just said, we were meeting many hit artists at the time so Carole could well be correct. I know Sonny and Cher were living in London at this time, so it makes sense. I mentioned this recollection while speaking to Carole again quite recently and she added, 'While you were talking to me earlier you suddenly excused yourself as you wanted to have a quick word with Pete Townshend, who was standing at the other end of the bar.' It sounds like the stars were out that night.

Another memorable gig we did at 100 Oxford Street was with The Spencer Davis Group, who were yet another successful Birmingham-born combo; along with Spencer himself, they featured the talented Winwood brothers, Steve and Muff. The band's big hit of the moment was 'Keep On Running' which had gone straight to No.1 and was the highlight of their 100 Club performance that night. (It brought the house down.) The following year, 'Somebody Help Me' and 'Gimme Some Lovin'' would do the same in the UK, and also help them break the lucrative and all-important US market. They were a good bunch of guys, too, and clearly deserved the accolades they were receiving.

They arrived at the gig immediately after recording a spot on BBC TV's *Top Of The Pops*, so were already pretty pumped up. Like Dave, their talented singer Steve Winwood would eventually emerge as a significant solo artist (his bluesy voice is so recognisable).

Sharing billing with bands we really respected undoubtedly raised our game too. It was a great feeling when everyone gelled perfectly and we all hit our marks, and we certainly did that night. By the time Spencer and his band took the stage the sold-out audience were buzzing and I knew we had done a good job.

Luckily, we supported quite a lot of acts we really liked and it was for gigs like this that we did it. There is genuinely very little to compare with the feeling you get after a good show – it's a different kind of adrenalin.

With The Spiders From Mars, David would also share billing with Spencer Davis in 1972 I believe, though the Winwood brothers had long since departed, Stevie to form Traffic and then Blind Faith (with Eric Clapton, Ginger Baker and Ric Grech) and Muff to become a much sought-after producer and A&R man. (He oversaw many hit albums including Sparks' *Kimono My House* and Dire Straits' first and hugely successful eponymous album, which of course included 'Sultans Of Swing').

During one of my later visits to the Marquee, after I had left The Lower Third, I met up with Spencer Davis again. I think they had just had their second UK No.1 single by then and were probably played every hour on the radio. It certainly seemed like it at the time. I only mention the constant radio play because Spencer said to me, quite earnestly, 'We're off to America soon, do you think we'll do alright? 'Yes,' I replied, 'I reckon you will.' I was really flattered that he asked my opinion. Not that I had to be any kind of musical genius to work out the answer to that one.

*

Something that was hard to forget, and I thought twice about even referring to it now, was the story that suddenly hit the country early in October '65. We were playing at an all-nighter somewhere on the coast and during our journey the radio was dominated with urgent, distressing news updates. Various child homicides had apparently been perpetrated by a young couple in Manchester, neither of whom were related to the children they had murdered. What was particularly shocking (although the truly heavy details were yet to come out) was that a young woman had helped kill the children. It just seemed unimaginable then. The pathetic people involved became known as the Moors Murderers.

I only mention this here to provide a timeline context. While we were doing our best to become successful, make hit records and entertain people, the radio and TV news often reminded us that the real world wasn't that far away and could sometimes be a pretty horrendous place. This dreadful story dominated my memory of that whole period and, apart from the journey, I have no recollection of where that particular all-nighter was or how it went.

*

On a far lighter note, October also saw David in a completely different mode, posing for a fashion feature in *Fabulous* magazine with a model named Jan de Souza. Dave was friendly with designer John Stephen (later dubbed 'The King Of Carnaby Street' by the media), whose shops we often visited, even if we couldn't actually afford to buy anything. Presumably it was through Stephen that Dave got this booking as a model, wearing some of John Stephen's own clobber, including a long-sleeved knitted shirt and ever so trendy 'elephant' corduroy slacks.

I think he was actually paid with clothes, which was pretty handy for a pop singer. I know Dave kept hold of the elephant strides and even wore them on stage a couple of times, but it was only years later that I found out that he had modelled at the time.

The dark grey and green tartan-patterned slacks Dave often wore when we played live, and the white jumper he wore for another *Fabulous* magazine photo session, were also both John Stephen's items. He hailed from north of the border (Glasgow, in fact), and tartan often featured in his bold designs, including his female clothing range.

Dave, ambitious as always, also had desires to design his own clothes, particularly after spending time with Stephen, and it was not long after this that he came up with the military jacket he was later much photographed wearing. I'm sure Stephen helped him get it made and there was talk that Dave was also going to create a range of matching clothes.

This jacket must have been made towards to end of '65, as he wore it for another pop magazine photo session in very early '66. He was definitely one of the first to pick up on the whole 'I Was Lord Kitchener's Valet' styling that became so emblematic around 1967. Our Dave, as you well know, was always pretty quick off the mark.

There's a curious bit of film footage you can find on YouTube of Dave working at John Stephen's Carnaby Street shop, showing clothes to customers for an NBC American news special about Swinging London fashion. It's a 'blink and you'll miss him' type of thing, but it's clearly Dave, resplendent in the military tunic he would eventually be photographed in for the cover of his first album. What the film doesn't convey is the loud pop music that used to blare out from John's shops, straight out on to the street. He used every trick going to attract eyes to his windows and eventually every shop in Carnaby Street was doing the same thing. This created a right din but also somehow added an element of showbiz glamour to it all. These were the pre-pedestrianised years, of course, and you could still drive down and even park in the street itself. We certainly drove up and down Carnaby Street (or 'Peacock Alley', as it was sometimes called) in the ambulance a few times, but it would have been too noisy for the boys to park there overnight.

By the look of that NBC footage and the style of Dave's hair, it was filmed a year on from when I last saw him, so the jacket was at least a year old by this time and was obviously still a cutting-edge look. John Stephen clearly tipped Dave off that the film crew was coming and I'm sure wanted him to be there, knowing he would look perfect for this important news feature. Just before it cuts off, Dave is showing a female customer one of John Stephen's tartan outfits. Whether Dave actually worked there at any time, I'm not sure, but it obviously proved to be a handy hang-out for him.

Stephen would also supply the white suit that Dave wore on TV while promoting our last single in early '66. But that's a story in itself.

*

Having mentioned that this *Fabulous* assignment and some other magazine modelling work Dave undertook around this time was unknown to myself or any of the band, I know now that this was how Dave operated through much of his life. I've found out quite a lot more about his personality and working practices in recent years than I thought I actually knew.

Although, as I've said previously, we did talk a lot about the things that were going on from day to day, and he could get as excited as any of us about something interesting that may or may not be about to come off (like a possible TV or radio appearance, or foreign tour, etc.), there was still a lot he would keep to himself and would never share with me or the others. In that sense, I didn't know him as well as I thought. But then again, I've yet to meet anyone who actually knew Dave who doesn't say something similar.

I think that must be why so many people find him so fascinating today. There is always something new and interesting to discover that he did, or something fascinating he may have appropriated, or hid somewhere in his lyrics, his personas, his videos...

CHAPTER EIGHT

DAVIE JONES IS BACK IN HIS LOCKER

R alph was, by this time, engaging with all of us as a group, as well as with Dave as an individual and would make announcements as to what we needed to do in certain aspects of our presentation, clothes and hair.

But the announcement that really triggered the birth of one of the most recognisable names in the rock industry came when Ralph informed us that we needed to change our name. More specifically, David had to change his stage name from Jones to something else. Ralph was concerned that he would get lost in the wash of other Davie (or Davy) Joneses who were better established than him in the business. Later on, I discovered that Ralph had just made contact with a successful West End manager and publicist called Kenneth Pitt, and it was he who advised the name change. But it would be over forty years until I found that out.

There were at least two other singer/performers of

that name at the time, one a black American singer, the other was British and was making a name for himself on Broadway in the musical *Oliver!* Some eighteen months later, this young British actor/singer joined the mega-successful Monkees, which made Kenneth Pitt's timely suggestion one of the most valuable David could have taken at the time.

Ralph also thought that The Lower Third sounded too juvenile and that we should find a different name. But, after much debate we were unsuccessful in coming up with anything that we all liked, so it was left unchanged. I thought maybe we could go out as The Toys, but that didn't entirely fit Ralph's criteria of a more grown-up name and, in any case, it turned out that there was an American female vocal group of that name who were already established. I wonder if David remembered this and was making an oblique reference to the rejected name when he titled his 2001 LP *Toy*? This album, which was ultimately unreleased at the time as it clashed with the release of new material (although it was leaked online ten years later), was David's reworking of some of his earliest penned songs and included updated versions of 'Baby Loves That Way', 'You've Got A Habit Of Leaving', 'Silly Boy Blue' and 'The London Boys'.

No such trouble for Dave, though, who turned up at our next meeting and announced that he had changed his stage name to Bowie. OK, I thought. I know who that is, or was. Jim Bowie was one of the guys that held out at the Alamo to the grim end, and he gave his name to a type of large hunting knife. If truth be told, it was more childhood stuff really (there was an American kids' TV show about Jim Bowie that was very popular at the time), but Ralph didn't seem to mind.

In hindsight, it turned out to be the perfect name for him and it soon grew on me too. So from then on we were to be known as David Bowie and The Lower Third, for it had also come to pass that 'Davie' had to go too. Such was the pace of change in our camp and Ralph's attention to detail.

This is the first time I ever heard David mention the name 'Bowie', by the way, it wasn't something he'd been messing around with previously. (I once heard that he almost became Tom Jones when he started out – this before the arrival of the Welsh Tom Jones, of course.) I have also since read that Denis had reacted to Dave's choice of 'Bowie' as a 'fucking stupid name', but I don't recall hearing him say that at the time.

It wasn't long after all this that Ralph started buying small ads across some of the music papers featuring the word 'BOWIE' (and nothing else). This was a kind of precursor to the issue of the next single.

*

It was Ralph who got us our next recording deal (the first one for which the Third had a written contract). This was a particularly exciting prospect, as this time our recording manager would be Tony Hatch. Tony was big time in the industry with a proven track record including a well-known TV theme tune and a selection of big-selling singles. He had written and produced the smash hit 'Downtown' for Petula Clark and also recorded The Searchers (and penned their No.2 UK single, 'Sugar and Spice'), so Tony, like Shel, certainly knew how to conjure up a hit.

In retrospect, considering his work with The Who and The Kinks, Shel Talmy was probably the better fit for our type of music. These were bands we clearly had more in common with than The Searchers or Pet Clark and this contrast in styles became more apparent during our next session with Tony, though I have to say that overall he was a bit more flexible in his approach. At the same time I would also like to make clear that, as different as they were, both producers were similarly accomplished at bringing out the best in the artists they worked with.

While we were indeed sad to say goodbye to Shel, he had had two attempts to get Dave a hit record and had also given him open-ended recording time in Denmark Street, from which nothing had really clicked thus far. So to be given a further chance by a different label with another established producer was a significant moment. I'm not sure we even realised exactly how lucky we were at the time, but what I do know is that it settled us all down, and for a short while at least all was good in our camp.

While Tony had been impressed with Dave's performance and stage presence, the fact that he also wrote his own material was what helped clinch this new deal. Hatch, it transpired, had been getting tired of sourcing original material for many of the acts he was producing, such as The Searchers. Working with a dynamic young performer who brought with him his own songs was exactly what he yearned for.

With this we became Pye recording artists and before we knew it (Friday, 19 November 1965 to be exact), were booked in to record at Pye's prestigious studios, ATV House, 17 Great Cumberland Place, Marble Arch, a building complete with elderly commissionaire on the door and a classy studio set-up with all the required bells and whistles (I use this as a figure of speech, though

I'm sure they actually had bells and whistles to record with, if required).

Dave went about choosing the possible songs to record and proposed a slightly controversial, recently penned one for the 'A' side, one that again seemed to dip directly into his own personal experience. 'Now You've Met The London Boys' (which is how he originally presented it to us) had already proven itself live a few times and seemed like the natural number to select as our lead option. As before, on the day of the recording we had time pre-booked Regent Sounds to hone the arrangement prior to recording. We always aimed to be fully prepared for these important sessions and that morning it felt like we really had something good to present to Tony.

When Dave rerecorded this song with The Buzz (the version that Decca released), he had toned the recording right down and given it a completely different feel, something more plaintive and ballad-like. The Lower Third's 'London Boys' didn't compare, it was much more up-tempo, much rockier and markedly different. Our recording would also become something of a mystery after the master tape went missing, but more of that shortly.

Following our run-throughs at Regent Sounds it was gear into the ambulance and over to Pye studios and our first taste of working with Tony Hatch. Ralph (who had known Tony from his days with The Moody Blues) warned us that he was a stickler for quality, so it was definitely a nervy time for us all. Ralph's cautionary insight would prove correct to some extent but was, I'm sure, also slightly inflated to help keep us on our toes. After all, it was the first recording deal that Ralph had made for us and something he also had a lot riding on.

As well as proving to be a highly professional musician and gifted record producer, you could definitely detect Tony's no-nonsense, professional attitude from the off. He immediately came across as more business-like than Shel, who acted more like a free spirit in some ways. But for all that Tony was still fairly cordial, generally put us all at our ease, and the song was recorded quite quickly and without a hitch in the end. So we obviously hit our marks that day, no doubt aided by our extra preparation and alertness in the studio.

I couldn't recall what we actually recorded for the B-side when I first started to make notes for this book. No one I knew seemed to know either. I thought it must have been another of David's London-centric songs, as the city seemed to be cropping up more and more in his work at the time. In fact, it turns out that it was a three-minute track called 'You've Got It Made'. I know this because, just after I thought I had finished writing this book the actual Lower Third 'London Boys' master tape suddenly came to light (some fifty-three years on from the day it was recorded). The appearance of this tape was the strangest thing. It felt like it was almost waiting for the very last minute of my book's preparation to reveal itself again.

Exactly what 'You've Got It Made' is like I have no clue, I'm afraid, as the recordings themselves are still under wraps, but what is curious is that this title is also to be found in the 'London Boys' lyric ('You've got it made with the rest of the toys...'). I can't imagine we would have recorded a variation of the A-side to back up the single so, just like so much of David's life and work, this currently remains a mystery. I'm very much hoping that by the time

Bit much

AFTER playing a South Coast club we confidently anticipated a week's residency, if we reached the mark.

We soared above this mark. Then the promoter unblushingly told us we were "too good"·

As a four piece, we keep our price low. After our week the promoter was afraid that he would have to pay far higher to get a group of our standard.

Prestige is all very well, but must we spend hours rehearsing, just to be told to lower our standards? **DAVIE JONES, The Lower Third, Bromley, Kent.**

Top left: David performing on *Ready, Steady, Go* on 4 March 1966. © *Michael Ochs Archives / Getty*

Top right: Me, Dave, Patrick Kerr and Johnny Kidd waiting for the Isle of Wight ferry, 31 July 65.
© *Denis Taylor*

Middle right: A copy of David's irate letter to *Melody Maker*.

Right: Graham and Denis with our beloved ambulance! © *Denis Taylor*

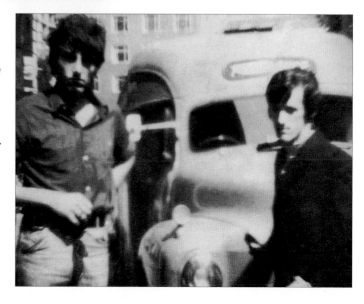

DAVIE CHANGES HIS HAIRSTYLE AND HIS GROUP

DAVIE Jones, who caused an uproar when he appeared on B.B.C. 2 in "Gadzooks, It's All Happening" when he was with a Maidstone group, has teamed up with a Thanet group on his next release.

The uproar came from the B.B.C. and Davie's fans. The B.B.C. said he couldn't appear with his hair so long, but his fans protested that he should go on and must NOT have his hair cut.

In the end, the programme director relented, and the show went on with Dave as the star, hair and all.

Davie's hair style now is a moderate "long back and sides," compared to his shoulder-length curls in the days of The Manish Boys.

His group, The Lower Third, wear the same "college boy" cut. Their only extrovert appearance seems to be in their silk ties—exotic in design and colour.

Ambition

Members of the group are: Dennis "Teacup" Taylor, born at Ramsgate 21 years ago. He plays lead guitar. Of his ambitions, he says his foremost is to become a good musician.

Graham Rivens, bass guitarist—according to the boys, "the beanstick" of the group at 6ft. 1in.—was educated at Dane Court Boys' School, Broadstairs.

Phil Lancaster ("My ambition is to make loads of money and keep playing"), the drummer, is the "foreigner" of the group, being a Londoner.

Associated

And finally there is Davie himself. Although he wasn't born in Kent, he has been associated with groups in the county for three years since he was 17.

"It was either full-time singing or commercial art," said Davie this week. "I was doing both at the time and I thought singing was more creative."

While Davie was singing with these Kent groups, The Lower Third were in Thanet playing in their home area "looking for some kind of foothold," said Graham.

In fact, they failed to find a foothold in Kent and moved to London for a few months to play at the Discotheque Club. Then they met Davie.

What does Davie and his new group think of the partnership? Davie feels it will be a success. "We have the same policies and fit rather well together," he said.

The disc that the group have recorded with E.M.I. is "You've Got A Habit Of Leaving" and "Baby Loves That Way." Both were written by Davie.

The number is the first on wax for The Lower Third, but Davie had a disc out called "I Pity The Fool" when he was a Manish Boy.

• • •

TOP TEN IN KENT

1 (1) "Help!," The

Davie, with new hairstyle, and new group—The Lower Third

CAN'T HELP THINKING ABOUT ME
PYE 7N 17021

DAVID BOWIE

MANAGEMENT
RALPH HORTON,
79a Warwick Square,
London, S.W.1
TATe Gallery 4706

AGENCY REPRESENTATION
Marquee Artists,
18 Carlisle Street,
Soho Square, W.1
GERrard 6601

Above: The new band – and David's new hair – made quite a splash when we appeared on the scene. © *Phil Lancaster Collection*

Below: An ad getting the Bowie name – and our single – out front and centre.
©*Kevin Cann Collection*

marquee artists

GERrard 6601   18 CARLISLE STREET. LONDON. W.1.

GER 6601   **DAVID BOWIE**   AND THE LOWER THIRD

WINTER GARDENS, VENTNOR
SATURDAY, AUGUST 7th

THE

PRETTY THINGS

with

JUGS O'HENRY

and

NEIL ANDERSON

plus

DAVY JONES AND THE LOWER THIRD

8—11.30   Fully licensed   Admission 7/6
LATE COACHES to and from Cowes,
Newport, Ryde

Top: A music press promotion from 1965.
©Kevin Cann Collection

Centre: Left to right: David Bowie, Brian
Pendleton & Phil May (The Pretty
Things), Denis Taylor & Phil Lancaster.
Also below is a concert leaflet from a
1965 gig. *© Denis Taylor*

David posing for shots at Ralph Horton's Warwick Square basement flat.

David's long locks seem tame now but, at the time, such styles were seriously unusual and caused quite a stir. Below he is pictured having a hairnet applied at the BBC centre before his performance with the Manish Boys on *Gadzooks*.

© Above: Hulton Archive / Getty /
Below: George Harris/Evening News/Rex

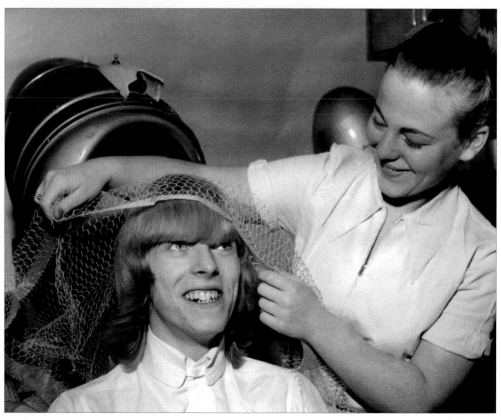

Above: The In Crowd front-man Keith 'Grocer Jack' West and me, chilling at Lew Davies' guitar shop in Charing Cross Road.

Right: My old school-friend, the artist Roger Seamark, remaking my old Lower Third drum head. And very nicely it turned out, too!

All photos © Phil Lancaster Collection

Left: A napkin signed by David, swearing he wouldn't get 'too big-headed' once he became famous. You know, I think he probably kept his word! © *Linda Stevens/Carlie Landygo*

I, DAVIE JONES HEREBY PROMISE NOT TO BECOME TOO BIG-HEADED WHEN I AM FAMOUS. SIGNED THIS GLORIOUS DAY 10TH MAY '65 IN THE PRESENCE OF

signed

Davie Jones

WITNESS

Below: The Lower Third, reunited outside La Gioconda coffee bar, 9 Denmark Street London, in 1983. Left to right: Graham Rivens, Denis Taylor and myself.

© *Ray Stevenson*

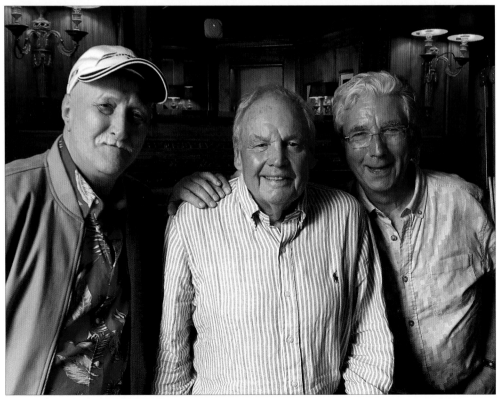

Right: Above: . . . and reunited again inside the Marquee club! © *Ray Stevenson*

Below: Yours truly, on the right, with Tony Hatch and Denis. © *Kevin Cann*

this book is published, I may have had the chance to hear these two fabled recordings once again.

Tony Hatch said years later that he did actually have concerns about David's London-inspired songs, and that he eventually asked him to come up with some different subject matter. This may have been partly due to a stage musical Dave wanted to do with Tony called *Kids On The Roof*, which he had based on a Victorian-themed London. This musical never came to pass in the end and I'm pretty sure we (The Lower Third) wouldn't have been involved even if it had, but I would have loved to have seen it completed. I later found out that Tony was going to do the score, so it sounds like Dave was looking more towards a Lionel Bart and *Oliver!* type of West End musical, complete with full orchestration, not an early rock opera innovation.

When we were finished at Pye we didn't have much time to spare as we were booked to play at the Marquee. Luckily the venue was only a few streets away from Pye HQ, so we didn't need to break a sweat to get there. We were sharing that Friday night's billing with fellow Marquee Artiste's The Summer Set, a five-piece south-coast outfit who specialised in the US surfin' sound. This band performed at the Marquee even more than we did and would share billing with David on more than one occasion. All of The Summer Set sang and harmonised well and came across with an impressive Beach Boys vibe. I've since learned that they were one of Keith Moon's favourite groups at the time, though today they are sadly pretty much forgotten.

With our first important Pye single in the bag, or so we thought, it was generally back to the odd live gig while we all once again dreamed of success and readied ourselves for the urgent promotional activity that would undoubtedly follow. Then after a week or so, news reached us that the board at Pye were unhappy with what we had recorded and had decided not to release the record after all. Not, we were told, because it wasn't good enough but simply because Dave's lyrics were too contentious. Disaster or what? We were definitely taken aback as Tony had quite a bit of sway at Pye and had clearly been very happy with our debut recordings.

David had referenced pill taking in 'The London Boys' (and not the type used for medicinal purposes either) and while it was an edgy, contemporary observation it was just too much for Pye's top brass to swallow (pun intended). So the decision was made to shelve it and, for a day or two, that is all we knew. Our disappointment was palpable, particularly as it wasn't clear what our future was with the label. It was left to Ralph to see if anything could be salvaged with both Tony Hatch and Pye while we all kept our fingers crossed.

The first time that you take a pill
You feel a little queasy, decidedly ill
You're gonna be sick, but you mustn't lose face,
To let yourself down would be a big disgrace
With the London boys...

We, including Tony, had thought our 'London Boys' recording had worked great on the day. There had been a lot of approving smiles on faces when we all listened to the playback in the control room. But at the same time we were all aware (and the matter was discussed in the studio) that the mention of illicit pill-taking might ruffle a few feathers along the way. Publicity, after all, is what we all wanted – label included – but in the end just not that type, apparently. On the day of recording we simply hadn't envisaged or allowed for such a negative outcome, particularly as Dave had taken care not to over-glamorise the drug scene and even considered the lyric more of a cautionary tale, rather than one of cool rebellion.

Many years later he recalled and reaffirmed that original reasoning, when he told a journalist, '"The London Boys" was another one about being a mod, it was an anti-pill song; though I wasn't particularly pro the thing [being a mod] after a bit.'

On reflection, I doubt the label bosses even listened to the song more than once at their meeting. We were just an unestablished band with an unknown writer/front man, working for a label that clearly had bigger forces at play. Pye Records was part of a larger company with a number of other lucrative business divisions to keep safe, profitable and unblemished, so I don't suppose it ever stood much of a chance of receiving board approval.

I recently wondered if it would have made any difference to the outcome of the band had it been released? We knew our small band of supporters had liked the song and often cheered as we hit the first few bars of it on stage. (When performing it live, after a short count in we would literally all start performing the song in unison, just as Dave sang: 'Bow Bells strike... another night... ') I don't suppose it would have been a hit, as nothing else had worked for Dave thus far, but it was nice to muse on this for a while.

Then, back at the Roebuck, Ralph delivered the news we had all hoped to hear: Pye wanted us to come up with another song. During the same briefing, Ralph also made it clear it was unlikely we would be given a third chance. No doubt the support and belief of Tony Hatch came to our rescue here. Tony had not only taken a shine to Dave 'the performer' (having seen us perform at the Marquee at least once before offering us the contract), he had also sensed great potential in his writing abilities too. It clearly made good sense for Pye to give us at least us one more chance to show them what we could do.

But that wasn't the last of 'The London Boys', of course. When Dave signed with Decca a year later, Pye agreed to give up any rights to the song, which allowed him to rerecord it with his new label. It might seem odd now that Decca should be OK about the lyric when Pye certainly weren't (and it's not as if society suddenly became more tolerant of songs that mentioned drug abuse in just one year). No, Decca already had some experience in this area.

In fact, they had already weathered a great deal of front-line controversy promoting a band who were more than happy to be considered the bad boys of pop, whose dalliances would soon venture further even than just rumours of recreational drug experimentation. This was a band whose name would become synonymous with illegal drug use, wild orgies, bisexuality, Satanism, crowd violence, cross-dressing and any other areas of general debauchery they could muster to ruffle the establishment's feathers. They were, of course, The Rolling Stones (and the Sex Pistols thought they were the first to upset parents!).

With this in mind, a Decca executive learning that David Bowie was 'feeling a bit queasy, decidedly ill' after downing a pill in one of his songs, would barely have raised an eyebrow.

*

So, geed-up and even more determined to come up with something good for Tony Hatch to get his teeth into, it was back to Regent Sounds to select and prepare two new songs. After trialling at least three or four, Ralph agreed that the proposed new A-side should be 'Can't Help Thinking About Me', and the B-side, 'And I Say To Myself', which we had just learned to play. We were all, I'm sure, a little relieved to work with less contentious lyrics too (with not even an aspirin mentioned this time).

While we diligently rehearsed 'Can't Help…', 'And I Say To Myself' and a couple of reserve numbers at the Roebuck the day before the session, Ralph reminded us that this would be the first release under the new incarnation of 'David Bowie and The Lower Third'. Both he and Dave were clearly putting all they could into making this a fully committed breakthrough. Ralph was also convinced he'd get some TV slots for us and certainly had all the right contacts in place.

So it was a great relief when we arrived back at Pye studios again after a slightly embarrassing false start. At least the quality of our initial recordings must have been good enough for the powers that be to think us worthy of another chance. Not a bad decision, as it happens, when you consider how much Pye (like Decca) must have made out of their Bowie back catalogue over the years.

When Dave presented a new song to us such as 'And I Say To Myself,' he nearly always strummed the tune on his acoustic, just la la-ing the words that he'd yet to come up with. This is something he did when he first played us 'Can't Help Thinking…' too. Most of the verses had yet to be written, though he boldly delivered the completed chorus: *'Can't help thinking about me, Can't help thinking about me…'*

The title had clearly been the main starting point of this particular song. Then, within the space of two or three run-throughs, while we all contributed our parts to help flesh out the song, he had pretty much completed the lyrics. I could never do that. He could work so spontaneously that I often wondered how he managed it.

Then, on the day of the session, while we were tuning up we could detect an air of panic in the control room, where things seemed more animated than usual. Just as we were trying to work out what was going on, a voice came over the talkback to ask if any of us had seen Dave's notebook. Apparently, he had forgotten to bring the lyrics!

Not now, I thought, as we all looked at one another in amazement before making a cursory search of the equipment bags and cases. He was normally glued to this notebook and constantly used it to scribble down lyrics, song titles and general ideas. But for some reason that morning it slipped his mind and he left home without it. As this mini-drama rolled on we wondered if we should start packing up the gear or whether Tony would want us to lay down the backing track.

After Dave realised that he'd definitely forgotten the lyrics he just smiled and said, 'Give us a minute. I'll write some new ones,' and did just that. Having run through it a few times the day before he probably remembered most of what he had written; the rest he just made up on the spot without breaking a sweat. He could work very fast in the studio, something I know he later became famous for, particularly with the many musicians and producers he would go on to work with.

Ralph had invited his keen financial backer Ray Cook to this session. Cook had recently become an investor in the band, or more likely, in Dave. The cash he put up was not the sort we ever saw, you understand, but money invested for promotion, equipment and other general expenses. This sadly didn't extend to a regular wage for the band, who struggled on earning a pittance.

A nice feature of one of our Tony Hatch sessions was a surprise visit from The Small Faces, who popped in to say hello, breaking off from their own session going on in the next studio. They recorded 'Sha-La-La-La-Lee' around the same time as 'Can't Help Thinking About Me' and it was released almost the same week. Steve Marriott was as cheery as ever and his presence helped remind us to enjoy what we were doing. I point this out as it's easy to forget, and for non-musicians not to appreciate, that these 'glamorous' recording sessions could often be quite tense affairs.

Steve also told us that the much-respected percussionist Speedy Acquaye was booked in with them that day. He also said something like, 'It's like a bloody pea-souper in our studio. We can hardly see each other because of the [marijuana] smoke,' which was quite funny. I had visions of Speedy behind his bongos in the corner of the studio, smoking a large bonfire-sized joint, dressed to the nines in his amazing, trademark African robes.

Speedy was born in Ghana and had come to the UK to make it as a performer, starting out as a fire-eater and cabaret dancer. When he found his niche as a percussionist he was finally set, and went on to spend many years as a top session player. He worked a lot live with Georgie Fame too, toured with John Martyn's band and doubled up on percussion in Ginger Baker's Air Force. I was lucky enough to see Speedy a couple of times working with

Georgie Fame but sadly didn't bump into him at Pye that day. Dave may have as he disappeared with Steve for a while during a break.

*

Like the rest of the band, Dave was still learning his trade and I'm sure equally felt the pressure to deliver on cue. Everything led to these important though fleeting hours in the studio and no one wanted to mess up. Graham, Denis and I were all in our early twenties by this time, while Dave was still a teenager but had already taken on key leadership responsibilities. What particularly impressed me was how resourceful he could be when he had to be: quickly rewriting forgotten lyrics while everyone waited on him was only one example of his strength of character and growing talent.

On our previous single, Shel Talmy had introduced Nicky Hopkins to reinforce and intensify our instrumental backing. On 'Can't Help Thinking About Me', Tony Hatch himself did the duties (he was also a damn good pianist). Denis played Dave's six-string guitar as well as his lead, which, along with Tony's piano accompaniment created a strong and resonant intro. While David sang his heart out he worked Tony's lucky studio tambourine – which encouragingly had 'Downtown Tambourine' written boldly on the skin.

For the vocal backing track, Graham and Denis sang harmony and David and I sang with his lead vocal. We had a number of goes at this, until Tony boomed over the intercom: 'Boys, for fuck's sake... It sounds like Saturday night at the Old Bull and Bush.'

Basically, in no uncertain words (and the inclusion of a

few choice expletives), he told us to get our backing vocals in order. Our Roebuck and Regent Sounds run-throughs hadn't thoroughly covered BVs, but after a quick rethink we seemed to get it together. Have a listen – what do you think?

On the B-side, called 'And I Say To Myself', the monks choir were once again called into action, and the recording also featured some very neatly melodic bass work from Graham. I have a feeling Dave had written a more detailed lyric for this one originally but had no notebook with him, so he had to work on it from memory.

Once again, girl trouble is at its core but this time it included a narrative led by Dave's sensible 'inner voice', which tries hard to alert him to the dangers of the latest femme fatale who has beguiled him:

> *You're a fool, fool, fool,*
> *She doesn't love you,*
> *She doesn't need you, this I know,*
> *She's got a trail of men that she takes wherever she goes...*

I guess that backer Ray Cook was there to evaluate the potential of his new investment, and watching Dave confidently record the new single seemed to impress him. He seemed a nice enough chap, if maybe just a little misguided in his production abilities.

During the playbacks when we, or rather Tony Hatch, was deciding if a particular take was good enough to keep, Ray unwisely thought he'd throw in his two penn'orth worth and make a comment about how it could be sung differently. I remember that there was a lot of chat going on about it when Tony suddenly blew a fuse. It is too long ago to quote verbatim what he said, but it was along the lines of: 'My recording… my studio… I'm the producer… I decide…' In other words, he wasn't about to let any visiting amateurs, however well meaning, interfere in his production.

When it all calmed down Tony did apologise to Ray for jumping down his throat, politely explaining that it was his ship and his overall responsibility. Everyone made up, of course, but it did make an eventful and memorable afternoon even more so.

Very soon after the recording was completed, Pye passed the single for release. With that, a comfortable feeling of familiarity set in as record launch anticipation began all over again. This time, with one failed single behind us, I knew that high chart recognition wasn't quite so straightforward, but still held a hope that we would at least get ourselves noticed.

And the good news continued. Marquee Artists had properly set about getting us work other than at their own venue, the Marquee Club, and these gigs included our most exciting to date. We were all chuffed to bits when Ralph told us we had been booked to play in Paris over the coming New Year's Eve holiday period. Again, it felt like we were finally getting somewhere at last – well, out of the country, at least. It really was exciting for all of us.

But before that we had a few gigs to fit in, including one at an RAF camp in Leicestershire on Christmas Eve. (This was yet another inappropriate booking, but a paying gig all the same.) Our type of show certainly wasn't best suited for Christmas dance parties, but what excited me about this date (and maybe impressed Dave too) was that we were playing opposite Alex Welsh and His Jazz Band. As I mentioned earlier, I had seen this band live a number of times at the 100 Club in Oxford Street and other venues. Alex Welsh was definitely a charismatic figure, a Scot who sang, played cornet and trumpet and specialised in Dixieland jazz. He was also a bit of a comedian and often told great gags between tunes. That said, even though we had a great showman fronting our band too, neither act complemented the other in any way; in fact, we were totally mismatched for this particular occasion. The end result must have been pretty confusing for our audience too – those we hadn't already cleared from the hall with our volume, that is.

Yes we – David Bowie and The Lower Third – were undoubtedly too loud for this type of festive dance evening, so much so that even Alex Welsh wasn't amused and took up the cudgel on behalf of the RAF to try and get us to turn the volume down. But our music just didn't work quiet and was never designed for that purpose (a little bit like the legend printed on the back of David's *Ziggy Stardust* LP: 'To be played at maximum volume'). It was meant to make your ears ring, so at least you couldn't forget about us the next morning! Thinking about it, it's pretty amazing that I'm not stone deaf today as we were nosebleed loud.

I don't think Dave let the RAF/Alex Welsh interference concern him too much, as he was somewhat distracted by the local talent, so to speak. During the break (we would generally do two sets a booking), by the time he returned from the ambulance with this attractive young lady in tow, his hair was still dishevelled and his face had a familiar, contented look on it. In fact, he looked very much like the cat that got the cream (as did she).

Whereas Dave's songs of this period mainly reflected

the problems he had with the girls he fancied at home, for all his woes he certainly didn't go without while out on the road.

*

In the small hours of Christmas morning we were back in London and, as was often the case, after Graham and Denis dropped us off where I had left my car, I then took Dave home to south London.

As we drove up Plaistow Grove, David spotted a light on in the house next door to his and was slightly curious. As we pulled up outside he started to double up with laughter before pointing out, 'The kids next door are already up in the front room opening their presents.' He thought this was hysterical, as it was about 3am.

We parted that memorable Christmas Day morning saying something like – 'Next stop Paris.' We were all pretty excited about the trip, Dave included, and about the new single and forthcoming promotional event at which Ralph was planning to relaunch David and the band. Thinking back on this now, and knowing how our musical relationship was all going to end only a few weeks after this, I wonder if Dave already knew that he would be separating from The Lower Third soon, and was maybe even contemplating it as we drove to his home that morning.

The following day, Boxing Day in the UK, I celebrated my twenty-third birthday. Oh, to be twenty-three again.

*

Before I move on, having now mentioned Dave's home at Plaistow Grove, a story about David's family comes to mind. I have to say they were always a bit of a mystery to me. By comparison, my family life seemed far less complicated. I knew he got on with his father, but I'm pretty sure it wasn't always so smooth with his mother.

I remember once we had to detour the ambulance on the way to a gig to drop Dave off for an urgent meeting with his father. The meeting was close to but not actually at his family home – I believe deliberately arranged, and having something to do with his mother, Peggy, who was upset and playing up about something or other. I recall that there was a definite whiff of 'trouble at mill' about it all and that Dave needed to keep his head down for a while. I guess Dave's father, Haywood (though everyone called him John), had to put up with a lot too, as his wife never came across as the easiest person to live with.

These more private issues Dave would keep very close to his chest. He could be a very private guy a lot of the time, as I think he had to deal with a lot of emotional games at home – though it can't have been that bad, as he relied on Plaistow Grove as his de facto base, generally returning there at the weekend when we were not working.

I was only ever in both Mr and Mrs Jones's company once, when Dave was signing his management contract with Ralph Horton in a West End pub. He had to co-sign this with his parents, as he was still under twenty-one. The whole band attended too, for some reason. I don't remember Dave's mum speaking to us, but I remember his dad always seemed an amiable man.

I think Dave's mother was generally wary of David's cohorts. Denis told me that Peggy thought he would lead her boy astray. This was something that David had told him; it wasn't just a general vibe he picked up from her. Coming from his mother it had the reverse effect, of course, and just made Den that much cooler in Dave's eyes. Dave was very fond of Den.

Another lifelong friend of David's also once told me that he thought David's mother didn't like him either, so Denis certainly wasn't alone. If truth were told, she probably wasn't that impressed with any of the musicians David hung around with. But then, mums can be very protective.

Dave never told me that he had a half-brother (Terry Burns), but he did tell me that he had a sister, who I later found out was called Annette and was a half-sister on his father's side. He told me that she lived in Egypt, which impressed me at the time.

There is another interesting family connection I can add in here, though I had no clue who this person was at the time. On a couple of occasions, an elderly lady would drop into our rehearsals at the Roebuck. Having already seen Dave's mother, we knew straight away it wasn't her. She would just sit by herself, politely smiling at the side of the room, tapping her foot to the song we were running through, and then Dave would go over and have a quiet chat with her for a while.

I guessed she had some family link, though Dave never introduced her (he might have said she was a friend of his father as I'm sure we would have asked him). I now know that the lady in question was David's father's first wife, Hilda Sullivan, who had been a talented singer and pianist herself back in the day. I do remember that she was living nearby to the Roebuck at the time.

Evidently, Dave's father had kept in touch with her and she was also quite friendly with David's mother too, so it wasn't anything secretive. It was Hilda who had raised

David's half-sister, Annette, so quite possibly she was also keeping David in touch with her activities.

On the subject of contracts, Ralph never did sign up the band in any way, just Dave, who he quickly made clear was his only interest. I don't remember querying why we weren't all signed up as well. It hadn't occurred to us that this might be a safer way of conducting business. Again, I think because we were looking rather naively to Dave to watch out for us, we didn't watch out for ourselves. But we did sign a recording contract, even though it never did us any good.

When we were to become Pye recording artists it was Tony Hatch who, very business like, issued contracts to all of us individually. That actually felt really good at the time.

But then – oh, for the power of foresight.

Not long after the Pye single came out and The Lower Third broke up with Dave (more details to come, of course), I moved on to join The In Crowd (more on them to come too). One day, while I was in our agent's office, he told me that Tony Hatch had been in touch and apparently wanted me to release him and Pye from the contract they had with me. As I was looking at the paperwork, the agent casually asked, 'Do you think the record will do any good?'

Having moved on to a new chapter in my career and still feeling pretty jaded with all that had happened, I barely gave it a thought and casually replied, 'Nah.' 'Well,' said the well-meaning agent, 'you might as well let it go, then.'

The release document was there so I signed it, and that was that. Denis and Graham later told me that they had done the same. I didn't think any more about it for years, but in that second I gave up my rights to any royalties.

Now, both singles I made with David have been reissued countless times in countless countries, individually, collectively and many times as part of larger compendiums of David's music. Even a recent 2014 career retrospective collection titled *Nothing Has Changed* included both of our 'A'-sides. Shel Talmy has also released a number of David Bowie/Lower Third alternative takes and demos on a Bowie retrospective album.

If we had been paid something for our efforts over the years, that would have been nice, however token, but I certainly never let it bother me. It was more important to me that I was part of something special, historic even, and I can certainly take that in place of cash.

The fact is that it was just nice to have been a part of David's output and to have witnessed, early on, what it took others many more years to catch up with and to fully appreciate too.

To add salt to my purely superficial but rather impressive 'Can't Help Thinking About Me' war wounds, Pye never did send me a copy of the single either. I had to buy my own. I've still got it, although I suppose it's quite apt that my prized record picked up a small nick on its edge during a house move.

To be honest with you, now I've reached this far of the book, and focused more on the near misses I experienced, I really can't help thinking about me too!

*

Following our run of popular Friday night Marquee Club residencies earlier in the year, Ralph now managed to conjure a Saturday afternoon season with pirate radio outfit Radio London. Pirate radio was still flying high in the UK, particularly as the BBC were slow to recognise and adapt to this rapidly expanding market.

Radio London had picked up a sponsor in the shape of Inecto, a fairly well-known hair product manufacturer, and had been duly hired to broadcast a sponsored programme every Saturday from the Marquee under their *Inecto Show* banner. This was primarily devised to advertise Inecto shampoo, a range I sometimes saw promoted in magazines at the time.

The Inecto broadcasting format was not that dissimilar to the Radio Luxembourg show (for which we had danced to our record in front of a studio audience at EMI House). By contrast, the *Inecto Show* was for any label and act that had a single in or around the Top 20. These artists would be interviewed about what they were up to, about their current hit release and would then mime to their record for the live, and hopefully lively, Marquee audience. This radio show may have been broadcast live, as I can't remember hearing it on the radio myself, and I often listened to Radio London. On the monthly A4-sized Marquee Club gig guides – the ones you could pick up free back then and now sell for great amounts of money – these afternoon gigs were listed as 'The Marquee Saturday Show'. We were never mentioned or listed as the house band on these flyers and 'Inecto' was never referred to either.

Presenters such as Earl Richmond would MC these shows, and there is even a recording knocking around of him interviewing Dave at the Marquee later, in 1966. This featured Bowie and The Buzz at a similar Radio London event.

But in December '65, David Bowie and The Lower Third were booked to keep these young audiences entertained and 'whipped up' before the star acts took the stage. We provided live music, banter and audience interaction, acting as the general warm-up act before and after these special guest appearances. We would often find ourselves waiting in the Marquee's band room (which was at the back of the auditorium, not behind the stage) with a multitude of interesting stars – ranging from The Who and Stevie Wonder to Helen Shapiro and Pinkerton's Assorted Colours.

On one of the earliest Inecto shows I recall (Saturday, 18 December to be exact), we were delighted to be reunited with The Who once again. Pete and the boys were no strangers to the Marquee, of course, and were easily the club's biggest draw at the time. Like many stars of the day, they owed much of their success to pirate outfits such as Radio London, who collectively broadcast night and day to many millions of listeners. It's hard to imagine now, but pirate radio was literally the life blood of the record industry for most of the 1960s.

It was great to catch up with The Who again, though this time they were all a bit subdued. While we were getting ready to go on stage, we on one side of the band room and they on the other, it soon became clear that all was not well. We could see that drummer Keith Moon had yet to show up. We told that he was off ill (we didn't enquire what was wrong, but I later found out he had bad whooping cough), and to fulfil all the engagements in their busy diary Viv Prince had been taken on as a 'dep' drummer. There was only one problem with this arrangement, it transpired: Prince was very unreliable.

At about the same time we learnt that Keith was absent, I heard Pete comment that Viv was late for his band call yet again and hadn't made contact with anyone that day either.

Evidently he had been making a habit of late arrivals and had caused the band all kinds of grief since they engaged him in early December. In fact, I'm not sure he even turned up that afternoon.

We were stood with Ralph as I pondered the situation, then said quietly to the boys 'I wonder if they need a drummer?' Denis immediately turned to me and said, 'Get in there, Phil,' though I could tell Ralph was not so enthusiastic. As I stood thinking about it, Ralph looked towards me and smugly commented, 'Look at his eyes, he's got pound note signs rolling in them.'

Denis, however, acted on my behalf straight away, writing down my telephone number and taking it over to Roger Daltrey. This time Roger didn't ask if he knew me, though I'm not actually sure he remembered me from our Bournemouth encounter either. I didn't take it to heart, as they were so busy and must have been meeting hundreds of people month on month.

I never did get a call from them. In fact, I think Keith returned to the band a few days later. But it was great warming up the audience for one of our favourite bands, and I'm also pleased to confirm that David and The Who did appear at the Marquee, at the same time, albeit for a daytime radio recording.

On a final note about this encounter with The Who. It had been a difficult few months for them, as Roger had fallen out badly with Keith during a backstage argument at a show in Denmark. Roger landed a heavy blow on Keith and nearly broke his nose, resulting in the band unanimously firing their lead singer. After a few days (when it became abundantly clear that they couldn't continue without him) he was invited back for a meeting, and following a sincere apology to Keith, Roger was reinstated once again.

If that wasn't enough drama, again not long before our Marquee encounter, at another Who show in Denmark, an overexcited audience invaded the stage almost as soon as the show began, wrecking the group's equipment and in the process causing over £10,000 worth of damage. So it wasn't that surprising that they looked a bit jaded when we saw them again.

Our afternoon show with The Who was also the final Inecto gig of the year, though we would continue with this weekly booking in early January, following our trip to the continent.

I have since learned that fledgling mega stars such as Elton John and Marc Bolan came to see us during those Marquee days, though Elton – who was still Reginald Dwight at the time – didn't seem to think that much of us, judging by the comments I've read anyway.

CHAPTER NINE

PARIS – THE BEGINNING OF THE END

Before I move on to recount what memories I still retain of our trip to gay Paris, I've a confession to make. It wasn't just The Small Faces who were dabbling with pot. Dave and one of our band also partook in a bit of weed from time to time – shock horror.

One day Denis, Graham, Dave and myself were walking along the street together, on the way for a West End meeting. We were all dedicated cigarette smokers, but on this day two of us were smoking marijuana. I don't know who supplied it but it was probably Dave who was given it, being the figurehead of the group.

Our band had never used pot before and I had thought that all of us were against any form of drugs. I must have believed that it was an unspoken rule within the group that we were all anti-drugs and that it was of no interest to any of us. To be honest, though, it was never actually discussed before this and I simply must have expected the other guys, who seemed sensible enough, to have felt exactly the same as I did. Dave's 'legal' drug of choice had been barley wine (don't laugh, he was sometimes wiped out on the stuff, it's pretty potent).

In case you are wondering, David and Graham were the miscreants with the joint. What's particularly funny now is how Denis and I took exception to this and chided them both for smoking the stuff as we walked along.

Denis and I were saying things like, 'We don't smoke dope, do we?' nodding to one another like a couple of pompous school kids. We wouldn't let it go, either. Self-righteous or what?

Saying all that, I have to admit I have since revised my views on these things and have even tried a joint or two. Sadly, the first one I ever attempted to smoke made me physically sick, and the second one didn't go down much better either. So, I just decided to stick to the crack and heroin instead (I jest of course).

Naturally, Dave and Graham were completely unmoved by any of our comments. I reminded Denis of this event recently, and asked him what he remembered. Apparently, Dave had already confided in him that he had spent a recent afternoon getting stoned with his friend Donovan (whom he had known about a year, since his days with The Manish Boys). So it was less of a surprise to Den. But, like me, Den just didn't want to go down that road. As I said, I did eventually try the stuff, but it never really floated my boat. I gave up the cigs many decades ago too, so I really wouldn't care to give it another go now.

Another 'potty' occasion was had when we were working with The Spencer Davis Group at the 100 Club. We all used to hang out in the dressing room together and before one particular gig we stood in a circle as a joint was passed around. On that occasion I, with some definite self-consciousness, simply passed it quickly on without taking a drag. It was almost like it would contaminate me if I held on to it for too long. I'm sure it was all pretty harmless in the overall scheme of things, but it wasn't for me.

I could go on about The In Crowd (my next band), and two band members in the back of my car popping amyl nitrate like children's Smarties, but I'll stop there.

*

We were to play three shows in Paris. The first night was at the Golf-Drouot at 2 Rue Drouot, Montmartre, the next at the recently opened Bus Palladium, 6 Rue Pierre Fontaine (near the Pigalle nightclub), then the last night back at the Golf-Drouot again. For this trip, Graham set about converting the inside of the ambulance. It had always been a bit awkward, having the partition between the driver's cab and the back so Graham opened it up, successfully integrating both.

By this time we had acquired a roadie-cum-road manager called Paul Williams. Paul, who was about the same age as us, was a quietly spoken guy, but was (as roadies sometimes could be) invisible when required. Actually, to be fair he wasn't that bad, but he could be a bit difficult at inopportune moments. We gained quite a feeling of status from his arrival, as only successful bands had road managers. Paul came as a result of the business liaison Ralph had recently struck up with Ray Cook, the chap whom Ralph had persuaded to put money behind David.

Paul Williams was, I thought, a friend of Ray's, and I can't say that any money was discussed for his services (though I have since discovered that some of Ray's money was used to pay him something). So for this Paris 'adventure', we were in an improved, open-plan ambulance, bolstered by the addition of a new roadie and a few francs' pocket money to go between us.

The night before we left for France we travelled down to Margate, and to the hometown of the original Lower Third. Denis's family still lived there, so we all slept in his mum's front room in preparation for the short drive to Ramsgate and the ferry to France early the next day.

At that time in the music world (or in any world), you couldn't go far without hearing something about The Beatles, and the end of this year was no different. Once again they had stolen a march with another ground-breaking album, their second in 1965. This one was called *Rubber Soul*. Our radio was full of it, even on some of the continental stations we picked up. The Fab Four had recorded it all in a month, too, just a few weeks before its release, and if that wasn't impressive enough, the track listing still reads like a greatest hits album.

They were also at number one in the singles chart as we made our way to Paris, with two tracks that weren't even included on this album, 'We Can Work It Out' and one that seemed almost apt for our journey, 'Day Tripper'.

Great records are very much the soundtracks of our lives and it's impossible for me not to picture these amazing moments in my life when I suddenly hear any memorable music from back in the day. I know I've mentioned The Beatles' importance quite often, but mainly because they were such a phenomenon at the time, and every new recording they made was a clear progression. On the radio, at least that December, we travelled to Paris and back with John, Paul, George and Ringo, and it was fab.

*

When we set off for Calais, I believe I was the only one in the band who had ever been abroad before, so was probably affected with a slight air of superiority. As soon as we landed on French soil we went to look for something to eat, and a short way along the road we spotted a café where we parked up. It already seemed like we were in the middle of nowhere, just surrounded by a lot of countryside. In fact, we were barely out of Calais and already hungry (even though we had stuffed ourselves with a big send-off breakfast at Denis's a few hours earlier).

After being a little bit bamboozled by the menu we all, I think, ordered steak, which arrived alarmingly bloody. Normal fare in France, but totally unknown to us at the time. It just felt great to be there, that our band was good enough to at least make it into Europe, and this first French meal was like a mini celebration. We were a success of sorts, and this proved it.

The only down side was the limited hot beverage menu. With only coffee and hot chocolate on offer, poor old 'T-cup' hadn't made allowances for the sudden lack of English tea and started to fret about how he was going to survive.

We couldn't believe the state of the khazi either, which was no more than a rudimentary plank of wood with a hole in it. On my previous visit to France I hadn't encountered this more rural type of toilet arrangement, so I wasn't able to warn anyone. Dave was not impressed at all, but we all had a good joke about it when we piled back

205

into the ambulance and started the final leg to Paris (albeit having to stop and negotiate our first French petrol station on the way).

The great thing on this journey was that Graham didn't have to drive, though he still wanted to take over every now and then. It felt strange having him with us at the back for much of the journey, and must have felt very odd for him too, being so used to driving the whole time.

It was on this leg of the journey that, no doubt encouraged by some of the wine we had consumed at lunch, Dave delved into his own songbook and out of the blue started to sing, 'And I say to myself you're a fool, fool, fool…' By the second line the rest of us were singing along with him at the tops of our voices, with dubious attention given to any harmonic quality.

As the song progressed someone adjusted the words and started to sing, 'And I say to the French, you're ze fool…' to which one of us immediately replied, with an even broader French accent, 'I'm ze fool?' And so it continued for a lot of the journey, with more and more daft, improvised verses. In the end our roadie Paul, myself, Graham, Dave and Den were all declared fools as the song petered out to complete nonsense. In turn, 'You're ze fool' also became the catchphrase of the trip.

For much of the journey we also seemed to adopt a quasi French/Cockney accent, spouting a lot of 'Oo la la's, 'Ça va biens' and 'Mercy boucups'. Being typical Brits, none of us thought to bring an English-to-French phrase book either, so ended up asking for things slowly in English, though added a slight French accent to the mix in the hope that this would help. When we were met with blank stares, which was often, we just pointed at what we wanted to buy. Luckily, I did have a bit more experience here, which probably helped a little.

Luckily, cigarettes were one thing we weren't short of, having hammered the boat's duty-free shop on the journey over. To get a better picture of what we were like on our first day abroad, just imagine a group of hyped-up school kids on a day trip and you won't be too far out. That duty free was the equivalent of our very own cut-price sweet shop. We definitely liked the cheap cigs and couldn't wait to get the boat back. (Although we were only stopping in Paris for three nights, we were leaving the UK in 1965 and returning in 1966, which had a nice feel about it.)

Now armed with more cartons of ciggies than we'd ever seen in our lives, we smoked for France and Britain combined. So much so that the ambulance was like a fog inside by the time we neared Paris. Wanting also to experience some of the local customs, we decided it would only be polite to pick up a bottle or three of cheap French plonk at the same time. This was also in the hope of making our journey that much more pleasurable and getting a feel for the country we were staying in (that's my excuse, anyway). This worked well, and I can genuinely say we were all, apart from our sober driver Paul, feeling thoroughly continental way before we even reached Paris.

As we closed in on the French capital, the empty bottles increased in number and began rolling across the ambulance floor, colliding with one other when we braked or took a corner. It was definitely an annoyance but none of us felt compelled to deal with it, so that's how they remained until we needed an urgent toilet break. That's when we realised why it was an acceptable French custom for men to just stop by the roadside and pee on the nearest tree. With bladders set to burst and no sign of any roadside stops, that's all we could do, and when Paul finally found somewhere safe to pull over and park, we were fighting to get out the back of the ambulance.

I can still picture the four of us now, standing in a row and looking out across a picturesque French field, moaning with relief as our bladders emptied and sharing the odd 'Ooo la la or what?'

Fortunately, we now had a couple of beds in the back so were able to take turns grabbing a couple of hours' sleep. That felt like sheer luxury too: our very own travelling bedroom. I'm sure Graham could have gone into business fitting out boats and vehicles if he had wanted to.

Roadie or not, we still arrived late in Paris as the distance between Calais and Paris had deceived us somewhat (I believe it took us something like eight or nine hours). Somehow, though, we miraculously navigated our way through the outer reaches of Paris to the even narrower Montmartre streets, and there we found our Marquee representative waiting for us on a street corner. I don't know how we found the right street, let alone Paris. All credit to Graham in the end, I believe, though Paul may have deserved a pat on the back too, it's hard to remember. All I know is, we got to the place.

Anyway this Marquee rep was very pissed off with us for being late (not that late, actually), and I got quite annoyed with him after what I thought we'd achieved in finding him at all.

With little time to waste we were directed to our hotel where we quickly tidied ourselves up, put on our stage outfits then set off for the gig. There was no time to relax, as it was straight to work.

That first night in Paris we shared the bill with twenty-three-year-old Arthur Brown, who just a couple of years later would score a massive hit with 'Fire' (No. 1 in the UK and Canada and No.2 in the USA). At this time, though, the soon to be 'God of Hellfire' didn't even steam a little bit. I can vaguely recall someone saying he could skip around the stage very nimbly indeed, however.

Arthur told me he had been a student before getting into the pop business, having studied philosophy and law. He was a pleasant enough chap, quite well spoken as I remember, and was clearly a larger-than-life character, though I can't recall watching his act that night. It had been a bloody long day, so I was probably half asleep in the dressing room at the time. I later found out that he had briefly moved to Paris to study acting.

When it was nearly time to go on I was standing at the side of the Golf-Drouot stage to prepare myself. An unidentified French guy (no surprise there) sidled up to me and nodded my attention towards an attractive, dark-haired girl who was standing nearby, asking me bluntly, 'Do you want zis girl over zer?'

Then, slightly unexpectedly, he began to physically demonstrate a number of moves from what looked suspiciously to me like the more basic offerings of the *Kama Sutra*. The geezer, who I have to say was a passionate salesman if nothing else, gradually mimed the girl's entire repertoire, just so I knew what was on offer. It was bizarre, comical and a little shocking, all at the same time. And while he's going through the specials, I'm doing my best to concentrate on the important gig we were about to do, while giving him the occasional nod of approval for sharing his sex face with me.

'I did zis wiz 'er last night,' says he, doing his best Marcel Marceau mime with slightly bent knees and thrusting hips, his hands holding onto her imaginary hips while she, I envisaged, was also standing and bent forward in a suggestive 'take me' position.

'She eez vewy good, I'm telling you,' he continued, now a little concerned that his mime and attractive menu wasn't quite hitting the mark.

'Thanks,' says I, 'but I've got to go on stage now.'

Of course, on reflection I realised that he probably meant I should avail myself of his offer later on, not actually there and then, by the side of the stage. Where David was at that precise moment I don't know, but he couldn't have been that far away back stage. Had he been stood where I was, who knows if this guy may have picked up a sale? David enjoyed mime.

*

We had been used to getting a good response at the Marquee by now, but the French kids went absolutely bonkers for us. It was a really frantic, well-received gig. Probably the best reception we had ever had.

As soon as our set was over and we were back in our dressing room, hot, sweaty and somewhat overwhelmed at our reception, almost immediately we were greeted with a god-awful pounding at the door, mixed with what sounded like a few dozen excited, determined screams from girls desperately trying to get to us. We had never experienced anything quite like this before, and looked at each other in amazement.

Representatives of the Golf-Drouot, including boss Henri Leproux (who, I recently discovered, died in 2014), told us later that we had received one of the best responses they'd ever had for a British band. Whether that's what they said to every visiting British band I don't know, but you certainly couldn't fake that hysterical audience response, no way. The club was also delighted we would be back for at least one more show in a couple of days. As it turned out, we were asked to do an extra afternoon matinée too.

As our dressing-room door was about to cave in under this growing onslaught, and eager not to become rock casualties following our first concert abroad, we adhered to the club's sage advice and swiftly made our escape down some back stairs to the Rue Drouot, where a couple of cars were parked and ready to go. We were all still sweaty and buzzing after our high-energy performance as we practically skipped down the steep, narrow staircase, led by one of the club's management who was shouting loudly ahead to alert the drivers.

Some kids had already made it outside and ran over to say goodbye, so we quickly signed some autographs, kissed a few eager (female) lips and then piled into the waiting vehicles. I was amazed at how our French driver just bashed into the cars parked in front and behind to get out, while our mini fan club excitedly waved and blew kisses to us from the pavement, with at least one shedding a tear. This really felt like pop-star treatment and, on arrival at our hotel, we ducked straight into the bijou hotel bar for a few beers and a much-needed wind-down. It had been some day.

As we'd made such a hasty retreat from Golf-Drouot, our equipment had to remain. We had asked roadie Paul if he would, as he was hired to do, pack everything up for us but he was having none of it.

'It's so crazy out there I'm not doing it. I'll collect it tomorrow when it's safer,' he said, rather pathetically. As the club was OK with that, Paul was able to escape with us, but Den, Graham and I were a bit miffed that he hadn't secured our valuable gear.

Of course, this amazing first night remains my main memory of this trip, and I can still picture a lot of that particular evening now. I have to say the Golf-Drouot could almost have been the Marquee when the lights were on us up on stage. It had such a similar vibe about it and it made great sense that there was this close bond between the clubs. Like the Marquee, the Golf-Drouot was a very popular teenage club and is still revered by those that remember it, as is the Marquee by those who used to go there regularly. No doubt this was down to a mutual admiration between the two skilled club proprietors behind these establishments, the Marquee's Harold Pendleton and the Golf's aforementioned local legend, Henri Leproux.

During our brief French capital sojourn, at least one of our contingent managed a memorable French connection. It didn't go unnoticed that Den had started to hang out with a very sweet-looking French girl, whom he met at the Bus Palladium and may even have been bilingual (lucky sod). I didn't realise they had remained in touch, but Den told me recently that after the band broke up he went back to Paris twice more to see her. They stayed in contact for quite a while.

My only other clear-ish memories are of some of our time off in Paris, running up and down some steps near the beautiful Sacré-Coeur Cathedral in Montmartre, and generally sodding about in the back streets. Trying to fathom out French menus in a couple of cheap Parisian cafés also comes to mind.

At one point, after admiring the Sacré-Coeur and its amazing views across Paris (where we spotted the Eiffel Tower for the first time), I know we wandered through a late afternoon Place du Tertre, the famous artist's square where, by night, the many surrounding bars and restaurants came to life. From there we must have wandered down and around Rue Lepic as we ended up in the Boulevard de Clichy, near Pigalle, facing the legendary Moulin Rouge.

As I write this, I'm smiling at how chuffed Dave and the rest of us were to discover, by chance, what must be one of the most famous theatres in the world, and have no idea that some thirty-five years on David himself would contribute a couple of songs to assist a remake of the film of the same name. One of those songs was a cover of Nat King Cole's 'Nature Boy', which I'm sure was recorded especially for the film. It's a beautiful version, which I sometimes include, along with a few other choice Bowie recordings, on my weekly radio show. I'd just never made that song and film link with our Paris trip before today.

I can still hear Dave telling us about Toulouse-Lautrec and how the wonderful posters he made were often drawn as the girls danced on stage at the Moulin Rouge. I loved the history of it all and Dave's great interest and knowledge of art helped make that little excursion something special.

There was a boy
A very strange enchanted boy
They say he wandered very far,
Very far, over land and sea…
('Nature Boy', first recorded by Nat King Cole)

I know we laughed a lot on that trip, and overall our amazing French reception (all the shows were a great success) gave us plenty to be happy about. We didn't make it up the Eiffel Tower, but then again, time was limited and we were mainly there to work.

In retrospect, we had a right result. David Bowie brought the house down on his first night abroad – and I don't suppose many acts can make that claim. I'm still very proud to have been part of it. But it wasn't all positive, I'm afraid to say, as it was while we were in gay Paris that Ralph ramped up his focus on Dave as a solo artist rather than as a member of the band. This is where it really started to hit home to us.

It was the first real sign of cracks appearing in the whole project, and it all started when Ralph arrived during rehearsals back at the Bus Palladium, where we were preparing to perform that night. It was quite an entrance too, as he was ominously attired in a brand-new, expensive looking, full-length black leather overcoat. In retrospect, he looked a little bit like an archetypal Nazi bad guy from an Indiana Jones movie. He was just lacking the jackboots and insignia.

On arrival, instead of catching up with us all collectively, as would have been polite and expected, he ignored us and urgently pulled Dave to one side and started to talk to him in private. This immediately dampened the mood, and felt particularly cold considering Ralph was supposedly there to represent us all. He didn't even want to find out how it had all been going. That felt really odd and pretty disrespectful too.

The excellent audience reaction that we, as a band, had achieved so far on this trip seemed to quickly dull. We had all been keen to let Ralph know how brilliantly things were going in Paris and were sure he would be relieved and want to share in our overall celebration. We could be a hit out here, we thought, given the welcome we had already received.

It was left up to Dave to tell us what was going on after rehearsals, which he did. Why Ralph was being so secretive we didn't know. It seemed more than a simple show of power, though that was probably all it was. Dave told us that all was still on course regarding the new single release and proposed TV appearances and things were now hotting up as the release approached. In fact, it had got so urgent that straight after the final gig Ralph would be taking him back to England to meet Vicki Wickham, the producer of the Associated-Rediffusion television pop show *Ready, Steady, Go!*

There had been talk before we left that Vicki, who also notably managed Dusty Springfield, would fly out to see one of our Paris gigs to make sure we were up to scratch. I wish she had – that would have been great and may even have changed what eventually happened regarding Dave's appearance.

We naturally had mixed feelings about all of this. While it looked highly likely that we were going to appear on our first TV show, why couldn't the meeting with Vicky Wickham wait until we were all back in London? It was, after all, our single too.

Our last two shows in Paris were back at the Golf and were once again incredibly well received. This time the club was much more prepared, though, and managed to keep an equally excited audience clear of our dressing-room door. It was a fitting end to our live debut in this amazing capital.

As per this last-minute change to the plan, Ralph flew Dave back to London; he had already packed and left when I woke up on our last morning (we shared kipping arrangements again in Paris for the usual economic reasons). This was also the first time Dave had flown. That probably gave us something to moan about on the way back to Calais too – 'It's alright for some, being flown home in style.'

Our gigs in Paris couldn't have gone better, but the Third returned to England after a short but action-packed adventure minus its lead singer and not a little deflated.

Ralph did come to our last Paris gig and we finally got to speak to him, but that wasn't very encouraging either. I was still so full of our positive French reception, I mentioned that it would be a good idea to build on it and return very soon. However, rather than share in any of our positive enthusiasm, Ralph coolly advised me that we should 'make it in England first', quoting the old (and in this case deeply annoying) adage, 'If you can't shovel shit on your own doorstep…'

He obviously had no particular interest in what we had to say or could do for him in the future (as we would soon discover), but I suppose he daren't push his disinterest and rudeness too far in Paris, as there were still bookings to be honoured.

*

Even so, our success in France still buoyed us up for a while, and we had some exciting, positive stories to share with family and friends. But we were also now aware that something had clearly changed in the group's dynamics and it would probably never be the same again.

On reflection, it could be said that the meeting Ralph so urgently swept Dave off to may have ultimately benefited us all. I just couldn't see it like that at the time, and my instincts were ultimately correct. In a way, Paris, with all its triumphs, was the beginning of the end of David Bowie and The Lower Third.

CHAPTER TEN

CAN'T HELP THINKING ABOUT ME

Not just relying on anything Pye Records could knock together for us, Ralph also engaged a publicity agent whose job it would be to get us noticed. Her name was Gaby Sturmer.

I was impressed with Gaby, who was in her early thirties, short in stature, business-like and very professional in all she did for us. I never actually had much to do with her on a one-to-one basis, apart from supplying some biographical information for her press release. Most of her planning was conducted with Dave and Ralph (Dave, of course, being an ex-advertising man and never short of an idea or two).

One evening, Ralph invited Gaby out with all of us to have dinner in Soho. We had duck à l'orange, of all things – a first for me. My main memory of that night – apart from flavoured duck – is of doing my Churchill impersonation at the table. I'm pleased to say it raised some laughter, even from Ralph, I think. The evening was a thank-you to Gaby and a rare treat for us too.

It wasn't long after this that Gaby set up another interesting promotion for us – aimed at getting us what column inches she could. We were gathered in Hyde Park for a photo session, together with a guy who had famously just had the snip to become a woman (though I haven't a clue now who it was). Various poses were assumed, the one abiding in my memory being of the four of us standing in a row, holding or carrying this newly made lady while she lay across our outstretched arms, lengthways like a roll of carpet. As I was the littlest, I guess I must have been at the feet end. It was quite hilarious, really.

Gaby wrote up some suitable copy to accompany the best of the photos taken and I'm sure tried to get the item placed in one of the red tops, or even somewhere like *Tit-Bits* magazine. I'm pretty sure it wasn't taken up by any of the press in the end. Someone would have flagged it up at the time. I don't think we even saw any of the photos that were taken, not that they would have been much use in the music press. I'd love to see them, though, so if anyone has some pictures of someone who looks suspiciously like David Bowie with three similarly dressed guys, holding what I can only describe as a well-made-up roll of human carpet, you know where to call.

Before that morning photo session got underway we discovered that we were too early or the photographer was running late, so Dave suggested we wander across Park Lane to one of the big hotels. We ended up in a very plush, mostly deserted hotel bar and ordered a single glass of Coca-Cola (the price of which would probably have paid for a couple of full English breakfasts at the Gio, plus coffee too). Sitting alone at the bar was a very attractive, glamorously made-up woman, sipping on a cocktail.

'She's a prozzy,' one of the boys said under his breath, so as not to embarrass her. As we all subtly looked across to confirm or question this observation (which may even have been meant as a joke), without saying a word Dave got up and walked straight over to the bar and perched himself on the padded bar stool next to hers. He was amazing like that. He didn't debate it or even ask us to dare him; he was gone. The young woman concerned, just like that married lady in Bournemouth that Dave casually chatted up while she made us breakfast a few months earlier, seemed delighted he had made the effort and spoke to him like they were old friends (they weren't, just in case you were wondering). It was just a bit of flirtatious fun, of course.

I did read an interview that Dave gave many years later when he mentioned that people would be surprised at just how shy he really was, and how he found attending parties particularly difficult and uncomfortable affairs. Well let me assure you, this shyness didn't extend to talking to the opposite sex. Dave was a natural. He was never short of female attention and had no concerns about chatting a woman up either. He could charm the proverbial birds from the trees.

I suppose what he meant by shyness was directed towards groups of strangers rather than individuals, though I still found it hard to see Dave struggling in any circumstances. I suppose he may have lost some of his younger confidence and bravado in later years. These things happen.

While mentioning what Gaby did for us in publicity, I should also mention a chap called Roy Carson too. We ran into him at, of all places, the Gio, he being a young journalist working for the music press. He wrote under the name of Roy S. Carson, presumably as there was another writer with the same name, and he liked what we were doing. There was no money in it for him, but he kindly offered to write up a band biography – this a few months before Ralph employed Gaby and when Dave was still David Jones. I still have a copy of his detailed, two-page, hand-typed biography of David and the band, with his address at the top of it: 44 Old Bond Street, W1.

In it, he wrote of Dave:

Insistently he claims the dubious honour of being Bromley's first 'Mod' but has since changed his philosophy to become a 'Rocker'. He plays tenor, alto and baritone saxophones, as well as a guitar, flute and clarinet – though never all at once.

Roy also managed to get a small news item about Dave and the band in *Record Mirror*, I think. There was a small photo of Dave with it, which I remember being taken by Roy at the end of Denmark Street.

I would sometimes see Roy's name pop up above mainstream press stories over the years. In later years, it seems he specialised in crime reporting, and relocated to Sweden.

While touching on the subject of photography again, another slightly more important photo session needs to be mentioned here too. It must have been Ralph who sought out photographer Nicholas Wright, as we soon found ourselves in front of his lens, wandering around Pimlico one Sunday morning looking for suitable backdrops to pout in front of.

Nicky was right up there in the cool stakes with us all as he had taken the moody photo of The Rolling Stones for their debut LP cover. It was an intriguing front cover design in many ways as it just had the Decca label in the top corner above the full-cover photograph, with no mention of the band or a title (though 'The Rolling Stones' was emblazoned on the back for those that needed a clue). It felt a bit like a conventional cover was quite unnecessary for this particular group. The smart designer was the group's own manager, Andrew Loog Oldham.

I know Dave would have been especially pleased about Nicky's Stones association. Not that that he mentioned the Stones much to me at the time, but we now know how important they were to him over the years. He had first seen them live somewhere in south London when he was still at secondary school, and later forged a close, career-long friendship with Mick Jagger.

Many of Nicky's photos of David and The Lower Third appear in this book, including the picture of Dave and I on the cover, so I am eternally grateful to him for that. Sadly he is no longer with us but I did run into him in later years, not long before his death, while I was waiting for work in Archer Street. One of the narrow backstreets in Soho's club and theatre district, this was a thoroughfare that my drum teacher, Frank King, had turned me on to. It was the place where all band musicians (of the dance-band variety) hung out looking for work – like a sort of unofficial musician's labour exchange. A lot of the capital's scratch-band bookings originated in Archer Street, as they had done for nearly fifty years. As a brief indulgence, here are a few lines of a 1924 poem by one Syd Gamage about this historical but now defunct musicians' market place:

Oh! what a sight is Archer Street,
Where all sorts of musicians meet,
You there will find a motley crew,
Who gaze expectantly back at you
With longing eyes, as if to say –
Got any 'dates' to give away?'

It was great to see Nicky again – a talented, laid-back guy and great to hang out with. He was keen to know how we were all getting on, though I could only give him a basic update. He mentioned that he had stayed in touch with David and worked on more photo sessions with him too, which didn't surprise me. Working with Nicky was yet another highlight of my time in the business, and particularly with David and the boys.

*

To announce David's first ever single as 'Bowie', Ralph and Dave had Gaby design an attractive four-page leaflet to tell the industry of his rebirth under the heading – 'Davie Jones Is Back In His Locker'. This glossy foldout promotion also included a short profile of each band member, along with our pictures. Here is some of Gaby's copy:

Davie Jones Is Back In His Locker... at the bottom of the sea. And instead we have David Bowie, a 19-year-old singer discovered by Tony Hatch. Why David Bowie? 'There were too many Davie Joneses' David explains. 'David Jones is my real name and when I turned professional two years ago my pirate-like character was just right at that time, and the name fitted in with the image I wanted to give myself.

Ralph and Gaby also arranged a record launch to be held in central London, with professionally printed cards, inviting guests to meet and greet:

David Bowie with The Lower Third
at the Gaiety Bar, Victoria Tavern,
Strathearn Place, Hyde Park –
Thursday, January 6th 1966

There is little doubt that some of Ray Cook's money was hard at work here. The Victoria Tavern was a polite buffet affair with a number of music-trade reporters and a few photographers milling about while Ralph and Gaby tried to interest them in talking to, and writing about, Dave. The venue itself was pretty upmarket, with the Gaiety Bar itself designed much like a mid- to late-Victorian theatre and reached via a tight staircase on an upper floor of the pub. The reception also spilt into the downstairs bar too and I'm sure a few guests didn't even make it much further than that. There was even a rumour knocking about that John Lennon might turn up. He didn't of course, but his fifty-three-year-old dad did, and that, more than anything else, made my day.

Alfred 'Freddie' Lennon had recently come out of the woodwork and had made a record with Pye, his sudden appearance naturally interesting the national newspapers, who sensed a good story when it showed itself. Mr Lennon was with a very young-looking manager (younger than Ralph) and they both looked a bit lost at the reception, so I took the opportunity to introduce myself.

It turned into the highlight of the whole afternoon for me when I got into conversation with Fred and he told me all about his fascinating life. He didn't hold back either, he was happy to talk about anything and everything, so I just sat back and listened.

You could definitely see the strong Lennon family resemblance too, particularly around the eyes (at one point when he smiled it looked like an older version of John himself sitting there), and of course Fred's Scouse accent and very particular nasal intonation was very similar to his son's. There must definitely be localised variations between individual regional accents, even within Liverpool I would say.

Fred first met John's mother, Julia, when she was fourteen and he was fifteen, and he told me how he had been at sea in the merchant navy for years. John was born at the start of the war and, as Freddie was sent away in the navy on the treacherous Atlantic convoys, he only got to see his wife and son once during this time when he was allowed back home on leave. It was me that added in the word 'treacherous' I hasten to add. Men like Fred Lennon wouldn't use such a dramatic word when talking about their war service, and his face told you that he hadn't had an easy life. It was a lottery if the ship you were on would complete the passage or get torpedoed, and if you were hit you had little or no chance of surviving the freezing north Atlantic water if you weren't quickly rescued. I think the stress eventually got to him as he went absent without leave in the last few months of the war, causing his family hardship when his cheques stopped arriving.

When he was eventually allowed home following the war, instead of being able to return to the family he had thought about every day, he was informed that his marriage was over and that he wasn't welcome in his own house. To make things even more unbearable, his wife was pregnant, carrying another man's child. It must have been devastating for the guy, particularly when he mentioned how much he adored his son and would have done anything for him.

Evidently it was this marriage split that had confused John, who would have been about five or six when his father returned from the war. Fred also said that the story going around that he had planned to kidnap young John and take him abroad during his marriage break-up was a load of rubbish and that there had been no such drama, though John had cried desperately when he was made to say goodbye to him by his estranged wife.

He was unable to properly defend himself, as it was his wife who kept custody of John, which caused a rift between the two that never properly healed. It sounded to me like John was unaware of exactly what had happened and had been fed some bad stories as he grew up.

He went on to tell me how John was now very suspicious of his motives and how awkward it was when they met after years apart, his son now a huge star, of course. 'I know John must have wondered if I was after this or that...' Freddie told me, putting his hand behind his back to mimic a 'back hander', 'but I wasn't,' he confirmed, with some sadness in his eyes.

I was very moved by his story, and how genuine he came across. It particularly struck me then, over twenty years after the end of the war, how people's lives were still being greatly affected by the turmoil it had left in its wake.

A photographer asked Fred to pose for a picture with the group, so we happily lined up together (minus David), even though Freddie was most concerned at how he'd look as he had lost his front teeth in an accident at sea years earlier. To illustrate his concern, he opened his mouth to show me that he had no teeth. But the picture was taken and I would love to have had a copy, though I never saw one used anywhere.

I mentioned that David wasn't in the photo. I'm really not sure why he chose to avoid it, but he quietly made it clear that he didn't want to be included and steered well away. Maybe he thought it would be disrespectful to John Lennon if he did pose with his father. However, Lennon hadn't a clue who David Bowie was then and I'm sure wouldn't have been at all bothered even if he did know of him. I was puzzled by Dave's decision, but then again, Ralph was being so protective over everything he was doing at the time, it may well have been a directive from up on high.

It was, however, a great experience for me and I was very pleased I spent some time talking to Freddie when no one seemed to be bothered to even go over and say hello. I suppose it was the juxtaposition of him, an absolutely no-frills, working-class bloke, talking in an ordinary way about the navy, the war and his son – a son who just happened to be one of the biggest music icons in the world. But it also showed the reality that, for all his great wealth and massive success, John was also just another casualty of a senseless war.

On a final note about Fred Lennon, his Pye single was aptly titled 'That's My Life (My Love And My Home)', and he co-wrote it. Ironically, it managed to do slightly better business than ours, I was told, which wasn't saying much. But having been pretty much snubbed by Dave at this press launch it was somewhat ironic that Fred probably got more out of it than Dave in the end.

So that was the highlight of the Gaiety Bar record launch, for me anyway. It was a pretty laid-back affair all in all, and the press weren't particularly set on fire by us, or by Dave. It was a shame that Tony Hatch couldn't make it, as that would have undoubtedly given photographers more saleable photo opportunities – like *'successful producer with his exciting new band'*. As it happens, I don't think I have ever seen any photos of Dave and Tony Hatch together, even from later on when The Buzz had filled our shoes.

But the record did thankfully get some favourable reviews, and I still have the odd cutting to prove it in my scrapbook. Other than that, not much came from the afternoon, though you couldn't fault Ralph for trying. He was doing all he could to get his boy noticed. It was just a shame he didn't feel the same about The Lower Third.

Now I look back, older and thankfully wiser, it's amazing to think that Dave was still just eighteen when this promotional event was staged. He seemed so much older and more mature in many ways. His nineteenth birthday was two days after this, on 8 January.

But what of 'Can't Help Thinking About Me'?

Well, the single did get into the charts and so was some kind of success for Dave, I suppose (though many believe that Ralph bought the single into the charts, no doubt with the money he should have been giving us). But it never went high enough to really mean anything – until much later on – and of course copies of the single today go for large amounts of money.

One or two of the reviews are worth typing up for posterity. *New Musical Express* was quite upbeat, if a little contradictory: 'David Bowie wrote the stormer 'Can't Help Thinking About Me' (Pye) which he sings with his group the Lower Third – absorbing melody, weakish tune.' *Disc Weekly* was even more direct: 'David Bowie wrote 'Can't Help Thinking About Me' (Pye). With enough ear bashing [it] could make it.'

Best of the bunch, though, was *Record Mirror*:

> *David Bowie: Can't Help Thinking About Me/And I Say To Myself (Pye 17929). Backed by the Lower Third, this is a Bowie penned top deck with a good beat, neat vocalist and a mass of enthusiasm. Artiste used to be known as Davie Jones – this underlines his promise.*

Someone else who picked up on the single (after seeing Dave perform live with The Buzz at the Marquee) was singer and journalist Jonathan King. He was impressed enough to write an article in the *Music Echo* titled, 'Bowie's Record Does Not Deserve To Die', revealing that he too could see Dave's great potential.

In 1983, David referred to this song as his first serious attempt at songwriting:

> *It was the first band where I'd started writing songs. I think the first song I ever wrote, there might be others, but this is the only one that sticks out was called 'Can't Help Thinking About Me' [breaks up laughing]. That's an illuminating little piece, isn't it? It was about leaving home and moving up to London.*

For all its disappointments, 'Can't Help Thinking About Me', did have some early merit. For example, it became Dave's first-ever US release, single or otherwise, issued by Warners during 1966. So at least he made it to America, even if he had yet to set foot there. This alone would have meant a lot to David. The track also featured on a 1966 Pye compilation LP (*Hitmakers Vol.4*), which was the first time David Bowie's name ever appeared on an LP. 'Baby Loves That Way', the B-side of our first single, had also featured on a European Columbia records LP compilation called *Beat 66*, which was the first album to include any of David's recordings (he was still Davy Jones then, of course).

David's meeting with Vicki Wickham in early January obviously paid off as he would shortly perform the single live on *Ready, Steady, Go!* But he didn't appear alongside the band he recorded it with. I suppose the clue to our fate was in plain view ever since we recorded the single; the song's title really summed it all up. The end of David Bowie and The Lower Third was closer than we thought.

*

It was arranged that I would meet Dave one afternoon at the trendy Le Macabre coffee bar in Meard Street, Soho – where the frothy coffee came with a horror theme that included skull ashtrays and coffin-shaped tables. I have no memory of why we were meeting. It may have been to hang out before a gig or just a social meet-up. When I got there, I found David sitting with a pretty girl – which wasn't, as we have seen, that unusual. He introduced me to the young lady and after a bit of chat she left.

David then told me, 'She was the first girl I ever had sex with.' Nothing amazing in itself, but it was the very respectful and tender way that he told me as he watched her walking up the stairs to leave. To him, as well as being a meaningful event it was also something very special. That impressed me, and stayed in my memory.

New Year 1966 marked our return to the Marquee and our first evening gig at our 'home' venue in a while. This was followed the next afternoon by the return of the Saturday afternoon Radio London Inecto shows. These appearances would not only be the last of these promotional afternoons gigs, they were among the last-ever shows for David Bowie and The Lower Third.

On the afternoon of 15 January, pop quartet Pinkerton's Assorted Colours arrived to fill Inecto's star-guest slot. A few weeks earlier they had been just another unknown band, but during the previous weekend their first single, 'Mirror, Mirror', had entered the UK Top 10. I can still see them today, standing quietly on the other side of the Marquee's band room waiting to be introduced on stage, all done up in stylish, double-breasted, needle-cord jackets and matching lined flares. Each of their neatly tailored suits was, as you would expect, designated a different primary colour.

Pinkerton's were one of Reg Calvert's bands. Later that year Calvert was shot dead in a dispute over a soured business merger deal. As well as band management, he had also owned pirate station Radio City (which broadcast from old World War II forts located on Shivering Sands in the Thames Estuary). It was partly due to the events surrounding Calvert's death that the BBC decided to launch their own dedicated pop music station in 1967.

Reg Calvert's most high-profile act had been Screaming Lord Sutch. The latter was another brilliant self-publicist whose act centered on mock-horror scenarios and characterization songs such as 'Jack The Ripper'. He had also been well known for growing his hair shockingly long in the early sixties, and Dave mentioned him once or twice in connection to his own long-haired men society in 1964.

In fact, there was a connection here. Dave did run into Lord Sutch often during these early years and apparently shared billing with him more than once, though I don't know exactly where and with which band. Sadly, it was never with us. During the 1980s, David even named a video character Screaming Lord Byron as a nod of appreciation to one of rock's more interesting and flamboyant early creations.

*

It wasn't only Pinkerton's Assorted Colours I can remember on the latter Inecto shows. While supporting Dave Dee, Dozy, Beaky, Mick and Tich, for example (who were promoting their Top 30 hit 'You Make It Move'), their drummer Mick Wilson asked me if he could use my kit for his stint. I didn't have a problem with this, knowing he was a very competent drummer. But the irony of this is, a few weeks later, Dave Dee and co. were on *Ready, Steady, Go!*, coincidentally at the same time as David. The Lower Third had now fallen by the wayside and David's new drummer, John Eager, was in my place. During Dave's dress rehearsal, to save time John asked Mick Wilson if he could use his kit for the run through and he obviously agreed (in *Any Day Now* you can clearly see Mick's name on the drum kit John is using behind David). I wonder if Mick thought John was me and was just returning the favour?

The Animals also stopped by for their Inecto moment (it was particularly good to see Hilton Valentine and Eric Burdon again). An amazing band, of course, and when they appeared on the bill with us that Saturday they were still very much on a roll and had been chalking up huge hits since 1964's 'House Of The Rising Sun' made No.1 in the UK, USA, Canada and Sweden. That afternoon they performed 'It's My Life', which would also climb nicely into the UK Top 10.

Animals bassist Chas Chandler left the band at its height the following year and moved into record production and artist management, to notable effect. He certainly had a good ear, because not only did he discover Jimi Hendrix while on his last US tour with The Animals, he brought him over to the UK, funded his earliest recordings (including 'Hey Joe') and helped make him the legend he became. Chas also recruited bassist Noel Redding and drummer Mitch Mitchell.

Among other great successes Chandler, who died in 1996, also picked up on Wolverhampton's most famous band, Slade, and helped to transform them from a skinhead group into Britain's biggest-selling pop quartet of the 1970s, both managing the band and producing all of their major hits.

Yet another interesting Inecto guest was Bethnal Green's very own songstress, Helen Shapiro, who also appeared one afternoon promoting 'Forget About The Bad Things'. Although I can't recall her performance, I can clearly remember her sitting by herself in the band room, keeping herself to herself. She had grown up in Clapton, just a short distance away from my own manor, and while still at school sang backing vocals in a fledgling school band called Susie and The Hula Hoops. I mention this because one of the Hula Hoops turned out to be an equally ambitious young chap (and at that point just the guitarist), called Marc Feld – later to be one Marc Bolan, and destined not only to be a cool English superstar like Dave, but also a friend and close contemporary of his.

I've mentioned Marc Bolan a couple of times in passing already, and his name is well connected to Dave's when studying this period in both of their careers. They had apparently met in Les Conn's office in late '64 or early '65 as Conn had been trying to get both of their careers off the ground. One day, with no live work to offer either of them on his books, Conn gave them a few bob each to paint his Denmark Street office.

It's hard to believe now, I know, but apparently manual labour didn't actually suit either Jones or Feld, and they soon decided they had better things to do. When Conn returned to check on progress he discovered that the two miscreants had long departed, leaving his office a shambles with barely a lick of paint on any his office walls. I'm sure there must be a useful moral that can be drawn from this sad tale, one that includes future superstar musicians and paint, but I've yet to come up with it.

Although I've read that Dave and Marc Feld were practically living in each other's pockets over this period, I can't remember ever seeing Marc around or hearing Dave mentioning him. We certainly didn't share any billing with Marc or any of his groups.

*

Ralph had been instructing the Third to be more animated on stage. I responded by waving my arms about and accentuating my movements. In retrospect, this probably more resembled that crazed Muppet drummer 'Animal' than anything else. But it seemed to do the trick for Ralph, as far as my presentation was concerned anyway. Whether this impressed the Pinkertons that day, or anyone else for that matter, I will never know.

It would have been wonderful if Ralph's request had inspired Den to shoot around the stage like Wilko Johnson once did so brilliantly with Dr Feelgood. Ralph would never have allowed anyone to upstage Dave like that, though, so I'm not sure what his instruction to Den and Graham actually was, and I can't say I detected any difference in their stage mannerisms at any time. So the joke was probably on me. Funnily enough, Den does actually remind me a little of Wilko for some reason.

Dave needed no such encouragement. In fact, one night, pissed on his favourite tipple, the dreaded barley wine, he came over to me mid number and bashed my ride cymbal with the microphone, Roger Daltrey fashion. He whacked it so hard that the bracket that held the cymbal on its stand snapped! My reactions were pretty quick back then and, as I caught the cymbal with the hand I had been playing it with, was able to reduce the loss of dignity slightly by just putting the cymbal down on the floor. I was mad at Dave, but it was Graham who, the next morning, contacted a now sober Dave to insist he pay for the repair. You know what, I'm not sure he ever did pay for it in the end.

*

During those final weeks together we apparently played as far north as Carlisle – one hell of a trek in our snail's-paced ambulance. I just can't remember our final shows that well – including that one in Carlisle and another a bit closer to home in Harrow.

Although I have no memory of Harrow as a gig, I do remember we performed at a public school, so that may have been the one. Travelling to that particular gig, I remember quite well what was played on the radio during the journey. I distinctly recall 'Michelle' by The Beatles, followed by 'My Ship Is Comin' In' by The Walker Brothers.

While the Walkers were playing, Graham started singing 'My shit is coming in', a reference to the regular, rather unpalatable news reports of sewage being washed up along the British coastline at the time. I can still see Graham laughing his head off as he was singing it, and all of us laughing out loud with him. It's funny the things that stay in your memory, but hearing either of those songs still remind me of that day, our uncontrollable laughter and some of the events that followed.

When we entered this hallowed private school to check out the hall, we couldn't help but get distracted by a long coat rack full of school gowns and mortarboards, all hanging neatly in a row. Of course, being the cheeky so-and-sos that we were, we naturally had to try them on for size; so Dave, Denis, Graham and I decided to dress up and arse around.

We soon got busted, of course. While we were pretend sword fighting and making general charlies of ourselves in the school's atmospheric, echoey corridors – all dressed up in our academic robes like would-be extras for a future *Harry Potter* movie – a slightly disgruntled house master suddenly appeared on the scene, clearly disturbed by the racket we were making. Not best amused at our childish antics, he soon brought things to order and cut us down to size.

Probably pushing our luck further than was wise, one of us then cheekily asked him if we could borrow the items to wear for that evening's performance. No prizes for guessing his rather direct, terse reply. 'And keep the noise down...' he said with a typical teacher's 'Do not test me, boy' look on his face. He then turned rather neatly on his heels and walked back quickly to class, no doubt well in the mood to throw a chalk board eraser at the first pupil who looked like he had misbehaved in his absence.

I have no memory of the actual performance, how it went or even if there were any females present (it was a boys' school). It was, however, yet another of our many slightly odd engagements.

I wonder now if the school had booked us in error? Maybe expecting Davie Jones and the Lower Third to be a pleasant young Welsh soprano, backed by an equally delightful prepubescent schoolboy choir. Not the slightly annoying, scruffy herberts whose illegally painted ambulance was now blighting the school car park. Herberts who, without any particular thought or consideration, would later inflict possible long-term hearing damage to sensitive, thoroughly unprepared young ears. Whatever the event, whatever the venue we, Davie Jones and The Lower Third, would guarantee to deliver the music with plenty of everything, particularly volume. I'm pretty sure our amps even went to eleven. I've no doubt most of those schoolboys didn't forget our appearance for a while. The ringing in their ears would have taken a few days to subside.

*

Sometime around this period with The Lower Third I attended a party at Jack and Pat White's place, where I met up with my old buddy Denis Payton. His band, the Dave Clark Five, had had a recent hit with, 'Catch Us If You Can', made No.5 in the UK); they had also just starred in a film of the same name, and were the next most popular British band to The Beatles in America). Anyway, Denis asked me how things were going with David Bowie, but there was no way I could compete, or offer any positive slant on it at all. I just shook my head with a resigned look on my face.

He asked if the group was likely to get anywhere. But given the amount of work we were getting by then and the ongoing problems with Ralph I simply replied, 'No, it won't do anything.'

In retrospect, it was an amazing thing to say, I know, given what David Bowie *did* go on to achieve over time. But I had probably included Dave in this whole 'doomed to failure' statement, as I wasn't able to see the wood from the trees at that point. But that's exactly how it was, I can't lie.

I do admit, there's a hell of a lot of irony in this whole story.

*

We knew Steve Marriott well by now and one thing I discovered was that you could count on his unpredictability.

On the afternoon of Saturday, 22 January 1966, both The Small Faces (Steve's band) and a fifteen-year-old 'Little' Stevie Wonder were appearing on the *Inecto Show* and therefore sharing the band room with us. Helene and I had only recently become engaged (David was indeed prescient a few months earlier when he called out to John Gee that Helene was my fiancée), and she was waiting in that back room enjoying the company with me. As we stood together listening intently to the amazing Stevie Wonder, who was doing an impressive warm-up on the upright piano in that small back room, we were all in our element. Helene and I particularly loved moments like these.

Some attractive black girl singers were next to Wonder, melodically doo-wopping along with him on these clearly impromptu numbers when Steve Marriott came over to me and cheekily said, 'I wish he'd fucking shut up, he's getting on my nerves.'

I was slightly taken aback at first, not realising straight off that he was joking, mainly because Helene was with me and it wasn't so usual to swear in front of females in those days. As Steve's face started to crack a smile I got the joke and it did make me laugh. Only Steve Marriott could have got away with that. I later thought how bloody funny Steve was in general – he seemed to enjoy himself the whole time and was always good fun to be around. A right cheeky chappy.

In this band room, high on a wall was a black-and-white closed-circuit TV monitor showing a live feed that was fixed on the whole stage. When we were waiting to go on, or had already been on as support, we used to watch the other bands via this a lot of the time. If there had been domestic VCRs available back then, a lot of valuable footage could have been recorded and kept. It wasn't HD quality, but it was good enough, and when you consider the incredible rare performances that stage witnessed over the years, it makes you wonder what might have been. It's a pity that there is absolutely no known footage of Dave performing with any of his sixties bands (excluding Ken Pitt's footage of Feathers in the promo film *Love You Till Tuesday*).

Regular gigs were a comfort, work-wise, as it felt like we belonged. These residencies produced little money but it was steady work. Hard to think of it now, but I remember the four of us once stopped off on the way to a gig and went into a pub where I bought a packet of five Weights (one of the cheapest cigarettes around then) and shared them out. I don't know who got the fifth cigarette. Probably Dave – he did love his cigs.

When we ran out of petrol, as you know we frequently did, with no money to fill up Graham would go into a garage and beg petrol – and incredibly he succeeded, sometimes.

Money remained an issue and ultimately became the undoing of the band. With hindsight, it's a bit easier to see what was probably going on, that things weren't necessarily all they seemed. It looks very much today as though we were all being given the squeeze, that we were probably fast becoming surplus to requirements. Dave was already thinking ahead to a different style of sound and presentation, and making that shift was probably the next thing on his agenda. Making the money even tighter was a clever way of giving the band the initiative to literally throw the towel in, without needing to give us any valid explanation.

Moving from band to band would later prove to be an important aspect of David Bowie's creative development. But none of that would have made any sense to us at the time, and in truth wasn't a particularly nice thing to do to anyone. It didn't seem to make any sense not to follow the project through properly, particularly as we seemed so close to breaking through.

At least our gigs at the Marquee paid out each week and our loyal fan base there made it particularly rewarding, performance wise at least. But the lack of funds was a constant concern and had already threatened to bring things to a head.

Ralph claimed he was dealing with expenses on our behalf and, while he had some reserve money, maintained he needed to hang onto it for something else connected to our advancement. Exactly what these plans were have gone from my memory now, so they can't have been that thrilling.

If anything, his coldness about money added to the overall stress of the situation. He just didn't seem to care about us. It was something we didn't feel comfortable talking to Dave about either. It wasn't his call anyway, and I know he often had to go cap in hand to Ralph for his own funding too.

Given Denis and Graham's situation, which was dire (they could barely eat some days and had resorted to living full time in the ambulance due to the lack of rent money), I cheekily said something like, 'Can't you just use some of this reserve money to pay the boys something?' I say 'cheekily', as I believe the reserve money Ralph had referred to was his own, presumably from his Radio Caroline earnings. However, in Peter and Leni Gillman's *Alias David Bowie* book, it was revealed that Ralph was still being funded by Ray Cook at this time, so now I'm not so sure.

On Saturday, 29 January 1966, we were to play two gigs: our usual afternoon *Inecto Show* at the Marquee and then on to the Bromel Club in Bromley for a special evening event. My dad came to see us at the Marquee that afternoon, which just so happened to be the time that things started to kick off.

It all began when Ralph made an announcement, some time that afternoon, telling us that there would be no pay coming to us for the Bromel gig that night. This, he explained, was because he needed money from the gig 'for expenses'. We – that is, Denis, Graham and I – were flabbergasted at this remark, particularly as he knew full well the conditions Denis and Graham were living under. I believe he also stated it was going to be a few days before any further work was available, which meant the boys had absolutely nothing to live on, in London, for over a week. Funnily enough, he offered no update about *Ready, Steady, Go!* either, which was quite clever considering he had apparently secured the booking.

On learning that we were not going to be paid for the next gig, my dad discreetly advised us to tell Ralph, 'No pay, no play.' The evening gig meant something special to Dave as it was on home turf and there would be a lot of familiar faces there. It may even have had something to do with his old school, but exactly what I'm not sure. We obviously felt that we would have some safe leverage there to at least get some of what was due to us. Whatever, I'm pretty sure it didn't matter to us by then – enough was enough and we were not in the mood to compromise, whatever the outcome.

Later that afternoon we duly turned up for the gig at the Bromley Court Hotel on leafy Bromley Hill, where the famed Bromel Club was based. This was the second time David and the Lower Third were booked to appear here. Before I joined them, Dave had managed to get the band a gig at the club, and the Third's first drummer, Les Mighall, did the honours. It was one of the first shows they ever did together too, so it was kind of apt that this was probably intended (by Ralph and Dave) to be the last.

It was a typical brisk winter's afternoon and was already dusk in Bromley when we arrived. All the way there we were getting more and more agitated about Ralph's increasingly belligerent attitude towards us. I felt a mixture of anxiety and also excitement as we reversed the ambulance towards the hotel's front doors, parked this way to reduce the distance the three of us had to carry the gear in (as we were the flunkies as well).

While I had an uneasy feeling in my stomach, I also felt that we, the band, were being used, unappreciated and short-changed. I couldn't hold back any more and wanted the high-and-mighty Ralph Horton, in particular, to know exactly how I felt.

As had been the case for some weeks by then, Dave travelled separately with Ralph in the Jag, no doubt adding even more fuel to the 'them and us' anger that was swelling.

We were in the car park unloading the equipment when Ralph and Dave pulled up, seemingly unprepared for what was about to follow. It felt like a scene from *High Noon*; there was no room for any small talk and the adrenalin was pumping. As he was getting out of the car one of us went directly over to Ralph and asked him straight out, 'Are we going to be paid tonight or not?'

His answer was still 'No,' so that was it. We stood together gave Ralph our 'No pay, No play' ultimatum, which he immediately took as the dissolution of our relationship. There was no hesitation in his reaction to our ultimatum either, so we later agreed that he had already made his mind up on the matter. As neither side was prepared to budge, that was it.

I suppose that there is also some irony in the fact that the last gig we did with Dave was a Radio London *Inecto Show*, not even a full-on evening gig where we could have gone out in style.

*

And so ended the band. David Bowie and The Lower Third were no more. Nothing unusual in bands breaking up, but this particular parting left a bad taste; there was something cynical and contrived about the way it happened. It was also a sad way to end things at such a promising time, and I also felt bad for Dave at the time, seeing his disappointment at not being able to play his old haunt that night. I still can't work out why Ralph didn't at least pay us for one last gig.

Recently, I have had reason to pass through Bromley a number of times for family matters. It had always stuck in my mind how David Bowie and The Lower Third had split up at the Bromley Court Hotel that dismal afternoon. So I drove into the hotel car park with my partner Christine, just to see if it was anything like I remembered. I had heard that the building and grounds had changed very little since that day, so I thought it was well worth checking out. I wondered if it would bring it all back.

After taking a few minutes to reacquaint myself with the layout, I was clearly able to picture where we were all positioned that night. I have to say, it was a very strange feeling.

I looked back from the hotel entrance, where we were unloading the band's gear, to roughly where David was standing, a bit childlike, balancing himself on the hotel's low car park wall, keeping well clear of the fall-out. As this imagery returned, I couldn't help but recall some of the feelings I had that afternoon when I desperately wanted Dave to suddenly step in and say something. I still didn't quite believe that he was OK about the band breaking up the way it did, when even a small token gesture of payment was all that was needed. It seemed so silly, so unnecessary.

While feeling sorry about the split, it also brought back how angry the three of us were at the way we were being used by then, with little regard for our feelings or overall situation. So it was a slightly bittersweet nostalgic meander, but I'm really pleased I went back.

As I stood there, I wished we had stayed with Dave for another six months, if nothing more. It would have been nice to have made another record or two with him. It was such a great experience in the studio, and you never knew what he was going to come up with. I felt he was always on the edge of something special, at any time, and I'm pleased to say I wasn't wrong. It's just that it took another six or seven years for him to properly work it out and finally make himself known to the world.

We then went inside the Bromley Court to see where we would have played. It was a hot day, so we went into the hotel lounge for a cooling drink. There, I immediately spotted a photo of David and The Lower Third on a wall. It was actually an album-sized EP cover set in a glass frame.

Next to the picture was some text about David having played there and some of his general local history, the hotel quite rightly proud of the association he had with the building. A side meeting room, which looks like it was once used as Bromel Club dressing room, has also been renamed the 'Bowie Room'.

So it was quite a poignant and rewarding visit for me in the end, particularly as I looked across the lounge that was once the area where these gigs were staged.

Well, I thought, looking at the photo on the wall, we did all make it in here after all.

*

Following our break-up in Bromley, now it was back to just The Lower Third again, without David Bowie. This was full circle for Denis and Graham.

Unbowed, the three of us resolved that night to continue, to give it a go, even without our charismatic front man. But in truth the spirit of the band was broken that afternoon and nothing would come of these well-intentioned plans. In any event, deprived of any upcoming gigs we would need financing while we got a new repertoire together, and there were no Brian Epsteins waiting in the wings to magically assist us. With this, we sadly drifted apart.

Saying that, Denis and Graham did actually try their best to keep The Lower Third going. As I had quickly found myself a new band to work with, they drafted in a new drummer called Ned Taylor. I never met Ned or heard of any of gigs they may have performed as a trio, though I have seen a photo of this last line-up. Apparently, Denis had taken over the lead vocal duties and sounded, in his own words, 'like a poor man's Ray Davies'. Den was taking on a lot here. Dave Bowie's shoes were by no means easy to fill. Within two or three months it really was game over and by the spring of 1966 The Lower Third were finally laid to rest.

Oh, I'm on my own
I've got a long way to go
I hope I make it on my own
I can't help thinking about me...

CHAPTER ELEVEN

BOWIE AND BEYOND

Shortly after The Lower Third broke up with David, he appeared on *Ready, Steady, Go!* – together with his new band, The Buzz. They were, of course, performing our single, 'Can't Help Thinking About Me'. It was pretty surreal to see this after all we had been through and, to be honest, felt just a little unfair. John Eager had taken my seat and I had to concede, he clearly looked like he knew what he was doing.

I'm sure Denis and Graham also found it hard to watch and were feeling just as I was, particularly as this TV appearance was dangled before us even before Paris, and mentioned again during the London press launch. It was pretty rough on us in the end.

David's friend, clothes designer and successful retailer John Stephen, had loaned him a finely cut, pure white suit, which seemed to glow under the bright studio lights. Stephen even got a look in himself during the broadcast when he was interviewed earlier in the show by host Cathy McGowan about his work and particularly about the special suit he had made for him. I read later on that the outfit was actually too bright for the cameras and that it caused the studio technical people some real difficulties, which was obviously why David looked like he had just consumed a whole box of Ready Brek (a British breakfast cereal whose early TV adverts featured radiantly glowing children, apparently full of this strangely radioactive porridge).

Well, what can I say? David performing the single we had worked hard with him to make – backed by strangers. No doubt we would have worked with David on this show had we not made the stand that we did at the Bromel Club but then, that would have also pushed us all into further financial distress, of that I've no doubt. The truth is though, *Ready, Steady, Go!* would have perfectly topped off our moment with David.

Horton must have been particularly pleased about our exclusion from this show, and that the mutineer 'hired help' had finally got their comeuppance. *Schadenfreude* is, I believe, the correct borrowed term to suitably describe that smug, self-satisfied feeling at another's misfortune which he no doubt enjoyed that night.

I was certainly well schadened, I know that!

This is not to say that the guys in the new line-up had done anything wrong. Far from it: at the eleventh hour, Dave had quickly assembled a competent, professional band. At least they performed the number faithfully. Their performance of 'Can't Help Thinking About Me' was mimed, but was reliant on a backing track they themselves had recorded earlier in the day, though Dave definitely sang it live when it was filmed. In some ways keeping it faithful to our original was at least a small courtesy to The Lower Third. All of the other bands appearing on the show, including Dave Dee, Dozy, Beaky, Mick and Tich (who performed their first Top 10 hit, 'Hold Tight') and The Yardbirds, who showcased another of Dave's future *Pin Ups* faves, 'Shapes Of Things', performed in the same way.

Directly after David finished and the audience were clapping, Cathy McGowan introduced The Small Faces, who then performed 'Sha-La-La-La-Lee' with vigour. Again, it was ironic to see Stevie perform straight after Dave, having got to know him quite well in the preceding months. Just another reason why I felt I should have been there.

Both Dave and Stevie performed with great confidence and I'm sure would have sold a few more records on the back of their performances that night. The Small Faces certainly did, I know.

*

David and Ralph were now well into planning the next phase of his career, which was most definitely solo approach focused. This, I'm reliably informed, was clearly expressed to David's new backing band, which Dave quickly named The Buzz. And, as history records, The Buzz lasted for about the same amount of time that The Lower Third did. It was the way that David worked most of his career. Changing groups enabled him to experiment, not only with different types of musicians, but also with different performance ideas and musical styles.

As he had done with us, he probably asked The Buzz guys if they would consider wearing make-up too.

One result of January's Gaiety bar press junket was Dave's biggest feature to-date in *Melody Maker* – the paper we all considered to be the foremost music publication of the day. Titled 'A Message To London From Dave', the interview was published on 26 February, so a bit late for Denis, Graham and I to get excited about at the time, but now it's well worth including in part, for posterity:

Without doubt David Bowie has talent. And also without doubt it will be exploited. For, Mr. Bowie, a 19-year-old Bromley boy, not only writes and arranges his own numbers, but he is also helping Tony Hatch to write a musical score, and the numbers for a TV show. As if that wasn't enough, David also designs shirts and suits for John Stephen, of the famed Carnaby Street clan.

And his ambition? 'I want to act,' says Bowie modestly, 'I'd like to do character parts. I think it takes a lot to become somebody else. It takes some doing.

'Also I want to go to Tibet. It's a fascinating place, y'know. I'd like to take a holiday and have a look inside the monasteries. The Tibetan monks, Lamas, bury themselves inside mountains for weeks and only eat every three days. They're ridiculous – and it's said they live for centuries.'

It should be stated that David is a well-read student of astrology and a believer in reincarnation...

'As far as I'm concerned the whole idea of Western life – that's the life we live now – is wrong. These are hard convictions to put into songs, though. At the moment I write nearly all my songs 'round London. No. I should say the people who live in London – and the lack of real life they have. The majority just don't know what life is.'

Every number in Dave's stage act is an original that he

has written. As he says, the themes are usually London kids and their lives. However, it leads to trouble.

'Several of the younger teenagers' programmes wouldn't play 'Can't Helping Thinking About Me', because it is about leaving home. The number relates several incidents in every teenager's life – and leaving home is something which always comes up.'

I needed to keep my work options open so took to dropping into the Marquee from time to time to see who was about and do a bit of networking. One afternoon, David was playing an *Inecto Show* with The Buzz, so I decided to check it out. Before the show I could see Ralph, who I was sure saw me but made no acknowledgment. I thought 'sod it' and went up on the stage to where Dave was sorting something out and said, 'Hello'.

I finally got my farewell handshake (and a friendly greeting) so I sort of felt like we'd made up, and said goodbye in exactly the right way. Basically, we were always friends and always would be – even though we wouldn't see each other again in person.

Denis also met up with Dave some months after the band broke up. They bumped into each other in Denmark Street in late '66. It was nice as Dave was very happy to see him and invited Denis into Central Sound Studio, which was housed in the basement at No.9, to play him his latest 45 release, 'Rubber Band'. I'm really pleased that Denis was able to meet up with him like this again (as I've said, they had also been genuinely close friends) and it proved to all of us that there really had been no hard feelings in the end.

As well as travelling and working with Mandy Rice-Davies, Den also formed another rock band called The

Rave. This short-lived outfit included ex-Merseybeats drummer John Banks, but never properly found its feet. He also briefly played in a band called The Dream, who managed to blag a twelve-day tour supporting The Who. In Coventry, Den watched from the wings in some distress as Pete Townshend smashed a brand-new Gibson guitar across the amps. 'It was a Gibson that had two necks, one with six strings, the other twelve. I would have loved a guitar like that, so it wasn't exactly fun watching him destroy it,' Denis recently told me.

The following morning, wise old Den was up with the larks and left the nearby hotel to return to the venue to see if he could find any parts of the guitar. To his surprise, Pete Townshend was already there, doing exactly the same thing, trying to beat the cleaners to claim any guitar fragments he could find. So Den joined in his search and soon discovered a splinter. 'I offered it to Pete and to my amazement he took it and put it in his pocket,' Den continued. 'He then explained that he was not supposed to be playing the Gibson at all as he had a deal with Rickenbacker. I've no idea why he smashed up such a lovely guitar if he had an alternative.'

So that was Den's final Who encounter, which was one more than mine. David, of course, remained particularly friendly with Pete and they recorded together in 1980.

Before giving up on the music business, Den also did some touring with another guitar legend, Duane Eddy. But by the late sixties Den had returned to Margate and set himself up as a professional photographer in the town, where he still resides.

Graham also kept at it for a while and picked up some rewarding work playing bass in Crispian St Peters's backing band (Peters was at his height, having enjoyed big hits with 'The Pied Piper' and 'You Were On My Mind'). This was an interesting turn of events, as Crispian's manager was Kenneth Pitt, who had coincidentally begun to co-manage David with Ralph shortly after Dave had split with The Lower Third. Not only that, but Graham fell in love with Ken's secretary, Diana 'Dinkie' Thompson, and later married her. For a while Graham continued working as a semi-pro musician while also establishing a pitch on Soho's Berwick Street Market, where he set up his own electrical supplies stall. This line of business earned him far more money than he ever made in music and soon led to a shop in Margate and, ultimately, a distribution warehouse in Broadstairs.

Graham eventually sold his business and left the UK for good, relocating to an island off Thailand, where he remarried and still lives very happily today.

*

After my meet-up with David at his Marquee/Buzz performance I never did see him again – live in concert or otherwise. I would have loved to have met up with him again for old time's sake, but didn't try. Graham Rivens did, however.

Graham went to see David perform at the Milton Keynes Bowl in 1983 and tried to get a message back to David to see if they could meet up. Sadly, he was met with complete indifference. The security guys apparently just stared at him when he told them who he was. They were totally uninterested and he never did get to say hello to Dave in the end. It was probably hearing that story that put me off ever trying myself. In fairness to David, though, big gigs like that are not set up for meetings with old buddies, unless you can get yourself on the guest list beforehand.

I shared my disappointment at parting with David with my local newspaper, the *Walthamstow Independent*, who had kindly run other news stories about me, the group and about our various antics. The headline said it all: 'Pop Group's TV Hopes Dashed', referring to our *Ready, Steady, Go!* let-down:

> The hopes of 23-year-old Walthamstow drummer Phil Lancaster of appearing on the coveted TV pop show, 'Ready Steady Go' was dashed when his group, The Lower Third, and their lead singer, Davie Bowie, broke up.
>
> Phil said the trouble started when their manager concentrated all his efforts on making Mr Bowie 'the leading light'.
>
> Phil explained: 'He only wanted Dave to make it, with us as a backing group. There was a lot of money trouble. We stood it as long as we could until we reached a peak and had a big bust up.
>
> Last Friday Davie Bowie appeared on TV alone.
>
> 'Everything for the best,' said Phil resignedly.
>
> Phil has just finished some work in Scotland with a popular group he has joined called the 'In Crowd'. Now, with this group, they are playing at a new underground London club in Oxford Street.
>
> 'I don't know what the future holds for me, but the In Crowd are quite optimistic. In this business you have to be prepared for anything,' he declared.

My next band, which also included another future superstar, made David Bowie and The Lower Third seem like choirboys by comparison. Already an established band with TV experience and a few Parlophone singles behind them, The In Crowd, whom I luckily joined just days after leaving David and the Third, were working regularly and were very good musicians too. I suppose it could be viewed as my good fortune that, as history would later prove, I had once again fallen into a band that included more stars of tomorrow. In truth it was only they that made fortunes in the long run – which is often how these things pan out – but it still proved an invaluable experience for me too.

Keith West, our singer, (whose real name was Keith Hopkins) was to have great success with his memorable record 'Excerpt From "A Teenage Opera"' (aka 'Grocer Jack') the following year. I remember Keith telling me once that his sister was dating Dudley Moore at the time. As you know, I was a big admirer of Dudleys, so that quite impressed me. Our lead guitarist was none other than the amazing Steve Howe – who also happened to be a mate of my pal, John Urquhart. Steve was another who would become a major star, he being one of the key members of seventies supergroup Yes. The other members of The In Crowd were John 'Junior' Wood on rhythm, and Simon 'Boots' West (no relation to Keith) on bass.

Early recognition of Steve Howe's brilliant guitar abilities came via a member of Bob Dylan's band, when we were playing a residency at Blaises, at 121 Queens Gate in South Kensington. Blaises was a club known at the time for drawing in the music elite, and on the night John Lee Hooker was headlining, Dylan came by to see him, and by default, us too.

After we played our set, one of Dylan's inner circle (probably his close friend Bob Neuwirth) came up to the stage and said to Steve, 'You sure play a bitch of a guitar.' Dylan was performing at the Royal Albert Hall, on the tour where he was using an electric backing band for the first time – and in doing so, upsetting many of his purist acoustic/folk followers. It felt pretty good performing in front of one of my heroes and it even briefly brought to mind David's excellent impression of Dylan that afternoon in the Gioconda. It also crossed my mind that he'd probably be quite jealous if he'd known I'd performed in front of the great Dylan.

My initial 'getting to know' The In Crowd repertoire took place at Steve's mum and dad's house in Holloway, north London, where Steve played me the mostly Otis Redding play list we would feature. The In Crowd had also recently released three singles for Parlophone, which of course were also included in the set and proved very popular with our audiences.

*

Thinking back on my time with The In Crowd brings back a whole mixture of feelings and emotions – some not that great, if truth be told. In many ways it was the polar opposite of working with David, Denis and Graham. I got on with them, one to one, but often when together, some of their activities were beyond the pale for me. For example, one of the guys would ring up random strangers using names he'd select from the phone book, and then tell them believable fake bad news (reporting a death in the family or a serious accident), just for the fun of it. He would then leave that often-distraught person believing the news to be true. That wasn't for me.

We did have quite a few genuine laughs, though. We were playing a gig, I don't remember where, and the stage had a full-length painted scenery panel set up behind us on the stage, which towered above us. I guess it was for a coming play or other similar entertainment there. Anyway, we were into a number when I noticed this huge backdrop slowly starting to move and tip over, in our direction. It seemed to happen in slow motion, just like it had been planned for comic effect.

I looked across at Steve, who had also clocked it, and we both started laughing as this enormous panel gradually reached our heads. We never stopped playing until the song was over, then various road crew and venue staff ran on to rescue us. Thankfully it didn't crush anyone; it rested on Steve's nut while he carried on doing his thing, smiling the whole time.

I used to often make the others laugh during the endless hours driving to and from gigs – particularly with my take off Armand and Michaela Denis (who were well known contemporary TV presenters in the David Attenborough/ wildlife documentary mode).

I sometimes hung out with Keith West down at Lew Davis's guitar shop in Charing Cross Road too (I just couldn't keep away!). In fact, I'm pleased to say I have a photo of us both hanging around there. Other than that, I didn't socialise with the band that much, but they would always tell me what adventures they had been up to between gigs, like getting friendly with some women in the van, only to find out they were men in drag – then saying, 'Oh sod it,' and carrying on.

One of the farthest gigs I did with The In Crowd was in Glasgow. John 'Junior' Wood and I couldn't be bothered travelling up in the van, so opted to fly there instead. The return flight tickets were £6 each – which was basically our fee for the gig, but we just couldn't face the drive. The trouble was, we hadn't worked out what we were going to do when we arrived and had made no arrangements whatsoever. This actually led to one of the most bizarre coincidences ever.

After landing at Prestwick Airport, we took an airport bus into Glasgow, eventually getting out in an area that looked suspiciously like the Gorbals. It was about 1am by now and it was looking pretty bleak, to say the least. In search of a place to stay we walked in what looked like the most promising direction but had no luck finding a cheap hotel of any kind. It was deserted and we were feeling pretty vulnerable and very much out of our depth in a strange, quite scary Scottish city. One that was particularly notorious down south (justified or not) for its gang violence. Being lowland Sassenachs did little to ease our nerves either.

After an hour or so of aimless traipsing we passed the entrance to a park and noticed a group of guys, about half a dozen or so, gathered near the entrance. By now we were getting a bit desperate, so approached them in the hope that they were not only of a friendly persuasion, but also able to point us in the direction of a cheap hotel or guesthouse. As we nervously began to ask for directions, it suddenly dawned on me that I recognised one of them in the park's low light. He was, I was sure, a musician. Then I recognised another. Incredibly, and I'm not sure what the odds would have been that this could happen, these guys actually turned out to be in one of Scotland's top groups, The Beatstalkers. Quite why the 'Scottish Beatles' (as they were dubbed locally) were gathered in a park at two in the morning I have no idea, but I'm sure glad they were.

The Beatstalkers had been on the same bill as myself

while performing with David and The Lower Third at Bournemouth Pavilion the previous year. Not only was it a huge relief to see some friendly faces, they immediately came to our assistance and drove us to their manager's apartment a few miles across town. I still can't believe the coincidence to this day.

Our next piece of good fortune was that their manager, who they had to wake and by rights should not have been at all happy about it, not only knew of The In Crowd but loved the band and was pleased to meet us. He kindly invited us both to stay, so Junior and I ended up crashing there for two nights, free of charge, with transportation laid on to and from the venue.

Out of all the people we could have bumped into on our first trip to Scotland, we met The Beatstalkers – and they couldn't have been more hospitable. I'm sure it wasn't just that we were fellow musicians – they were just really great guys. Somebody was looking out for us that day for sure.

Funnily enough, shortly after we ran into them in Glasgow, The Beatstalkers began spending more of their time in London, where they had started to make a name for themselves. It was there that they had, and here's another cool coincidence, befriended David Bowie and started recording some of his songs. For a while, David's new manager Kenneth Pitt also managed The Beatstalkers.

Beatstalker bassist Alan Mair became very good friends with David. Alan also designed and made cool clothes, and David sometimes worked on his Kensington Market stall to earn a few extra pounds when cash was particularly tight. Alan later became a member of punk outfit The Only Ones, with whom he recorded the cult classic 'Another Girl, Another Planet'.

The only other thing about that eventful In Crowd trek to Glasgow was on show night itself. While we were preparing to go on stage, word travelled to our dressing room that 'The Fleet is in'. The Fleet, we were informed, were one of Glasgow's most notorious razor gangs. Not the most welcome piece of news we could have received.

I'd like to think it was the quality of our performance that night, or that they seriously dug our music, but whatever it was, The Fleet behaved themselves and the show went off without a hitch. Saying that, I've just remembered that Keith West's beautiful green suede jacket, his favourite for stage, went missing that night. So maybe The Fleet weren't so saintly after all?

*

I generally enjoyed my time with The In Crowd, but I didn't stay long – less than a year, I think. Our lifestyles were just too radically different, and anyway, that allowed Twink (real name John Alder) of the Pink Fairies, to take over my job. He was always hanging around the band, waiting for the chance to take my seat and was probably a better fit.

Saying that, not long after Twink joined them, The In Crowd sort of dissolved and, with some personnel changes, were rebadged and become Tomorrow. Label owner, DJ and general mover and shaker John Peel would champion the group in a big way.

Tomorrow found their own scene too, and became particularly known in 1967 for their psychedelic concerts, notably at the UFO Club in Tottenham Court Road. Around the same time, Keith West (who had also split away) reached No.2 and was dominating the radio waves with 'Excerpt From "A Teenage Opera"', or 'Grocer Jack', as it is more commonly known, and David Bowie released his first album on Deram – backed on many of the tracks by The Buzz. It was great to see this sudden burst of activity and success, old friends and colleagues doing well at last. But I have to admit to feeling a certain amount of frustration at the same time. Like them I'd been working my backside off but each time it looked interesting something happened and I just seemed to miss out on the prize.

No, it's too late for your sympathy now, though I'll give you the full details of my, 'Show your support to Phil Lancaster' crowdfunding page at the end of this book.

*

And the coincidences continued.

A couple of years after the demise of the Third, while on a ferry to Stockholm to meet my future mother-in-law with my intended (as I said, David's effort to marry me off to Helene came true), we bumped into an old friend. While we were up on deck taking in the sea air I turned around and there was, of all people, 'T-cup'.

Ever the troubadour, Denis was off, guitar in hand, to try his luck playing in Sweden. It was great to see him again and we spent much of the journey catching up, including hearing his stories of working in Israel with Mandy Rice-Davies at her club, Mandy's. Denis had also recently run into David again too. David had told him he was auditioning for a part in the stage musical *Hair* and seemed in great form. It was a real blast from the past.

*

I couldn't forget the time I had with David and the boys, and hearing about Dave's debut album reminded me of that. The Lower Third set up was exciting and I really missed that journey. With David we were hungry for success and felt that, with his writing talent and our sometimes surreal choice of material, we were really creating something unique. Our Wardour Street audiences certainly seemed to agree.

But that band had gone and, while others I had worked with were starting to get some recognition, I had to settle back into playing as a workaday musician with residencies at places like the very posh Quaglino's Restaurant in St James's with people like David Frost and Dave Allen in cabaret, and at The Lyceum in the Strand and The Empire, Leicester Square, opposite Joe Loss. The work included the early *Come Dancing* BBC TV show, something Miss World founder Eric Morley had created in 1950. Joe Loss and his orchestra did the TV bits and we did the filler sections to keep the dancers and audience entertained (similar to the way David and The Lower Third played at those Marquee Inecto shows). During one of these *Come Dancing* events, John Urquhart and I got a direct bollocking from Mr Morley as we apparently blocked one of his cameras during a televised section.

It wasn't exactly what I had planned and it often meant a trek to Archer Street, but for all that I was still able to do the thing I loved the most: play music.

I did many nights with both David Frost and Dave Allen at Quaglino's. I didn't really get to know them well, but I practically got to know their sets by heart, as I would watch them each night from the side of the stage. Both had their own unique way of delivering a joke and obviously, as performers with very contrasting styles, structured their sets differently. Dave Allen was the consummate joke teller and skilfully lured his audience into the punch line, whereas David Frost worked more with his audience, often feeding off them and adapting his set accordingly. But watching both men at work at close proximity, one thing was clear: apart from working with quality material, in the end it was as much down to their perfectly timed punch line delivery that made them great at what they did. It really isn't as easy as those guys made it look.

It was at Quaglino's that I got to know folk singer Roger Whittaker quite well too, another of their regular name cabaret artists. He was a really nice guy and I can't believe now that I actually gave him some career advice. He was clearly a very talented performer. I was equally impressed with his personable, laid-back stage manner and could definitely see him doing well on television. Chatting with him in the restaurant one evening I said, 'You ought to be on TV, you should have a show like Rolf Harris has. You'd be great at it. Your whistling songs would work really well too, they are very good.'

But it seems Roger had already tried to break into British TV and received a few knock-backs. 'Television producers don't want me,' he replied, matter-of-fact like. Of course, those who remember the late sixties will know that he did eventually become a regular face on British TV, and he did get his very own show, not too many years after my prediction. I believe he eventually did manage to leave old Durham town too...

I obviously took on a lot of varied opportunities as they came along around this time. One job I did which will always remain clear in my memory was to dep at Raymond's Review Bar in deepest Soho; the first and only 'adult' club I ever worked in (honest). I turned up with my trusty snare drum, ready to use the regular drummer's kit, which was already set up on the stage – it being customary to take your own snare drum when depping.

Clubs didn't always place musicians at the top of their consideration list, so when I discovered the venue's drum kit was set up away from where the other musicians were sited I realised that this was a gig with a difference. My fellow musicians were actually below me and beside the stage while the drums were sat on the stage itself. In other words – I was in among the action.

So the night kicked off and we started our set. One number we were given early on to do was a favourite of mine, it was 'Marina', from the puppet series *Stingray*. As we hit the first chords of this number I suddenly noticed a bright light go on at the other end of the room and an enormous aquarium light up. It looked very impressive, but that wasn't all as, lo and behold, an attractive mermaid then plunged into it. Of course, this being the Raymond Revue Bar is probably clue enough to tell you that the attractive young lady concerned, who swam so skillfully in this aquarium complete with exotic fish tail, was topless. She swam like a fish too, and kept her eyes open the whole time while smiling and looking out at the audience.

Later it was time for the main event – the Revue Bar's famous strippers. I, of course, was sat on the stage with them. No complaints there, though it did come as a bit of a surprise.

The second girl on then casually strolled out on stage next to me and did a fun routine with a powder puff. With a follow-spotlight on her the whole time she delicately dabbed herself and teased the audience, and very soon most of her clothing was scattered around the stage. Then she must have noticed me sitting next to her. 'Mind your cymbal,' she said giggling, giving me a naughty look and wink as she sashayed about, pretending to nearly hit my cymbal with her naked bottom.

Then she must have clocked the little beard I had and, with the spotlight now firmly on me, proceeded to involve me in her act by powder puffing my chin, and her rather impressive exposed bosom, in time to the beat. It was actually very funny, certainly for the audience, but for me I felt a strange mix of unexpected embarrassment and glee.

*

My full circle came with the final two venues I regularly played at (the Lyceum and Empire, Leicester Square) where I was at last playing in a 'proper' band once again, this time with my old childhood pal John Urquhart. I also eventually got together with Denis Payton again, after The Dave Clark Five had disbanded. We were into writing and recording for a while, so it was sort of back to my roots with my old school pals again. It was great to be working with them once more, particularly now we had all had some decent individual experience of the music business.

Denis had had the most thrilling ride, of course. The Dave Clark Five had been massive in America (chalking up seventeen Top 40 hits in the US alone and no less than eighteen appearances on the *Ed Sullivan Show*). But to John and I he remained the same old Denis, if maybe a little more financially comfortable than he had been back in the early days.

At the Empire, in Leicester Square, we played sedate afternoon tea dances – the type where it was more appropriate to play most numbers with brushes rather than drum sticks, you know the type. An odd mixture of people attended these dances, I would discover. In among your everyday general public would be professional ballroom dancers and (so I was told by my colleagues) ladies of the night.

The professional dancers were actually a real pain in the backside, as they would regularly complain about the tempos we kept. Now I had been taught to play the likes of the foxtrot, quickstep, tango and so on – in fact, those tempos were literally 'drummed' into me, so to speak. We also closely followed the count-in by our bandleader, Dave Holgate, who also had plenty of experience. To counteract these irritating barbs, Dave brought in a metronome and placed it in clear view of the auditorium, setting it to suit the pace of whatever style of music we were asked to do next. From then on, whenever a disgruntled pro-dancer tried to blame us for his own bad timing, Dave would just nonchalantly refer him to the metronome – which couldn't lie and soon shut them up. As for the ladies of the night, who were working the Empire by afternoon, they were no bother at all.

It felt odd, though, working on afternoon shows like this, particularly on warm, sunny days. Inside the Empire it was very dark and often smoky, and going outside following a set to be met by bright daylight felt very strange for a normally nocturnal muso like myself (a bit like going to see a film on a summer afternoon and it still being light when you leave).

Dave Holgate deserves more of a mention here too as he was a very interesting man. As well as being an excellent bandleader and talented double bass player, Dave was also a consummate sculptor. He became very well known in his adopted Norwich for his great craftsmanship (among many other qualities) and two of his beautiful statues, of Mother Julian and Saint Benedict, remain as a testament to his skill and can be seen on either side of the door on the west front of Norwich Cathedral. Dave died in 2014 and characteristically told a friend shortly before he passed away, 'If I could die an impressive death, I wouldn't mind so much the dying. I like to impress.' He certainly did that.

*

As the years progressed, I wasn't surprised to hear my old pal David Bowie's name mentioned on the radio or TV from time to time. When I saw pictures of David dressed and made up as a white-faced mime one day I thought, what's he up to now? It was such a jump from rock music in every way. I must admit I thought he'd suddenly become a bit affected. I couldn't quite see the point of it and it even crossed my mind that he'd finally kicked into touch the idea of being a musician once and for all and was looking for a different stage career.

He, of course, knew exactly what he was doing, that it was just another performance discipline to learn and something he could add to his stage repertoire. I've since read of the work he did with Lindsay Kemp and how Lindsay even helped him to project his voice, as they didn't use any vocal amplification when he sang his songs during their theatrical shows.

It was working in different areas of the arts like this, sometimes even with non-musicians like Kemp, that really helped set David apart from the rest. There aren't many rock singers who would have considered that kind of training back in the day, but it was because he was smart and prepared to experiment like this that helped make him the huge talent he became. As I'm sure I've said elsewhere in this book already, he simply approached things in a different way. The commonplace bored him.

I didn't know Dave was still singing during his years with Kemp, I thought it was just mime set to classical music and sound effects. But evidently Lindsay loved David's album so much he wanted him to perform some of the songs from it, set to his own unique choreography.

Funnily enough, I've also read that Lindsay Kemp never thought of himself as a mime artist at all, more as a dancer and master of movement. I can't say I know much about Lindsay's work myself, but close friends of mine tell me how brilliant he is. I wish I'd seen one or two of the shows he did with David now; it would have been an education at least.

Of course, with the benefit of hindsight, David's interest in mime and movement made perfect sense. He was already spreading his performing wings when he encouraged The Lower Third to dance a song, rather than play it. David's later work on stage and video show how his apprenticeship with Lindsay Kemp added many more skills to his repertoire, and he finally got to experiment with make-up on stage too.

And I've not even touched on the fact that he was performing as a different character on stage for the first time. No doubt the famous characters such as Ziggy Stardust and the Thin White Duke owed much to his time with Kemp too – so what a great move by David, then.

So much for being affected.

It wasn't too long either before I heard David being played on the radio again, though it's hard to get the chronology exact all these years on.

Yes I did hear 'The Laughing Gnome'. *Ha ha ha, hee hee hee.*

I thought, here we go he's trying to find something new here, a new direction. And though I found 'Laughing Gnome' funny, I did wonder what was going on with whoever was producing him and what the general plan of action was. Of course, it was just another one-off experiment in the end and although I know some people take the mick out of him because of it, it's not that bad a record.

But then came a monster: 'Space Oddity'.

The first time I heard the song, it was quite a moment. I can still remember when it lifted off from the radio at my home. Now this really was different, this was special. I was knocked out with it and genuinely pleased for David. At last, I thought, he is getting somewhere, and I'm sure it wasn't even in the charts at that point. I just knew it would be a big hit, no doubt, it sounded so different from anything else going on at the time. Whenever it came on after that I thought, 'I knew he could do something special, I used to play drums with that guy.' I was really proud of the association.

With 'Space Oddity', he finally realised his talent. Although it was only about four years since I had worked with him, it already seemed like much longer. So much was going on all the time and the business was changing so quickly, it felt like I'd worked with Dave in a different era by then. He was already entering a glamorous new time, and only two or three years after that he would be heading out front, pretty much leading the field.

On reflection I guess it all started with 'Oddity', though I know the next hit record took a couple more years to arrive.

By then, my second child Jenny had been born and I had a growing family to support. As much as my heart was in music I had to be realistic and ensure I brought in a regular pay cheque, even though the musician in me wanted to be both out on the road and back in the studio, performing and making music.

While David was travelling from continent to continent, and planet to planet with his Spiders from Mars, I was raising a family and sadly just couldn't afford to take any chances on the road any more (though I would have probably gone for it had he come knocking on my door. I would even have brought my own lipstick!).

But the husband and father in me said it was time to wise up and do the right thing. So it was back to civvy street for me and I went into office work for the first time. A pianist I gigged with managed to get me into the place where he worked during the day. I still worked with scratch bands for the odd one-night booking (as ever, with no rehearsal and often not even knowing the other musicians), though sometimes there was a face I recognised. This often meant late nights, but we really needed the money, plus it kept my hand in at the same time and could sometimes be very enjoyable.

I carried on playing semi-professionally until, lo and behold, I was offered a professional residency at a gig in a Covent Garden nightclub. I took the job but annoyingly, and unexpectedly, it only lasted six weeks following a sudden disagreement between the band's manager and the club.

Out of work again, I quickly found myself another day job, and then resumed work on the semi-pro scratch band circuit. This included also depping once more at Quaglino's restaurant for a while.

It was also around this time that I experienced some serious déjà vu when I was invited to a south London pub to work with an old friend. Amazingly, I did a rock gig with Ted Hatton, my old mucker from the Eddie Ricardo Trio at the Van Gogh. With this booking I'd pretty much come full circle and returned to the band I had cut my professional drumming teeth on, so to speak.

My daytime, nine-to-five office job was based in Sloane Street. I must have had a nice smile or something because I was talent spotted to become a company salesman and took that on – which is more or less what I did for the remainder of my working life. But it was really music, music, music, whenever possible. It was, and still is, such a big part of my life and I lived for it.

*

From 1965 on it seemed that David Jones wasn't too far from anything I was doing, and it wasn't long before people started to search me out to ask me about my time working with David Bowie and The Lower Third.

In the early to mid-1980s I began to get calls from people wanting to interview me about David Bowie and this led to some ongoing contact with the producers of *Starzone*, a glossy, quality Bowie fan magazine. I got to know Kevin Cann, David Currie and Gina Coyle from the magazine; dedicated Bowie fans, and clever people in their own right.

Kevin Cann wanted to regroup the band for a reunion – he was working on a detailed article about the group and asked if I would come. I agreed and it was arranged that we would all meet at the Gioconda, a fitting venue for the get-together.

It was great seeing Graham and Denis again, and Kevin, Gina and David couldn't have been more charming facilitators. Unbeknown to me, Kevin had invited David Bowie, who wasn't that far away at the Dorchester at the time, leaving information on times and place and so on. Of course, we all knew that it was highly unlikely that he would join us and he didn't arrive. He was probably busy anyway, but we later found out that he always had very fond memories of the band, though he did also say that we probably played a bit too loud. I know this was true, but that was The Who's bad influence on all of us. I have to say that David was equally complicit in the volume levels at the time.

I recall that Denis Taylor's sister came to see us once at the Marquee and had to go outside mid-way through because our loud music made her feel unwell. That probably gives you some idea of the unregulated decibel level we hit back in the day.

It was a fascinating morning at the Gioconda and it was hard to believe that we would all sometimes crash out in the ambulance outside that café overnight. The band's universe seemed to revolve around that street.

It was a real treat to see some fascinating old 8mm film footage of David briefly walking from Regent Sounds to the Gioconda café, with a carefree and engaging smile to camera. These few frames of colour film were only discovered and made public a few years ago. It was an amazing find, randomly shot in 1965 by a visiting tourist who clearly had no idea who David was. We could well have been in the café waiting for him while it was shot, after all the Gio was pretty much our static base. That short clip immediately brought to mind the film that Ralph took of us down in Bournemouth that same summer, and also the little film premiere of it he treated us to that night at Warwick Square. Nice memories.

*

Returning now to the early 1980s, after our trip down memory lane at the Gioconda we all decided to have a wander across to Soho and to the Marquee, which was particularly nice for me as my children, Stefan and Jenny, were with me. It was great that they could see where their old man used to go and what he used to get up to in the sixties, not only as the famous venue would close its doors a few years later but also because it got burnt down and lost forever. Photographer Ray Stevenson, who worked a lot with David himself in the sixties, accompanied us that afternoon and took photos throughout. One or two grace the pages of this book.

I met Denis and Graham a couple of times more after that. Once when I went down to Margate and once when we got together at a Bowie event at The Fridge in Brixton, where Mick Ronson and Angie Bowie were performing.

Peter Gillman, who had interviewed me for his book *Alias David Bowie*, was also at the Fridge with his wife and co-author Leni. It was interesting to hear from Peter that night what he had uncovered in his research. He was able to give a base to my feelings of all those years ago when it seemed that Ralph was separating Dave from us. It had been Ralph's plan to turn David into a solo artist, quite rightly in retrospect, and his one-time suggestion to the Third to try and form their own identity now made sense. All water well under the bridge, but interesting nonetheless.

I was very pleased when I heard that David was performing 'Can't Help Thinking About Me' again in the late nineties. I often wondered what he thought of the early material he worked on with us, particularly as he had moved on so much in the years since.

He featured the song with terrific conviction in a showcase for the VH1 TV series *Storytellers* – a show in which the artist not only performed songs from their back catalogue but also provided some of the song's history and general back-story at the same time.

Dave started his reminiscences about that period of time, including 'Can't Help Thinking About Me', with a nice memory of his friendship with Steve Marriott, relating how one day Marriott suggested that they form a band together called David and Goliath (of course, that never happened). Dave goes on to explain how Marriott then described his new band, The Small Faces, to him shortly afterwards), before leading on to an amusing introduction about the first solo record he recorded:

'It's probably the first song I wrote and recorded as a solo artist,' he begins, 'and it's a beautiful piece of solipsism called "Can't Help Thinking About Me", and it does contain – though some might disagree – two of the worst lines I have ever written. I actually have to sing this:

> *My girl calls my name, Hi Dave…*
> *Drop in, come back, see you around if*
> *you're this way again…*

'You don't think that's the worst line, no?'

*

I still play drums today when I can (though I've long retired professionally). Whenever I visit my daughter

Jenny in Canada I often get asked to 'sit in' with local groups, which is good fun. And I'm still able to show off as these days I play music to the public in a different way: I am a presenter on Channel Radio. It was something that happened completely out of the blue, actually.

It all came about from a radio interview I did for Kevin Cann, who is a director of the station and who invited me to the studio. From that interview came an offer to do my own show. I might say I'm in good company on the station too. The show that's broadcast just before mine is presented by a lovely man who is quite a legend in his own right, the actor and writer David Barry. David presents a show called *Imaginarium*, and in case you don't immediately remember his name, David played the one and only Frankie Abbott in the popular *Please Sir!* and the *Fenn Street Gang* TV shows, and appeared in lots of other things too. We also have Boy George presenting his own 'club' show, and every other week or so a famous face or two drops into the studio to appear on someone's programme.

I picked up guitar playing years ago, having spent a lot of time with all the guitarists I worked with over the years, so songwriting then became another means of creative expression for me. I've quite few songs of my own up on the net that you can check out if you fancy it. Once music is in your bones, particularly as a performer, it never seems to leave. Thank goodness.

I even picked up some impressive moves (he says so humbly) from those years with Dave Bowie and the like. If I ever get up for a jig about somewhere, like at a party, I'm generally using a mix of David Bowie and Keith West stage moves. Sitting behind great performers provided me with the perfect vantage to take in all of their best performances.

I liked both David and Keith's stage moves a lot, though David's will always remain the most memorable for many reasons.

*

When my old drum teacher Frank King passed away, his partner phoned to tell me. I hadn't been in touch with Frank for a while, but the news broke me up. She told me that she kept finding papers that had 'Phil Lancaster, star pupil' written on them, so thought she should contact me. I was amazed and so proud that he had thought of me like that, one of his success stories. When I married Helene, Frank came to the reception at my parents' house. He bought us a kettle as a wedding gift, which was most welcome. I'll never forget Frank King.

*

If, by some means, someone finds out I knew and worked with David Bowie, they always tend to ask, 'What was he like?'

Well, I'll tell you. He had a great sense of humour, could be aloof at times, was extremely focused on what he wanted to do and he had two streaks running through him: one of innate kindness and, occasionally, one of cold ambition. Not a bad combination to get yourself noticed in the entertainment world. He was also absolutely non-judgmental of people, something quite mature at such a young age and something that stood him in good stead for life.

CHAPTER TWELVE

SUNDAY, 10 JANUARY 2016

Over the Christmas holidays of 2015, I was in Canada enjoying the festivities with my daughter Jenny and her family. During the early hours of 10 January, I was awoken by my mobile phone ringing. Thinking it must be someone calling me from the UK who had not realised the time difference, I ignored it, turned over and went back to sleep.

Some little while later, I woke again at the buzz of a text coming in. This time I opened my phone to read a message from a friend and neighbour at home briefly saying how sorry she was about David Bowie's passing. In my semi wakefulness, I thought it was a strange thing to say and what did it mean? It obviously couldn't be true.

Then I received a text from a newspaper reporter who said he had tried to ring me and would I like to comment on the passing of David Bowie. My god, it must be true then.

I woke my partner Christine to tell her. By now the rest

of the house was rising and gradually the terrible news began to crystallise. Like many people, a sense of disbelief immediately set in, a kind of knowing but denying it. Then floods of texts and messages started to arrive on my phone... condolences. This felt strange and a bit fraudulent for me, as I had not been with or seen David for decades, but maybe people that cared felt it was one little step closer to David to be able to express their sadness.

It affected me greatly as I honed in on the fact that David had actually gone. Then I got upset. I thought, like everyone else, what a loss; it just wasn't right.

He was an icon, for sure, but also a guy I spent many, many hours with way back when, and now he was gone. By lunchtime the internet was full of the news.

Should I say something? I had answered the reporter, giving him my reaction, but wondered if there was something I should do online. Kevin Cann had, by now, written a lovely tribute on Facebook, so I also put my thoughts on there – and said goodbye to the most fascinating man I was ever likely to encounter.

What was particularly poignant for me at the time was that a year or so before this I did have contact with David again, via his cousin Kristina. David had paid me a really lovely compliment when she mentioned my name to him – it meant the world to me when I heard this.

Writing this book has actually been a revelation to me in so many ways. As I first started to think more about and then note down the main memories I had of Dave and our band's antics, I also listened again to the recordings we made and quite a few others that Dave did later too (*Pin Ups* was particularly fascinating and an album I'm so pleased he recorded). There was also so much media coverage after his death that I suddenly discovered, rediscovered and sometimes linked together things that I had only partial knowledge of before. This is often the way in any of our lives, when it comes to important friendships and/or relationships. But documenting something like this that I know means a lot to many, many people, and to be encouraged to add in more detail about my own life both before and after Bowie has made this a particularly special project for me.

But even when I thought I had finished recounting pretty much all there was to say about David Bowie and The Lower Third, I got a call from the BBC. Not that it has been that unusual to be contacted by the media since David's death, but this was rather different. Director Francis Whately asked if he could interview me and Den for a forthcoming BBC TV David Bowie early years documentary. The timing was perfect for both Francis and I, as I had only just finished wracking my brains for every memory and detail while working on this book and things were still very fresh.

This culminated in a fascinating day of filming in London in June 2018 with Denis and our old Pye Records producer, Tony Hatch. But that wasn't all. Francis had selected the beautiful Victoria public house as the interview location, a venue not too far from Hyde Park where we had launched 'Can't Help Thinking About Me' over fifty-two years earlier. The attractive Gaiety Bar where we held that original reception (and now an unnamed events room on the top floor) was the setting for our interviews. The room seemed different to how I remembered it, but it felt great to be back all the same.

Also invited to this shoot was Butch Davies (ex-member

of The Riot Squad, a band David performed and recorded with in 1967), and also George Underwood and Geoff MacCormack, David's oldest childhood friends, who were also ex-members of some of David's 1960s and 1970s bands.

Filming was conducted in situ in this upper bar during one of the warmest days of that humid summer, stretching into the early afternoon (I also did a separate interview with Francis a few days before). It was so good to see Tony Hatch again, and he Denis and I shared what memories we had left of those distant sessions. Tony had flown from Spain just for the interview that day.

This documentary is the third and final instalment of Francis Whately's *Five Years* project, and by good fortune is due to be screened a week or two after the publication of this book. All of this, together with the magical reappearance of the master tape of 'The London Boys' at around the time Den and I met with Tony Hatch again, ensured that 2018 was a most interesting and rewarding year.

During a quiet moment while Francis and his production team were setting up the shoot, I briefly tried to picture David as he was back then in 1966, immaculately dressed in his black suit and heavily lacquered mod haircut, looking on at us now, bemused and amazed. I'm convinced he would never have believed that, half a century on, the BBC would be celebrating his early career in such a considered way.

He's not here now to see the massive appreciation that there has been for both himself and his work, and I'm also sad I can't share this book with him now. But I know all of his old friends and colleagues that were gathered in the Victoria that afternoon probably felt as proud as I did on his behalf.

*

I don't have my original set of drums any more, the ones I used with David. I sold them in the 1970s to Geoff Britton, who just answered a 'for sale' advert I'd placed in *Melody Maker*. Geoff turned out to be Paul McCartney's ex-drummer, so I'm very pleased they went to a good home.

While looking up information on Geoff for this book, I noticed that he used to be in The Wild Angels. What a small world. In recent years, I became friendly with Mal Gray, charismatic leader of The Wild Angels. Sadly Mal died a week ago as I write this. I wish I could have told him he probably played in the band with my old Bowie drums.

The funny thing about working on this book is, I've realised I must be one of the few sixties musicians who actually remembers the 1960s. I'm not sure if that's an accolade or not!

It's also occurred to me as I write this, that David's passing was exactly fifty years to the month from he and the band splitting up. In every way, January 2016 proved to be a very unhappy anniversary.

*

My good fortune, along with my friendship with Denis Taylor and Graham Rivens, is to have shared such wonderful times with David. He was an inventive, highly creative man even then, back in the mid-sixties when he was desperately hunting for his own unique sound and style.

And, just as important to me – and this is something I will never forget – we shared so much hearty laughter while we batted about the country in our homely ambulance. It was a very special time in my life and I can't imagine better company.

AFTERWORD

As you know well by now, following our parting of ways with Dave he quickly drew together a bunch of very competent and talented musicians who would soon go on to back him on his debut album. My seat was taken by John Eager, who admirably helped adapt our old material to suit David's new, mellower approach, while adding in his own deftly professional feel. Although I wouldn't have admitted it back then, this guy clearly knew what he was doing and so I am delighted that, all these years on, with all rivalry asunder, John has agreed to add a short afterword to my humble tome. It feels good to leave you with a bit of a buzz:

*

Amazingly enough, I have never met Phil, but I feel we have some things in common. This is through our shared experience in two different backing bands, The Lower Third and The Buzz.

Of course, I suppose the main thing is we both knew David Bowie, musically and socially (I mean, you can't spend hours on the road without getting to know somebody). We were (and still are) both drummers, all part of the great powerhouse of the engine room. It also seems we both have a penchant for old, retired ambulances (used as bandwagons, I hasten to add!).

Like so many people of our age, the other thing we would have had in common at the time (apart from chasing up wages from our permanently broke manager, Ralph Horton) was sharing in the heady times of the 1960s. Anything was possible and only limited by your imagination. In our band, The Buzz, formed by Dave for a specific style he wanted to explore, this vision of hope and success was imbued by Dave himself, who we saw as having something quite special. I am sure this was also the case with the guys in The Lower Third.

From the recordings, there was a fairly pronounced difference between Phil's drumming style and my own – Phil's style being much heavier. Whilst I was able to play in that style too, I never quite had what he had. It's something that particularly strikes me when I think of 'Can't Help Thinking About Me'.

I often think now of those times fifty years ago, and I am sure Phil does as well. Dave was an unknown at the time, but through his own genius became the David Bowie we all got to know. No doubt this book will bring back valuable memories to those who both worked with and came to see Dave back in the day – and hopefully inform and entertain those who were too young for it to have registered.

John 'Archie' Eager
Drummer – David Bowie and The Buzz

APPENDIXES

DAVIE JONES AND THE LOWER THIRD – GIG TIMELINE

17.5.65	Littlestone, New Romney, The Grand Hotel
6.65	Birmingham, The Tower Ballroom
6.65	Bilbrough Top, York, The Boulevard
4.6.65	Bournemouth, The Pavilion Ballroom (Phil Lancaster replaces original drummer, Les Mighall)
11.6.65	Brighton, The Starlight Rooms
6.65	Bromley, The Bromel Club
6.65	Weybridge Hall, Hi-Fi Hop
14.7.65	London W1, Bata Clan Club (minus David)
17.7.65	St Leonards-on-Sea, The Witch Doctor
23.7.65	Bournemouth, The Pavilion Ballroom
24.7.65	Isle of Wight, Ventnor Winter Gardens
25.7.65	Bournemouth, The Pavilion Ballroom
30.7.65	Bournemouth, The Pavilion Ballroom

31.7.65	Isle of Wight, Ventnor Winter Gardens
1.8.65	Bournemouth, The Pavilion Ballroom
6.8.65	Bournemouth, The Pavilion Ballroom
7.8.65	Isle of Wight, Ventnor Winter Gardens
19.8.65	London W1, 100 Club
20.8.65	Bournemouth, The Pavilion Ballroom
26.8.65	London W1, 100 Club
9.65	Birmingham, Elbow Room
4.9.65	Cheltenham, Blue Moon
5.9.65	Bournemouth, The Pavilion Ballroom
7.9.65	London W1, 100 Club
14.9.65	London W1, 100 Club
18.9.65	Morris's Ballroom, Shrewsbury (final gig as Davie Jones)

MORRIS'S BALLROOM * Shrewsbury

SATURDAY, SEPTEMBER 18th

Parlophone Recording Artists

DAVIE JONES & THE LOWER THIRD

PLUS THE CLUBMEN

MONDAY, SEPTEMBER 20th

Package Show featuring Decca Recording Artist

BERYL MARSDEN

Columbia Recording Artist

STEVE ALDO with THE CREWCUTS
PLUS THE ASTRONAUTS

DAVID BOWIE AND THE LOWER THIRD – GIG TIMELINE

21.9.65	London W1, 100 Club
8.10.65	London W1, Marquee Club
10.65	London, Streatham Ice Rink
31.10.65	Portsmouth, Birdcage Club

5.11.65	London W1, Marquee Club
13.11.65	The Barn, Brighton
19.11.65	London W1, Marquee Club
10.12.65	London W1, Marquee Club
11.12.65	London W1, Marquee Club (afternoon performance)
11.12.65	Brighton, Cadillac Club, Florida Ballroom (evening)
18.12.65	London W1, Marquee Club (afternoon performance)
24.12.65	RAF Camp, Leicestershire
31.12.65	Paris, Golf-Drouot
1.1.66	Paris, Golf-Drouot (matinée)
1.1.66	Paris, Bus Palladium (two shows)
2.1.66	Paris, Golf-Drouot (matinée and evening shows)
7.1.66	London W1, Marquee Club
8.1.66	London W1, Marquee Club (afternoon performance)
15.1.66	London W1, Marquee Club (afternoon performance)
19.1.66	Birmingham, Cedar Club
1.66	Newmarket
1.66	Carlisle
1.66	Harrow
22.1.66	London W1, Marquee Club (afternoon performance)
28.1.66	Stevenage, Town Hall
29.1.66	London W1, Marquee Club (afternoon performance)
29.1.66	Bromley, The Bromel Club (cancelled evening show)

Sadly, this timeline is incomplete. Many Lower Third appearances with David remain undocumented.

RECORDINGS

1. 'You've Got A Habit Of Leaving'/'Baby Loves That Way'
Davy Jones – Issued: 20 August 1965
(Parlophone R 5315) UK

2. 'Can't Help Thinking About Me'/'And I Say To Myself'
David Bowie with The Lower Third – Issued: 14 January 1966
(Pye 7N.17020) UK

'Can't Help Thinking About Me'/'And I Say To Myself'
David Bowie with The Lower Third – Issued: March 1966
(Warner Brothers WB 5815) US

Davy Jones & The Lower Third's 'You've Got A Habit Of Leaving',
'Baby Loves That Way', coupled with The Manish Boys' 'I Pity
The Fool', 'Take My Tip'; first released by EMI: NUT (7") EP
Series, EMI 2925; and issued as a 10" EP in 1982 by See-For-Miles-
Records / Charly.
All EP tracks produced by Shel Talmy in 1965. UK

APPENDIXES

COMPILATIONS (Selective listing)

Hitmakers Vol. 4 – including **'Can't Help Thinking About Me'**
'Can't Help Thinking About Me' also featured on this compilation
LP, released in late 1966. It was the first time a track by David
Bowie had featured on a UK album.
(Pye NPL 18144) UK

VH1 Storytellers – **a live album by David Bowie** including **'Can't
Help Thinking About Me'**
Recorded in August 1999 and released in 2009, David included
'Can't Help Thinking About Me' as the earliest example of his
songwriting during this television showcase – though admitting
some embarrassment at the lyrics, including the line, 'My girl calls
my name, Hi Dave...'

Toy – **'You've Got A Habit Of Leaving' and 'Baby Loves That
Way'**
In 2000, David rerecorded a selection of his 1960 compositions for
an officially unreleased album project titled *Toy*. Included on it
were reimagined versions of 'You've Got A Habit Of Leaving' and
'Baby Loves That Way'.

Nothing Has Changed: The Very Best Of David Bowie
Official Parlophone compilation. The luxury 3-CD edition
including **'Can't Help Thinking About Me'** and **'You've Got A
Habit Of Leaving'**. Released in 2014.

The Many Faces Of David Bowie
A compilation CD set including **'Can't Help Thinking About
Me'**. Released in 2016.

DEMO ISSUES

David Bowie – Early On (1964–1966)
A compilation CD issued in 1991 on Rhino.
Featuring unreleased Lower Third backed demo recordings, **'I'll Follow You'** and **'Glad I've Got Nobody'**, a demo with David accompanied by Denis Taylor on lead titled **'I Want My Baby Back'**, plus two other contemporary numbers from that time, **'That's Where My Heart Is'** and **'Bars Of The County Jail'** – both of which are just David on vocals and acoustic guitar. All are from Shel Talmy's archive.
(Rhino R2 70526) US

Making Time: A Shel Talmy Production
A compilation CD issued in 2017 on Ace Records. Features one previously unissued Davy Jones & The Lower Third mix of **'You've Got A Habit Of Leaving'** (with noticeably different vocal, guitar and bass overdubs).
(Ace DCHD 1497) Europe

UNRELEASED MATERIAL

Around 2016, some additional unreleased Davy Jones and The Lower Third acetates came to light, including the fabled **'Born of the Night'**. These recordings were made in either May or early June 1965 and feature the band's original drummer, Les Mighall. A previously unknown recording called **'I Don't Mind'** was among the discs found (a very slow-paced ballad which was actually a cover of a James Brown song, recorded by James Brown and The Famous Flames and released in 1961) and also another early cover, this of the more familiar Yardbirds number **'I Wish You Would'** (a song we would sometimes include in our live set). This Yardbirds cover is actually not that different from the version David would record eight years later for *Pin Ups*, and again features David quite prominently on harmonica.

Over the page is the text from a rare 1965 press release/band biography issued by EMI Records to support the release of 'You've Got A Habit Of Leaving'. The original incorrect spellings are retained – including mention of the comparatively unknown Jimi Hendrix as 'Hendricks' by EMI's press department.

EMI Biography
DAVIE JONES & THE LOWER THIRD
– For The Record –

'We're not a "scream" group. We like our audiences to be quiet while we're performing a number, and then to give us a healthy response when we finish.' So says Davie Jones, who recently teamed up with The Lower Third and is heard with them on the group's first record, 'You've Got A Habit Of Leaving'.

Davie was about 17 when he became a full-time singer: 'It was either that or commercial art. I was doing both as a semi-pro and at that time I thought singing was more creative. I joined the King Bees and was with several more groups until meeting The Lower Third.'

While their future vocalist was singing with other groups, The Lower Third were playing in the Thanet area of Kent, where they lived at the time. They are now based in London. They were, as bass guitarist Graham Evans said, 'trying to find some sort of foothold.' Three months ago they moved to London and played for a few weeks at The Discotheque Club before meeting Davie. Since then they have played at Bournemouth Pavilion and at a seaside club where membership increased from 50 to 2,000 during their stay.

What do Davie and his new group think of their partnership? Says Davie: 'We like each others [sic] ideas. We have the same policies and fit rather well together. All of us like to keep to ourselves and we like things rather than people.'

First record by Davie (who wrote both sides) and The Lower Third is 'You've Got A Habit Of Leaving'and 'Baby Loves That Way' on Parlophone R 5315. Release date was August 20th, 1965. With the Manish Boys, Davie previously recorded 'I Pity The Fool' on Parlophone R 5250.

APPENDIXES

Davie Jones and The Lower Third line-up as follows:-

DAVIE JONES born at Brixton on January 1st, 1946. Sings and plays harmonica. Likes – painting; dislikes – 'in crowds'. Favourite artistes – Graham Rivens, Sammy Davis Jr.; food – rump steak; drinks – barley wine, vodka and lime. Ambition – 'the group's ambition'. Has blonde [sic] hair, green eyes, is 5ft 11 ins. and weighs 9 stone.

DENNIS [sic] (Teacup) TAYLOR born at Ramsgate on July 6th, 1944. Plays lead guitar. Likes – women with kinky boots; dislikes – 'in crowds', big heads. Favourite artistes – Frank Sinatra, Sophia Lauren, Carroll Baker; food – spaghetti Bolognese, Chinese; drink – rum, cider, stout. Ambition – to be a good musician. Has grey-blue eyes, dark brown hair, is 5ft 11 ins. and weighs 10 stone.

PHIL LANCASTER born at Walthamstow on December 26th, 1942. Plays drums. Likes – rain, reading Jack Kerouac and John Steinbeck; dislikes – hypocrisy. Favourite artistes – Sammy Davis, Lambert, Hendricks [sic] and Bevan; food – cod and chips; drinks – lager and lime. Ambition – 'to make loads of money and keep playing'. Has blue eyes, brown hair, is 5ft 8 ins. and weighs 9 stone.

GRAHAM RIVENS born at Plaistow on October 10th, 1942. Plays bass guitar. Likes – big cars, guitars; dislikes – traffic wardens, taxi drivers. Favourite artistes – Phil Lancaster; food – curried prawns, fresh fish and chips; drinks – vodka. Ambition – 'to end up with a line of garages and pubs'. Has blue-grey eyes, dark brown hair, is 6ft 1in. and weighs 10 stone 11lbs.

WITH THE COMPLIMENTS OF:
Martin Ross, The Press Office, EMI Records

ACKNOWLEDGEMENTS

I may have said this before but this whole book writing experience has been extremely cathartic and I thank you from the bottom of my heart for staying with it up to end. I just hope it didn't prove too tortuous!

Many years ago a lot of friends were telling me that I should write down my David Bowie story. Eventually, after a few more years passed, I got down to it. But for quite a while that was how things lay, until I was reunited with Kevin Cann. Kevin is a writer of acclaim who had recently published his consummate work called *Any Day Now* – which covers David's early career up to the mid-1970s. So it is with great humility that I acknowledge here my tremendous thanks to Kevin for his tireless effort and for his general assistance, for editing this book and for his priceless advice and encouragement. Couldn't have done it without him.

I would also like to thank my lovely partner Christine for her support and encouragement, my special children Stefan and Jenny, and also mention my soul mates Jack White, John Urquhart, Roger Seamark and the late Denis Payton, all of whom pop up in my story – and without whose friendships I would never have had such a wonderful life, both in and out of music.

Many thanks also to Andy Neill, whose *Anyway Anyhow Anywhere: The Complete Chronicle of The Who 1958–1978*, co-written with Matt Kent, is a definitive and quality work on the band. By pooling research notes, Andy and Kevin have been able to confirm the exact date of our Marquee appearance with The Who, which isn't bad considering it's now fifty-three years after the event.

Thank you: Denis Taylor, John Eager, Tony Hatch, Timothy White, Linda Stevens and to Reto Stocklin, for kindly playing me the most recent band acetate discoveries.

At John Blake publishing we would particularly like to thank James Hodgkinson for his belief in this book and for his sage editorial assistance. We would also like to extend the same to Rob Dimery for casting his eye over the completed text with an eagle eye for detail, and to Hannah Naughton, for designing the cover of the book.

Finally, not forgetting of course – Denis 'T-cup' Taylor and Graham Rivens (the other two-thirds of the Third). And to David Jones, our leader, friend and mentor – it was indeed an honour and great pleasure to have known and worked with you.

Thank you all.

ACKNOWLEDGMENTS

David's 1965 passport photo.

Photos and memorabilia courtesy of
Phil Lancaster, Denis Taylor and Kevin Cann.

You can hear Phil Lancaster's weekly radio show
every Saturday afternoon on Channel Radio:
www.channelradio.co.uk

Original songs by Phil Lancaster can be heard at:
www reverbnation.co.uk

INDEX

INDEX

INDEX

INDEX